The Hebrew Bible,
the Old Testament,
and Historical Criticism

The Hebrew Bible,
the Old Testament,
and Historical Criticism

Jews and Christians in Biblical Studies

—— · ——

JON D. LEVENSON

Westminster/John Knox Press
Louisville, Kentucky

© 1993 Jon D. Levenson

All rights reserved. No part of this book may be reproduced or transmitted in any form or by any means, electronic or mechanical, including photocopying, recording, or by any information storage or retrieval system, without permission in writing from the publisher. For information, address Westminster/John Knox Press, 100 Witherspoon Street, Louisville, Kentucky 40202-1396.

Scripture citations from *The New English Bible* are copyright © The Delegates of the Oxford University Press and The Syndics of the Cambridge University Press, 1961, 1970, and are used by permission.

Quotations from *Tanakh* are copyright © 1985 by The Jewish Publication Society, 1930 Chestnut Street, Philadelphia, PA 19103, and are used by permission.

Book design by ediType

First edition

Published by Westminster/John Knox Press
Louisville, Kentucky

This book is printed on acid-free paper that meets the American National Standards Institute Z39.48 standard. ∞

PRINTED IN THE UNITED STATES OF AMERICA
9 8 7 6 5 4 3 2 1

Library of Congress Cataloging-in-Publication Data

Levenson, Jon Douglas
    The Hebrew Bible, the Old Testament, and historical criticism :
Jews and Christians in biblical studies / Jon D. Levenson. — 1st
ed.
    p.   cm.
    Includes bibliographical references and index.
    ISBN 0-664-25407-1 (pbk. : alk. paper)

    1. Bible. O.T.–Hermeneutics. 2. Bible. O.T.–Criticism,
interpretation, etc. 3. Bible. O.T.–Criticism, interpretation,
etc., Jewish. 4. Historical criticism (Literature) I. Title.
BS476.L48 1993
221.6'01–dc20   92-33118

To some friends from our years in Chicago together:

John Burgess	*Lewis Glinert*
Robert Cohn	*Moshe Gresser*
John Collins	*Menahem Herman*
Arthur Droge	*Coert Rylaarsdam*
Randall Garr	*Lawrence Sullivan*

Contents

Abbreviations

CBQ	*Catholic Biblical Quarterly*
CJR	*Christian Jewish Relations*
ET	*Evangelische Theologie*
HBT	*Horizons in Biblical Theology*
HSM	Harvard Semitic Monographs
HTR	*Harvard Theological Review*
JAAR	*Journal of the American Academy of Religion*
JAOS	*Journal of the American Oriental Society*
JBL	*Journal of Biblical Literature*
JES	*Journal of Ecumenical Studies*
JQR	*Jewish Quarterly Review*
JSOT	*Journal for the Study of the Old Testament*
MJ	*Modern Judaism*
MQR	*Michigan Quarterly Review*
OBO	Orbis Biblicus et Orientalis
OBT	Overtures to Biblical Theology
OTL	Old Testament Library
PCTSA	*Proceedings of the Catholic Theological Society of America*
RE	*Religious Education*
SBLMS	Society of Biblical Literature Monograph Series
SBT	Studies in Biblical Theology
SH	Scripta Hierosolymitana
SNVAO	Skrifter utgitt av det Norske Videnskaps-Akademi i Oslo
TKT	Texte zur Kirchen- und Theologiegeschichte
TT	*Theology Today*
UNDCSJCA	University of Notre Dame Center for the Study of Judaism and Christianity in Antiquity
VTSup	Vetus Testamentum Supplements
ZTK	*Zeitschrift für Theologie und Kirche*

Acknowledgments

The earliest forms of four of the chapters in this book were given as invited lectures. Chapter 1 was delivered at a conference on "The Future of Biblical Studies" at the University of California at San Diego in April 1984. I thank the conference organizer, Professor Richard E. Friedman, for the invitation and the arrangements. Chapter 4 was given at a conference at the University of Notre Dame entitled "Hebrew Bible or Old Testament? Studying the Bible in Judaism and Christianity," in April 1989. The conference organizers, Professors John J. Collins and Roger Brooks, and my respondent, Professor Joseph Blenkinsopp, deserve my gratitude. Chapter 5 was the presidential address at the annual conference of the New England region of the Society of Biblical Literature in April 1992. Thanks are due to the membership for their vote of confidence and to Professor Thomas R. W. Longstaff, the secretary, for his deft arrangement of the conference. Finally, the earliest version of chapter 6 was first given as the Aaron Kriwitsky Memorial Lecture at the Maurice Greenberg Center for Judaic Studies at the University of Hartford in April 1988. My gratitude goes to Professor Jonathan Rosenbaum for the invitation and the hospitality.

The thinking behind these essays has developed in conversation with more colleagues and students than I can possibly list. I should be remiss, however, if I failed to recognize those who were so kind as to read drafts of one or more chapters and to give me of their counsel. Abundant thanks are owing to Professors Tzvi Abusch, Gary Anderson, Robert Cohn, John J. Collins, Arthur Droge, Moshe Gresser, Lynn Poland, J. Coert Rylaarsdam, and Lawrence Sullivan, and to Dr. John Burgess, Rabbi Joel Poupko, and Father Paul Mankowski. It is perhaps unnecessary to add that wise counsel is not always heeded, and these scholars cannot be held accountable for my wrongheadedness.

I must also thank those expert typists at the University of Chicago and at Harvard who proved so adept at deciphering my hand — Michelle Harewood, Wendy Lee, Brian Murphy, Heidi Swarts, Bruce Krag, and the late Sara Hazel. Mr. Murphy, whose contribution to the manuscript extends well beyond the category of typing and into that of editing, deserves a double expression of gratitude. I am also grateful to my research assistant, Carey Walsh, for aiding in editing, proofreading, and other tasks essential to the production of the book.

To Professor John B. Carman go my thanks for providing the precise wording of the title to chapter 4 and thus also of the subtitle to the whole volume.

Finally, let me thank my editor at Westminster/John Knox Press, Jeffries Hamilton, for all his help in seeing this project through to publication.

Grateful acknowledgment is made for permission to reprint the following copyrighted material:

Chapter 1 is a revised version of a chapter by the same title originally published in *The Future of Biblical Studies: The Hebrew Scriptures,* ed. Richard Elliot Friedman and H. G. M. Williamson (Atlanta: Scholars Press, 1987), and is used by permission of Scholars Press.

Chapter 2 is a revised version of "Why Jews are Not Interested in the Bible," originally published in *Judaic Perspectives on Ancient Israel,* edited by Jacob Neusner (Philadelphia: Fortress Press, 1987), and is used by permission of Jacob Neusner.

Chapter 3 is a revised version of an article by the same title published in the *Journal of Religion* 68:2 (April 1988). Used by permission of the University of Chicago Press. © 1988 by the University of Chicago. All rights reserved.

Chapter 4 is a revised version of a chapter by the same title originally published in *Hebrew Bible or Old Testament? Studying the Bible in Judaism and Christianity,* edited by John J. Collins and Roger Brooks. © 1990 by the University of Notre Dame Press. Used by permission of the University of Notre Dame Press.

Chapter 5 is a revised version of "The Bible: The Unexamined Commitments of Criticism," originally published in *First Things* 30 (February 1993) (New York: The Institute on Religion and Public Life).

Chapter 6 is a revised version of "Exodus and Liberation," originally published in *Horizons in Biblical Theology* 13 (1991) and is used by permission.

Preface

The essays that follow represent my thinking over the last several years on the relationship between two modes of biblical study, the traditional and the historical-critical. This is a relationship crucial not only to the intellectual history of biblical scholarship, but also to the profession of biblical scholarship in our time. It is, however, also a subject that has attracted remarkably little systematic reflection, especially as it applies to the Hebrew Bible/Tanakh/Old Testament. One of the reasons for this dearth of attention is itself a recurrent theme in these essays: liberal Protestantism, which has always dominated the distinctively modern study of scripture, tends to advocate the *replacement* of traditional interpretation with the historical-critical method. My claim is that this is unsound in both theory and practice. The theoretical deficiency is a blindness to the inability of a self-consciously universalistic and rationalistic method to serve as the vehicle of any particularistic religious confession. The practical consequence has been the development of a host of historical-critical interpretations that are really only rewordings or recastings of traditional Christian views. This, in turn, has meant that the continuity of the Hebrew Bible with the ongoing Jewish tradition (and not with the church alone) has been denied or, more often, simply ignored. And so, we are too often left with Christianity trying to pass as historical criticism and with historical criticism severely distorted by unacknowledged religious allegiance.

Awareness of the problem moves us in two seemingly opposite directions. On the one hand, it requires us to view with suspicion any unqualified claim of continuity between the Hebrew Bible and the religious traditions that derive from it, Jewish as well as Christian. In the name of intellectual honesty and a sense of historical change, we are compelled to adopt an interpretive stance that is rigorous in its resistance to religious tradition. On the other hand, in privileging *historical* context the historical-critical method shortchanges the *literary* context defined by the completed Bible, Jewish or Christian. Having decomposed the Bible into its historically diverse constituent sources, its practitioners lack the means to do justice to the Book currently in our possession as a synchronic, systemic entity. The closest they can come is to provide a diachronic description of how the completed Bible came into being. But the Bible (under any definition) cannot survive methods that are themselves unable to transcend the limitations of historicism and empiricism. For such methods can at best only describe a range of canons and cultures but can never explain why we should concentrate on one rather than another. Indeed, a historicism afraid to acknowledge normative judgments about suprahistorical truth eventually deteriorates into historical relativism and experiences mounting difficulty articulating the transhistorical value of historical study itself. This is the dead end to which, in my judgment, the secularization of biblical studies has delivered too many of its practitioners. Ironically, those eager to adapt biblical studies to the modern university now find their own discipline plunging into the crisis that has engulfed the entire university. At the heart of that crisis lie the loss of a transcendent goal for learning and the weakening of the communities and practices that can sustain the faith and belief upon which all learning — and not only biblical studies — depends.

I make no claim to have resolved the obvious theoretical opposition between modernism and fundamentalism that has riven modern religious life, both Jewish and Christian. My essays, if they are properly understood, will not meet with the approval of those traditionalists who can only ignore or explain away the new evidence about the composition of biblical books that has expanded exponentially over the last few centuries. But the same essays will also disappoint those who believe that modern study supersedes traditional interpretation and that nothing essential is lost when historical criticism is awarded a monopoly in the interpretive process. Although the more extreme advocates both of religious traditionalism and of modern rationalism wish it otherwise, neither tradition nor modernity can credibly dispense with the other. When biblical studies ignores this point, it becomes impoverished and endangers its future. My own intuition is that the two seemingly opposite directions in which these essays move are each indispensable avenues to the larger and more encompassing truth. The dignity both of

Chapter 1

————— • —————

The Hebrew Bible, the Old Testament, and Historical Criticism

> What could be more glorious than to brace
> one's self up to discover New South Wales
> and then realize, with a gush of happy
> tears, that it was really Old South Wales.
> G. K. Chesterton, *Orthodoxy*

• I •

If there has ever been a book that has thrived in a plurality of contexts, it is surely the Hebrew Bible. In the Jewish tradition this book,
known as the Tanakh or the *Miqra'*, is properly placed alongside the
Talmud, Midrash, and medieval rabbinic commentaries. These books,
highly diverse and delightfully argumentative, establish a pluriform yet
bounded context of interpretation for the Tanakh. In the church, the
Hebrew Bible, known as the "Old Testament," appears as the first of
the two volumes of sacred scripture, the "Bible," and interpretation is
not complete until volume 1 is related to volume 2, the Old Testament
to the New, so as to proclaim together Jesus Christ. In both the Jewish and the Christian traditions even as they were constituted before
the Enlightenment, there is substantial precedent for searching out the
meaning of a passage in the Hebrew Bible apart from the meanings
directly suggested for it by the books that mark out its traditional contexts of interpretation. At least from the eleventh century C.E., the "plain

1

sense" (Hebrew, *peshat*) was much prized. It is important to remember that this "plain sense" was itself culturally conditioned and a matter of communal consensus and that among rabbinic Jews and Christians, it was not pursued with the intention of undermining the normativity of the larger context. A plain-sense exegete (*pashtan*) like Rabbi Samuel ben Meir ("Rashbam," Northern France, twelfth century) could be uncompromising both in his pursuit of the plain sense and in his allegiance to halakhah (rabbinic law), which often bases itself on the biblical text in a way that contradicts the *peshat.* He is paralleled by those Christian exegetes who recognized a "historical sense" to the Old Testament without relinquishing a Christocentric interpretation of it. In both the Jewish and the Christian cases, the unity of the overall religion was maintained, even though it was not seen as operative in all forms of exegesis. There could be concentric circles of context, but the smallest circle, the plain sense, finally yielded to the largest one, the whole tradition, however constituted.

In the last three centuries, there has arisen another context of interpretation of the Hebrew Bible, the *historical* context: no part of the book is to be read against literature, either internal or external, that cannot be reasonably presumed to have existed at the time. To be sure, historical criticism has affinities with the pursuit of the plain sense and builds upon the half millennium of *pashtanut* that preceded its emergence. They differ, however, in that historical critics place all the emphasis on development and historical change and fearlessly challenge both the historicity of the foundational events (e.g., Sinaitic revelation, the resurrection of Jesus) and traditional ideas of authorship, for example, that Moses wrote the Pentateuch or that the Gospels were written by the evangelists to whom they are ascribed. Historical critics take the text apart more ruthlessly than traditional *pashtanim,* and, qua historical critics, they lack a method of putting it back together again. They reconstruct history by concentrating on contradictions, which they then allow to stand. The traditions, of course, often recognized the same contradictions. The difference is that traditionalists had a method that could harmonize the contradictions and, in the process, preserve the unity of the text and its religious utility. Consider, for example, the contradiction between Exod 12:15, which mandates the eating of unleavened bread during Passover for a full seven days, and Deut 16:8, which specifies six days of observance for the same commandment. Below, we see one way that the rabbis of the talmudic period handled the contradiction:

> How can both these passages be maintained? The seventh day had been included in the more inclusive statement and then was taken out of it. Now, that which is singled out from a more inclusive statement means to teach us something about the whole statement. Hence, just as on the seventh day it is optional, so on all the other days it is optional. May it not be that just as on the seventh day it is optional, so on all the rest, including the first night, it is optional? The scriptural passage: "In the first month, at evening ye shall eat unleavened bread" [Exod 12:18] fixes it as an obligation to eat unleavened bread on the first night. (*Mek.*, Pischa' 8)[1]

The assumption of the rabbis here is that the Deuteronomic law is not independent of that given in Exodus. On the contrary, the operative law is to be discovered by taking *both* passages into account. The unity of the Mosaic Torah requires that *all* its data be considered. The two laws do not compete; together, they enable the ingenious exegete to discover the truth. The law that emerges, and is halakhah to this day, reflects neither the seven days of Exod 12:15 nor the six of Deut 16:8, but only one day.[2] In short, rabbinic exegesis of the Torah here yields a norm for which, prima facie, the Torah provides no evidence at all. If this seems absurd, consider that the alternative is simply to choose arbitrarily and subjectively one Torah verse over the other, as if they were not of equal sanctity. If one assumes, with the rabbis, that they are of equal sanctity and that they exist in the same mind (the mind of God) at the same moment (eternally), then one is required to undertake just the sort of exegetical operation in which the rabbis are here engaged, an operation that is, in fact, in continuity with the redactional process that helped produce the Hebrew Bible itself.[3] In the minds of historical critics, this operation is a historically indefensible homogenization of the past. By harmonizing inconcinnities, the tradition presents itself with a timeless document, one that appears to speak to the present only because the historical setting of the speaking voice or the writing hand has been suppressed, and all voices and all hands are absorbed into an eternal simultaneity.

The historical critics have a different way of handling the contradiction between Exod 12:15 and Deut 16:8. They feel no compulsion to see the two verses as derived from one synchronic reality, but readily consign them to different historical periods or to different locales or to different social sectors. Whereas the traditionalist begins with the assumption that the tradition (and certainly its most sacred texts) has a stable core and that there is a unified, if variegated, religion that can be derived from it — "Judaism" or "Christianity" — the historical critic begins with no such assumption of stability and continuity, but with a commitment to restore the texts to their historical contexts. Passages are to be read against their age, not against the book into which they eventually came (not, that is, unless it is the period in which the finished book was produced that we are seeking to interpret). Knowledge of that age is to be gained by excavating within the text, but also by means of archaeology and the extrabiblical texts and forgotten biblical manuscripts it unearths, without the traditionalist's concern that the resultant picture will depend upon an illicit mixture of sacred and profane sources.

In an important sense, historical criticism of the Bible thus resembles psychoanalysis. It brings to light what has been repressed and even forgotten, the childhood, as it were, of the tradition. But if Wordsworth was right that "the Child is the Father of the Man," it is wrong to think that the man will be happy to meet the child within him whom he thinks he has outgrown. Like psychoanalysis, historical criticism uncovers old conflicts and dissolves the impression that they have been resolved rather than repressed. It is only reasonable to expect both to encounter "resistance" in those to whom they are applied. Although most historical critics of the Bible consider themselves still somehow adherents of the Jewish or the Christian traditions, it must be conceded that the position of the majority of traditionalists who fear historical criticism and doubt its appropriateness is not groundless. Later, we shall examine ways in which some eminent Christian critics have dealt with the dissonance between two contexts, that of the Hebrew Bible of historical criticism and that of the Old Testament of Christian faith.

I have argued that the price of recovering the *historical* context of sacred books has been the erosion of the largest *literary* contexts that undergird the traditions that claim to be based upon them. In modern times, the multicontextuality of the Hebrew Bible has been the source of acute dissension. Much of the polemics between religious traditionalists and historians over the past three centuries can be reduced to the issue of which context shall be normative. When historical critics assert, as they are wont to do, that the Hebrew Bible must not be taken "out of context," what they really mean is that the *only* context worthy of respect is the ancient Near Eastern world as it was at the time of composition of whatever text is under discussion.[4] Religious traditionalists, however, are committed to another set of contexts, minimally the rest of scripture, however delimited, and maximally, the entire tradition, including their own religious experience. Their goal is not to push the Book back into a vanished past, but to insure its vitality in the present and the future: "The word of our God endures forever" (Isa 40:8). Their interest in the past is usually confined to an optimistic examination of how the vitality of yesteryear can energize the present. The discontinuities with which historical critics are preoccupied are of little or no use to traditionalists.

In recent years, increasing numbers of scholars have been asserting the validity of both the historical and the literary (or canonical) contexts. Some have sought to develop a hermeneutic that respects the integrity of the received text for purposes of literary analysis or theological affirmation, without in the process slipping into a fundamentalistic denial of historical change.[5] In this, the "second naiveté" of those touched by historical criticism is to be distinguished from the innocence of the orthodox believer who has never become aware of the historical context and who does not feel the claim of historical investigation. In truth, the literary interests of these scholars of the "second naiveté" have little in common with the search for proof texts so important to the growth of both Judaism and Christianity and to the establishment of their normative statements.

Underlying the literary context affirmed by religious traditionalists is the conviction that the text is somehow the expression of a reliable God. Harmonization is the exegetical counterpart to belief in the coherence of the divine will. The uniformity of scripture reflects the uniformity of truth. The alternative to this traditional religious position has never been stated more boldly than it was by a great pioneer of the historical criticism of the Christian Bible, Baruch (Benedict) de Spinoza (1632–1677), when he wrote that "great caution is necessary not to confuse the mind of a prophet or historian with the mind of the Holy Spirit and the truth of the matter."[6] For Spinoza, the excommunicated Jew who never became a Christian, the idea of inspiration was simply another shackle constricting the exegete. No longer need exegesis take place within the believing community. Scripture must be followed wherever it leads, come what may. The author of a biblical text will be the person who wrote it; its meaning will be what *that person meant,* not what *God means,* and no intellectually responsible exposition of it can take place without locating the text unshakably within the historical circumstances of its composition. Jews and Christians can participate equally in the Spinozan agenda only because its naturalistic presuppositions negate the theological foundations of *both* Judaism and Christianity. Ever since

Spinoza, those Jews and Christians who wish both to retain historical consciousness *and* to make a contemporary use of scripture have been, at least intellectually, on the defensive.

· **II** ·

The concept that the Bible has many authors rather than one Author has been as brutal to the New Testament as it has been to the Hebrew Bible. It was not long before scholars noticed that the four canonical Gospels contradict each other not only in details (e.g., Did Jesus say "Blessed are the poor" or "Blessed are the poor in spirit"?), but even in theology. In fact, the New Testament, too, soon ceased to be a single book in the minds of critical scholars. For example, they noted that for Paul, Christ is "the end of the law" (Rom 10:4), whereas the Sermon on the Mount in Matthew denounces those who set aside "even the least of the law's commandments," for "not a jot or a tittle will disappear from the law until all has been fulfilled" (Matt 5:17–20). No wonder Matthew's Jesus commends obedience to the Pharisees, who "sit in the chair of Moses" (Matt 23:2–3).[7] Now, if "the law" in the Sermon on the Mount means the Mosaic Torah, then St. Matthew's Gospel, or at least this document in it, is guilty of the heresy of "Judaizing," for the Pauline position that redemption in Christ means exemption from the Torah (see Galatians) became normative. And so the possibility emerges that the church has canonized a heretic — and his Gospel! If, on the other hand, the position of Matt 5:17–20 is valid, then what is to be said to all those Gentiles who believe, with Paul, that Christ allows them to come into the very bosom of Abraham while bypassing the Mosaic Torah? And even if Matt 5:17–20 refers not to the Mosaic Torah but to Jesus' own Torah or to his particular exposition of Moses', then the Pauline doctrine of justification through faith by grace alone, so central to Protestantism, still stands indicted *sola scriptura,* "through scripture alone." In short, the reason these various theological positions, including the heresy of "Judaizing," have kept turning up throughout the history of the church is that they can all make a plausible claim to be biblical. Martin Luther at the Diet of Worms could still express a commitment to "scripture and plain reason" rather than "the authority of popes and councils, for they have contradicted each other."[8] Historical criticism has now abundantly shown that scripture, too, is contradictory, a potpourri drawn from what are, in fact, different religions. In the process, historical criticism of the Christian Bible has shattered the Protestant dream of an orthodox church founded on biblical authority alone.[9]

The relationship between theological heterodoxy and the critical study of history is thus reciprocal. The historian soon discovers that orthodoxy hangs from a thread that is very thin, if it exists at all. Some of the traditionalists' heroes were heterodox; alive today, they might be accused of heresy. On the other hand, persons of heterodox leanings are driven to the study of history, in part because they can use history and historical documents, even the Bible, in support of their "heresy." The suppressed or forgotten past provides precedents helpful in dissolving the current consensus: historical criticism is invaluable to the venerable liberal (and, in my view, illogical) argument that the inevitability of unwilled change legitimates willed change, that the historical reality that the tradition was, de facto, always changing validates, de jure, contemporary efforts to alter it. In this way, just as fundamentalists suspect, historical criticism of the Bible aids in the rehabilitation of heresies, for the dismantling of the (orthodox) canon (a sine qua non of historical biblical criticism) and the normalization of heterodoxy imply each other. The frankest admission of this of which I know is the last paragraph of James M. Robinson's presidential address to the Society of Biblical Literature in 1981:

> For Jesus to rise in disembodied radiance, for the initiate to re-enact this kind of resurrection in ecstasy, and for this religiosity to mystify the sayings of Jesus by means of hermeneutically loaded dialogues of the resurrected Christ with his gnostic disciples is as consistent a position as is the orthodox insistence upon the physical bodiliness of the resurrected Christ, the futurity of the believer's resurrection back into the same physical body, and the incarnation of Jesus' sayings within the pre-Easter biography of Jesus in the canonical Gospels. Neither is the original Christian position; both are serious efforts to interpret it. Neither can be literally espoused by serious critical thinkers of today; both should be hearkened to as worthy segments of the heritage of transmission and interpretation through which Jesus is mediated to the world today.[10]

In reconstructing these various Christologies, Robinson uses not only the canonical literature, but also documents such as the *Gospel of Thomas* and Q. The last-named source is especially germane to a discussion of his method. Q (for German *Quelle*, "source") is the material that is common to Matthew and Luke but not to Mark. The theory of most critical scholars is that Mark and Q served as two sources for Matthew and Luke. Of course, Q, a collection of Jesus' sayings (or sayings attributed to him) without narrative, is hypothetical. It is found only in Matthew and Luke. But the probability that it existed independently has increased in light of the discovery of the *Gospel of Thomas*, which is a very similar collection. Robinson does not ignore the fact that the surviving tradition does not recognize *Thomas* and subordinates Q to a different genre. On the contrary, these moves he views as simply stations on the way to orthodoxy. His claim, however, is that historical excavation of a literary kind (to recover Q) and of an archaeological kind (to recover *Thomas*, which was found in a jar in the ground in Egypt) enables us to recover the alternative as it stood before it was branded with the stigma of heterodoxy. Historical study cuts the Gordian knot that holds together the canon and even individual books within it. As a result, the long-suppressed and forgotten Gnostic position becomes a "worthy segment[] of the heritage of transmission"! The assumption is that one of the traditional obstacles that Christians must overcome in their effort to hear the gospel is the proto-orthodoxy of the Gospel redactors themselves. If the redactors are orthodox, Jesus is a heretic.

One of the Gordian knots that some Gnostics tried to untie was the one that binds the Hebrew Bible and the Christian documents together as one (Christian) Bible. The idea that the two are linked is, of course, internal to the books that came to be called the "New Testament." Chief among the devices that connect the two is the idea that what the Hebrew Bible, soon to become only an "Old Testament," predicts is fulfilled in the putative events reported in the New Testament. Thus, for example, Matthew interprets the "voice crying in the wilderness" of Isa 40:3 as John the Baptist (Matt 3:1–3), and taking the poetry of Zech 9:9 ("humble and mounted on an ass / on a foal, the young of a she-ass") literally, he has Jesus ride into Jerusalem on *two* animals (Matt 21:1–7)! A related technique can be found in Gal 4:21–27, in which Paul understands Ishmael, the son of the slave girl Hagar, to be Israel according to the flesh, that is, the Jews, and Sarah's son Isaac, who is born of the promise (Gen 21:1–8), as the church. Here, Hagar stands for Mount Sinai and the slavery that Paul thought to be its legacy. Sarah suggests the heavenly Jerusalem and the freedom from the Torah that Paul considered characteristic of it. One son, the Jews, is a slave; the other, the church, is free. Hence, a Christian who observes toraitic law trades freedom for slavery. Although Paul's technique is based not on the idea of prediction, but on allegory, he, like Matthew (and the apocalyptic Jewish sects of the time), sees the real meaning of scripture as something in his own time. In and of itself, the Hebrew Bible is incomplete. As the Pauline theology of the Law became increasingly normative in the postcanonical era, such allegorical or typological interpretation of the Old Testament became all the more necessary. The church father Origen (d. 254 C.E.) put it nicely: on a plain-sense reading, without allegory, the Old Testament commands the sacrifice of calves and lambs![11]

Christian exegesis requires that the Hebrew Bible be read ultimately in a literary context that includes the New Testament. To read it only on its own would be like reading the first three acts of *Hamlet* as if the last two had never been written. Christian theology cannot tolerate exegesis that leaves the two Testaments independent of each other, lest either the Marcionite Gnostics or the Jews win the ancient debate. But the two anthologies cannot be collapsed into one, either, lest the newness of the New Testament be lost. For the New Testament is not simply the continuation of the Old, but its fulfillment, not simply another volume in the same series, but the climax and consummation of all the preceding volumes, the one that tells what the others mean. For by the time the books of the New Testament were being composed, almost all the books of the Hebrew Bible were already considered authoritative. The thrust of Christian exegesis, thus, is to present the "Old Testament" as somehow anticipating the New, but only anticipating it. The "Old Testament" must be made to appear essential but inadequate.

In modern times, the question of how to bring about such a treatment, how to relate the Old and the New, has once again become a crisis, for the old techniques seem discredited. Critical scholars rule out clairvoyance as an explanation axiomatically. Instead of holding that the Old Testament predicts events in the life of Jesus, critical scholars of the New Testament say that each Gospel writer sought to exploit Old Testament passages in order to bolster his case for the messianic and dominical claims of Jesus or of the church on his behalf. Today, only fundamentalists interpret Old Testament passages as historical predictions of New Testament narratives. Allegory has fared no better. To most biblicists, it seems woefully arbitrary. It is difficult to imagine Paul's interpretation of Genesis 21 persuading anyone who needed persuading. Although most Christians continue to accept the theology of Gal 4:21–27, its exegetical basis in the Torah has lost all credibility among historical critics.

The question arises whether a practitioner of historical criticism can speak of an "Old Testament" at all, whether the concept, like the term (the issue is not merely taxonomic), is not anachronistic. Whereas in the Middle Ages Homer and Virgil were regularly given an *interpretatio Christiana,* today the Hebrew Bible is the only non-Christian book still commonly given a Christian reading. What is at stake is the very existence of the Christian Bible in nonfundamentalistic minds. The challenge to historical critics of the Old Testament who wish to be Christian and their work to be Christian has been to find a way to read the Old Testament that is historically sound but also lends credibility to its literary context, its juxtaposition to the New Testament to form a coherent book. The following pages are devoted to an examination and critique of the ways some influential Christian critics have sought to meet the challenge.

• III •

Perhaps the most important synthesis of the experience of ancient Israel is that devised by Julius Wellhausen (1844–1918). The son of a German Lutheran pastor, Wellhausen became the great pioneer of the historical-critical study of both Testaments of his Bible. In his classic work, *Prolegomena to the History of Ancient Israel* (1878), Wellhausen divided the history of Israel's religion into three stages, each marked by a document or set of documents, which, woven together, eventually came to constitute the Pentateuch now in our hands. In the first stage, to be inferred from the Yahwistic history (J) and the closely related Elohistic source (E), religion is natural, free from law and the compulsiveness that Wellhausen associated with it. The sacred feasts are natural in character, tied unobtrusively to the cycle of the agricultural year, without any precise mathematical dates. The priesthood is universal, and one may sacrifice anywhere. In the next phase, known from the Deuteronomic strand (D), the festivals have begun to be detached from nature. Mathematical calculations begin to determine the dates of their celebration (e.g., Deut 16:9; cf. Exod 23:16). The priesthood becomes exclusively Levitical (Deuteronomy 18), and tithing begins (Deut 14:23). Most importantly, whereas in the earlier centuries any place could serve as the locus of a legitimate sanctuary (Exod 20:24), now only one shrine is permitted (Deut 12:1–7); the connection with the soil and the rhythm of natural life has been dealt a severe blow.

In the third and final stage of the religion of Israel, represented in the Pentateuch by the Priestly source (P), the festivals are fixed on precise days of a calendar (Leviticus 23), and a new festival, unattested in the earlier calendars of JE (Exod 23:14–17 and 34:18, 22–24) and D (Deuteronomy 16), the Day of Atonement, intrudes (Leviticus 16 and 23:26–32). "Just as the special purposes and occasions of sacrifice fall out of sight," Wellhausen wrote, "there comes into increasing prominence the one uniform and universal occasion — that of sin; and one uniform and universal purpose — that of propitiation."[12] The priesthood becomes limited to the clan of Aaron, all non-Aaronite priests having been demoted to the status of minor clergy (Ezek 44:9–16), and tithing becomes a matter of great concern (Numbers 18). Finally, in Wellhausen's view, in the fiction of the Tabernacle (*'ōhel mô'ēd*) of Moses' age, the cultic centralization and unity for which D had fought are simply assumed. With the triumph of P, Wellhausen insisted, the last trace of connection to the soil, the last trace of naturalness, has disappeared. The period of the wilderness becomes normative, as one should expect for a people uprooted in the exile of the sixth century B.C.E. "With the Babylonian captivity, the Jews lost their fixed seats, and so became a trading people."[13] The term "trading people," of some utility for aspects of medieval and modern Jewish history but of none for the biblical and the rabbinic periods, shows Wellhausen's estimation of the outcome of this long process of development. "Judaism" is Israelite religion after it has died: "When it is recognized that *the canon* is what distinguishes Judaism from ancient Israel, it is recognized at the same time that what distinguishes Judaism from ancient Israel is *the written Torah*. The water which in old times rose from a spring, the Epigoni stored up in cisterns."[14] In short, the Torah defines Judaism, and Judaism is the ghost of ancient Israel. "Yet it is a thing which is likely to occur, that a body of traditional practice should only be written down when it is threatening to die out," wrote Wellhausen in one of his most striking observations, "and that a book should be, as it were, the ghost of a life which is closed."[15] The ultimate apparition of this ghost, according to Wellhausen, was the Pharisees of Jesus' day, who were "nothing more than the Jews in the superlative"[16] — narrow, legalistic, exclusivistic, obsessive, compulsive, and hypocritical.

It has often been suggested that the major influence upon Wellhausen's three-stage evolutionary reconstruction was G. W. F. Hegel, who is thought to have interpreted world history in terms of a dialectic of thesis, antithesis, and synthesis.[17] To be sure, there is an analogy to be drawn between the two. It was, after all, Hegel who wrote of Jesus' reception by the Jews that "[h]is effort to give them the consciousness of something divine was bound to founder on the Jewish masses. For faith in something divine, in something great, cannot make its home in excrement. The lion has no room in a nest; the infinite spirit, none in the prison of a Jewish soul; the whole of life, none in a withering leaf."[18] Wellhausen simply sought to document the stages of the historical process by which so spiritual a thing as the religion of Israel came to be the ghost he called "Judaism." On the other hand, there are remarkable differences between Hegel and Wellhausen.[19] The latter's evolutionary model, for example, was degenerative, whereas the former's was one of increasing manifestation of the Spirit. Thus, Wellhausen's P (Judaism, Pharisaism) is in no sense a Hegelian synthesis of JE and D. Furthermore, the state plays no great role in Wellhausen's schema, whereas it is the manifestation of the Absolute for Hegel. But most significantly of all, Wellhausen, in point of fact, reconstructed more than the three stages that dominate the *Prolegomena.* In his *Israelitische und jüdische Geschichte,* Wellhausen treats a fourth stage, the gospel. His conclusion is, "[The gospel] preaches the most noble individualism, the freedom of the children of God."[20] For Wellhausen, of course, that freedom was the Pauline freedom from the Law, every jot and tittle of it. No wonder he described Paul as "the great pathologist of Judaism"[21] and made Rom 2:14 ("Not having the Law, they do the works of the Law by nature") the motto of part 1 to his *Prolegomena,* and Rom 5:20 ("The Law came in between") the motto of part 3, "Israel and Judaism."

The personal motivation for Wellhausen's reconstruction of Israelite history can be discerned in an uncharacteristically revealing passage in the introduction to his *Prolegomena:*

> In my student days I was attracted by the stories of Saul and David, Ahab and Elijah; the discourse of Amos and Isaiah laid strong hold on me, and I read myself well into the prophetic and historical books of the Old Testament. Thanks to such aids as were accessible to me, I even considered that I understood them tolerably, but at the same time was troubled by a bad conscience, as if I were beginning with the roof instead of the foundation; for I had no thorough acquaintance with the Law, of which I was accustomed to be told that it was the basis and postulate of the whole literature. At last I took courage and made my way through Exodus, Leviticus, Numbers. . . . But it was in vain that I looked for the light which was to be shed from this source on the historical and prophetic books. On the contrary, my enjoyment of the latter was marred by the

Law; it did not bring them any nearer to me, but intruded itself uneasily, like a ghost that makes a noise indeed, but is not visible and really effects nothing.... At last, in the course of a casual visit in Göttingen in the summer of 1867, I learned through Ritschl that Karl Heinrich Graf placed the Law later than the Prophets, and almost without knowing his reasons for the hypothesis, I was prepared to accept it; I readily acknowledged to myself the possibility of understanding Hebrew antiquity without the book of the Torah.[22]

In essence, Wellhausen tells us, the Law provoked a bad conscience in him, which ever-more attentive involvement in the Law could not assuage. The Law "makes a noise" but "effects nothing." Only the possibility that the Law is later than the rest of the Old Testament saved the book for him. Discovery of this point of chronology thus proved to be the great liberating experience of Wellhausen's intellectual life. It is fair to say that all his conceptual works on Israelite religion and Judaism are merely a footnote to that experience in the summer of 1867.

To any student of the Christian Bible, Wellhausen's autobiographical story has a familiar ring:

What follows? Is the Law identical with sin? Of course not. But except through the Law I should never have become acquainted with sin. For example, I should never have known what it was to covet, if the Law had not said, "Thou shall not covet." Through that commandment sin found its opportunity, and produced in me all kinds of wrong desires. In the absence of the Law, sin is a dead thing. There was a time, when in the absence of the Law, I was fully alive; but when the commandments came, sin sprang to life and I died. The commandment which should have led to life proved in my experience to lead to death, because sin found its opportunity in the commandment, seduced me, and through the commandment killed me. (Rom 7:7–11)[23]

In this text Paul, Wellhausen's great "pathologist of Judaism," offered a pathologist's analysis of himself as a Jew, or at least as Paul the Christian would like to reconstruct Paul the Jew, his dead self. It is not that the Torah is bad; on the contrary, Paul asserted that it is "holy" (Rom 7:12). The injunctive elements of the Torah, the commandments, however, lead only to death. They define its negative side. If the holiness and value of the Torah are to be associated with life, then means must be found to suspend the obligations that its commandments announce. In many places, Paul developed an exegesis of the Torah that he hoped would persuade his correspondents that its commandments have become dispensable. One such passage, the allegory of Gal 4:21–27, we have already examined. In Romans 4, Paul gave a kind of chronology of Torah "history" in support of the same point: since Abraham could be reckoned righteous through faith without the Mosaic Torah (Gen 15:6), which had not yet been given, then the possibility exists for others likewise to be so reckoned without the Sinaitic commandments. Paul saw the Christ event as the mechanism by which this theoretical possibility becomes real.

There are, then, essentially three stages to the sacred history of Pauline Christianity: righteousness without the Torah (Abraham), sin and death through the Torah (Moses, Sinai), and the restoration of righteousness without the Torah (participation in Christ). These correspond to the three stages of Julius Wellhausen's personal experience of the Old Testament: enjoyment of the nonlegal sections, the intrusion of the Torah or at least its most legal books (Exodus, Leviticus, Numbers), and enjoyment of the Old Testament again, with a clean conscience now that the Torah has been shown to be later in origin. In his intellectual life, Wellhausen reenacted Paul's experience, which Lutheran tradition had long taken to be autobiographical and normative.[24] Göttingen was his Damascus. For all his problems with the church over his use of the historical-critical method, Wellhausen's deepest instincts remained profoundly Lutheran.

In light of the influence of this Pauline archetype on him, Wellhausen's reconstruction of Israelite and Jewish religion becomes more readily understandable. JE was his Abraham, righteous and secure without the Torah. P was his era of the Mosaic Torah, dead and death-dealing, "pharisaical" (D is only intermediate between JE and P). Finally, the gospel was for him, as for Paul, that which liberates from toraitic tyranny, restoring the innocence of the distant past, Adam (before the Fall) or Abraham for Paul, and JE for Wellhausen. But note what Wellhausen did: he historicized Paul's exegesis. Instead of *individuals* within one book of unitary authorship, Wellhausen wrote of *historical periods*. JE and P both write on Abraham. It is not Abraham who was the ideal for Wellhausen, but the historical period of JE. Not being a fundamentalist, Wellhausen did not accept the Pauline exegesis as it stood. Instead, he converted it into historical categories, producing critical history that witnesses to the truth of salvation-history. The Torah in its entirety is no longer the norm; *it has been replaced by the historical process that produced it.* Scrutiny of that historical process discloses what is essential to the Torah and what is dispensable. What is dispensable is law, "Judaism." In short, Wellhausen decomposed the Torah into its constituent documents, reconstructed history from those components, and then endowed history with the normativity and canonicity that more traditional Protestants reserve for scripture. Biblical history replaces the Bible, but biblical history still demonstrates the validity of the biblical (i.e., Pauline) economy of salvation and thus serves to preserve the literary context of the Hebrew Bible. Its conjunction to the New Testament as volume 1 of the Christian Bible is logical after all. The historical context replaces the literary context, but without casting into doubt the anti-Judaic and antitoraitic thrust of Pauline-Lutheran theology. The Hebrew Bible remains only an "Old Testament."

• IV •

Wellhausen's *Prolegomena* appeared at the last moment at which its method and its conclusions could have seemed sound. To be sure, the Documentary Hypothesis, upon which so much of it is based, retains the support of the overwhelming majority of critical scholars, whatever the religious communities from which they hail. And many of the details of his reconstruction, such as those involving the centralization of the cult and the evolution of the calendar, remain, for the most part, a matter of consensus. But already in the decades following the publication of the *Prolegomena* in 1878, archaeological excavations produced an exponential growth in our knowledge of the biblical world, much of it as lethal to Wellhausen's reconstructed evolution as it is to the traditionalist's cherished belief in the uniqueness of Israel.[25] In our century, any critical scholar who wishes to address the religion of biblical Israel must treat the cultures of its neighbors as well. There are now far more materials available for a description of the ancient Near Eastern world than was the case when the *Prolegomena* appeared in 1878. For Wellhausen, no choice between historical description and normative theology was necessary, since he thought history showed a development toward the theological affirmation that claimed his allegiance, the anomian individualism that he considered to be the essence of Christianity. In this century, however, the relationship between historical description ("was") and normative theology ("ought to be") has become a pressing problem. Among students of the Bible, only fundamentalists, who do not think historically, and those critical scholars who lack religious commitment will fail to feel its claim.

In 1933, Walther Eichrodt, Professor of Old Testament and History of Religion at the University of Basel, Switzerland, published his *Theologie des Alten Testaments* with the announced determination to break "the tyranny of historicism in OT studies." Eichrodt wrote that there was only one way to "succeed in winning back for OT studies in general and for OT theology in particular that place in Christian theology which at present has been surrendered to the comparative study of religions." This could be accomplished "*by examining on the one hand [the OT's] religious environment and on the other its essential coherence with the NT. . . . The only way to do this is to have the historical principle operating side by side with the systematic in a complementary role.*"[26] Herein lay an admirable intention to navigate between the Scylla of fundamentalism and the Charybdis of positivism, in the hope of producing a religious affirmation that is historically accurate and intellectually honest. Eichrodt's goal was to combine the historical context of the Hebrew Bible ("its religious environment") and its literary context in Christianity ("its essential coherence with the NT").

The unmistakable implication of Eichrodt's methodological program is that the historical and the systematic principles only work in tandem and never at cross purposes. A historical inquiry into the "religious environment" of the Old Testament that casts doubt upon "its essential coherence" with the New must be disallowed. The consequence of this for Judaism is no less clear: the postbiblical Jewish tradition is a denial of the religious message of the Hebrew Bible not only according to the claims of Christian faith, as one would expect, but even according to the results of historical investigation.

If, in fact, the Hebrew Bible speaks univocally in favor of its Christian recontextualization, it is a great historical conundrum why the Jewish tradition endured at all. How could a people have so thoroughly missed the point of its own scriptures? Conversely, if the Hebrew Bible points univocally to rabbinic Judaism, it is puzzling that there ever should have been — and still remain — nonrabbinic traditions (including Christianity) that, in various ways and degrees, also lay claim to the Hebrew Bible. In sum, the historical evidence suggests that the Hebrew Bible speaks less univocally than Eichrodt thinks: it is to some degree coherent and to some degree incoherent with *all* its recontextualizations — Jewish, Christian, and other. The privileging of one of these over the others depends on something very different from dispassionate historical inquiry. It depends upon something more akin to an act of faith. This is not to impugn the act of faith, but only to say that it is highly problematic when it becomes regulative for historical study.

The lack of univocality in the Hebrew Bible is nicely illustrated by an analysis of the familiar words of John 3:16: "God so loved the world that he gave his only son so that everyone who has faith in him may not die, but have eternal life." This passage and others like it in the New Testament build rather obviously on texts in the Hebrew Bible, the only Bible the authors of what became the New Testament knew and recognized. The idea that God has a son can be found, for example, in Ps 2:7, in which YHWH tells his viceroy enthroned on Zion that "[y]ou are my son; this day I have begotten you." The idea that a father must give over his firstborn son appears in Exod 22:28, and the verse that follows is powerful evidence that the "giving" in question refers to sacrifice (v. 29). That the father should give his son over for sacrifice out of motives of *love* is familiar from the story of the binding of Isaac in Gen 22:1–19, in which Abraham is commended and the promise to him renewed precisely because of his exemplary willingness to sacrifice Isaac, his beloved son (vv. 2, 15–18).[27]

This brief analysis of the ancient Israelite background of John 3:16 supports Eichrodt's conviction that the Hebrew Bible stands in "essential coherence" with the New Testament. That with which Eichrodt's claim does not reckon is the element of incompatibility between the messages of the two books. Texts that imply the sonship, biological or adoptive, of the human king are exceedingly rare in the Hebrew Bible and in tension with a thoroughly nonmythological, instrumental concept of monarchy, evident, for example, in Deuteronomic tradition (e.g., Deut 17:14–20; 28:36; 1 Sam 8:10–22). The concept is also in tension with the pointed assertion of the fundamental difference between human beings and God that one finds in several passages (e.g., 1 Sam 15:29; Hos 11:9). Indeed, the concept of a human being who stands in descent from a god is conspicuous for its absence in the Hebrew Bible. It is, in fact, an idea that seems to have had a much clearer way among Canaanites and Egyptians, for example, than among Israelites.[28] It is striking that in the Hebrew Bible, YHWH has no children at all (except metaphorically, as in Deut 14:1), no parents, and no wife (except, again, metaphorically, as in Hosea 1–3). The assumption that giving him a divine son would in no way compromise the essential message of the Hebrew Bible is very much open to doubt. The doubt grows exponentially when, as in orthodox Christianity, the divinity of the son is so emphatically affirmed that prayer can be addressed to and through him.

The idea that God would sacrifice his son, even out of love for the world, is equally problematic. Despite the few texts in the Hebrew Bible that speak positively of child-sacrifice, biblical law explicitly prohibits the practice in its various forms (e.g., Exod 13:13; 34:20; Lev 20:2–5), and prophets vehemently condemn it as incompatible with the worship of YHWH and emblematic of idolatry (e.g., Jer 7:31; Ezek 16:20–21). In this, biblical law and prophecy stand in marked contradiction to the cult of the Canaanite god El, in which the sacrifice of children seems to have had an important place. Indeed, a Phoenician source tells us of El's own sacrifice of two of his sons, Yadid and Mot, and in Ugaritic myth, the divine father El hands over the younger god Baal for bondage but also, in another text, rejoices when Baal is raised from the dead.[29]

All this demonstrates that the Christian affirmation in John 3:16 not only stands in continuity with the Hebrew Bible, as Eichrodt's method presumes and requires; it also stands in *discontinuity* with the same book and with the ongoing Jewish tradition that also regards that book as sacred scripture. The greatest of Eichrodt's failures is not that he cannot do justice to Judaism, but that he cannot do justice to the theological diversity of that most unsystematic book, the Hebrew Bible. By treating that volume as an "Old Testament," Eichrodt's method forces him to focus only on its continuities with Christianity and prevents him from fulfilling the historian's task of listening to the multiple voices of the text itself.

The thematic continuity that Eichrodt developed was based on the notion of "covenant." Whatever other weaknesses this idea has, it again raises the possibility that the Jews are at least as much the heirs of the Old Testament as the church and perhaps even more so. For whereas Christian theology has generally held that the stipulations of covenant were, to one degree or another, made void through Christ, Judaism retains those stipulations (*mitsvot*) and rests more structural weight upon covenant than does Christianity.[30] Or, to put it differently, to the extent that "covenant" survives as a meaningful term in Christianity, it does so without the specificity and concreteness of *mitsvot,* upon whose observance almost every book of the Hebrew Bible insists. To avoid conceding defeat by the Jews, Christian covenant theologians must do one of three things: (1) they must reassert the classic New Testament claim that covenant does not require observance (i.e., that, in good Pauline fashion, the Mosaic/Sinaitic dimension is actually dispensable); (2) they must show that the Jews have perverted the covenant faith of their ancestors, so that Judaism is *more* discontinuous with the religion of Israel than Christianity (another New Testament theme, found especially in Hebrews); or (3) they must develop a dual covenant theology, that is, a position that somehow upholds the covenantal status of the people Israel and of the church equally. This last option, though approximated by a few of Eichrodt's contemporaries, is of the three the least consonant with traditional Christian theology. It is thus hardly surprising that Eichrodt chose only the first two possibilities. His effort to substantiate the second of our three theoretical options is particularly problematic but also particularly revealing of his method. Judaism, he said, has only "a torso-like appearance . . . in separation from Christianity."[31] "It was not," he wrote, "until in later Judaism a religion of harsh observances had replaced the religion of the Old Testament that the Sabbath changed from a blessing to a burdensome duty."[32] It is in the Mishnah (promulgated ca. 200 C.E.) that "real worship of God [was] stifled under the heaping up of detailed commands from which the spirit has fled."[33] In Judaism, he informed his readers, "the living fellowship between God and man . . . shrivelled up into a mere correct observance of the legal regulations."[34] In short, in Judaism "the affirmation of the law as the revelation of God's personal will was lost."[35]

In making these statements, Eichrodt capitulated in toto to the pole of his method defined by the New Testament; critical historiography did not inform him here at all. He accepted New Testament caricatures, stereotypes, and outright perversions of Judaism in the same manner as would the most unlettered fundamentalist. For example, what literary source in "later Judaism" (by which he means early Judaism) ever saw the Sabbath as "a burdensome duty" rather than a blessing? Volumes are spoken by Eichrodt's silence about the numerous passages in the Talmud and Midrash that describe the Sabbath as a pearl, as Israel's bride, or the like (e.g., *Ber. Rab.* 11:8; *Shocher Tov* 92:1). The likelihood is that he did not know they existed and had no interest in learning what spiritual treasure, what wealth of love, joy, camaraderie, and spiritual reflection, the observant Jew found (and finds) in the Sabbath.[36] Christian anti-Jewish polemics were so much more readily at hand and, especially in the Germanophone world of 1933, so much more readily accepted. Eichrodt's idea that the personal will of a gracious God fell out beneath rabbinic legalism fares no better. It cannot survive a confrontation with the numerous rabbinic sayings that present observance of *mitsvot* as a response to God's grace (e.g., *Mek. Bachodesh* 5).

In one instance, however, Eichrodt did cite a rabbinic text in support of his antirabbinic theology:

This means that for the heathen, being sinners without the Law, the only real possibility is God's punitive righteousness; and this state of affairs is not altered by Aqiba's fine saying: "The world is judged by the measure of God's mercy."[37]

Eichrodt's footnote to this quotation from the Mishnah reads:

Pirqe Aboth 3.16. The continuation, "and everything is done according to the multitude of works" proves conclusively that here, as in Wisd. 12.15, the only idea is one of resignation in the face of resistless and overwhelming Omnipotence.[38]

An examination of the complete tannaitic dictum shows that Eichrodt simply did not understand Rabbi Aqiba's point:

All is foreseen, but freedom of choice is given. In goodness the world is judged, but all is according to the amount of work.

So far as I can determine, the Jewish tradition has always understood the last word of Rabbi Aqiba's dictum as a reference to human efforts, not God's action. In other words, Rabbi Aqiba (d. 135 C.E.) here states two paradoxes — the coexistence of divine providence and human free will, and the importance of both divine grace and human effort in God's judgment of the world. Works are neither sufficient nor dispensable; they are essential but ultimately inadequate. The point is one that a Calvinist theologian should be expected to understand immediately. But for Eichrodt to have understood it and to have rendered it accurately would have been to forfeit his argument that the Jews lost sight of the nature of the divine-human relationship, substituting a legalistic works-righteousness for the more paradoxical and nuanced biblical stance. And to forfeit that argument would have been to forfeit the claim that historical-critical scholarship is compatible with the Christian tenet that the Hebrew Bible is *best* approached when it is within the same covers as the New Testament, that the Hebrew Bible, examined historically, speaks univocally in favor of its Christian recontextualization.

Our examination of the theology of Walther Eichrodt shows that his anti-Judaic remarks were not incidental to his theological method. They were owing not simply to social prejudice, but to his intention to show that the covenantal religion of ancient Israel is of a piece with Christianity. His willingness to accept traditional Christian slurs at face value both contributed to and was influenced by his apparent inability to read the rabbinic sources. In this, he resembled Wellhausen, who confessed his lack of knowledge of Jewish literature, especially the Talmud, and his consequent dependence on Greek sources,[39] but did not allow this handicap to prevent him from presenting a very negative picture of Judaism throughout his career. The disastrous effects on both Wellhausen and Eichrodt of ignorance of literature in postbiblical Hebrew underscore a truism that much of the scholarly world still evades: one cannot be a competent scholar of the Christian Bible without a solid command of rabbinic literature and rabbinic Hebrew (and Aramaic). Hebrew did not die on the cross.

· **V** ·

If Eichrodt's assertion that the same theme dominates each half of the Christian Bible is unlikely, even the lesser claim of thematic unity throughout the Old Testament has proven problematic. This search for the unity (or the center) of biblical theology is, in a sense, reactionary: it aims to diminish the impression historical criticism leaves that, at least with respect to the Bible, Heraclitus's dictum is correct — "everything flows." For, approached historical-critically, biblical theology seems to be like Heraclitus's river: one cannot step into the same one twice. A less reactionary response is to be found in the work of Gerhard von Rad, especially in his *Theologie des Alten Testaments,* first published in 1957. Making a virtue of necessity, von Rad saw the reappropriation and reinterpretation of the legacy of tradition as a precious theological asset. Behind that reinterpretation lay a continuing history of salvation (*Heilsgeschichte*), at the onset of which was a promise for which "there was, oddly enough, never any satisfactory historical fulfillment and consummation." Therefore, "the Old Testament can only be read as a book of ever increasing anticipation."[40] The fluctuation of tradition is to be seen theologically as Israel's effort to keep that promise and the hope for its fulfillment alive. For example, the Yahwist (J) has reinterpreted the promise of land to the Patriarchs as a reference to the conquest under Joshua generations later (Gen 15:13–15).[41] And the great anonymous prophet of the exile, writing when the promise of grace to the House of David seemed to have been voided, reinterpreted "the sure grace to David" as applying to the entire people Israel (Isa 55:1–7).[42] Thus could the Davidic covenant be saved at a time when the messiah was seen not in a scion of David, but in the Iranian liberator, Cyrus (Isa 44:24–45:3). If Old Testament theology recognized this process of recontextualization and reinterpretation of the promise (which, despite the changes, remains valid), then in von Rad's words, "[T]he material itself would bear it from one actualization to another, and in the end would pose the question of the final fulfillment."[43] For him, of course, this final fulfillment was Jesus as the Christ. The difference, for example, between Israelite messianism and New Testament Christology therefore need not be denied or minimized. The New Testament simply continues the traditionary process of the Old, which was itself always in flux. Thus could von Rad, on grounds very different from Eichrodt's, oppose, like him, those who take "the Old Testament in abstraction as an object which can be adequately interpreted without reference to the New Testament."[44]

Von Rad's method allowed the texts of the Hebrew Bible to speak more in their own voices than did the historicism of Wellhausen or the dogmatism of Eichrodt. His ear was more finely attuned to the plurality of notes sounded in the Hebrew Bible, and his mind was, relative to theirs, less inclined to force external schemes onto the texts themselves. The fact remains, however, that von Rad's effort to preserve the bifurcated Bible of Christianity without deviation from historical criticism was deeply flawed. Brevard Childs is surely right that

> a major problem with von Rad's *Old Testament Theology* is that he has failed to deal with the canonical forces at work in the formation of the traditions into a collection of Scripture during the post-exilic period, but rather set up the New Testament's relation to the Old in an analogy to his description of the pre-exilic growth of Hebrew tradition.[45]

In other words, already by the time of the New Testament documents, Israelite tradition had developed a strong notion of sacred scripture. The claim of the primitive church was not that its gospel was yet another link in an ongoing chain of tradition, but that it was *the* fulfillment of canonical writ. Von Rad thus preserved the bifurcated Bible by destroying the bifurcation. The New Testament is only the continuation of the Old. But if tradition in the sense of recontextualization is what legitimates the more recent past and binds it to distant antiquity, then von Rad's exclusive focus on the Christian continuations is unwarranted. Why did he not consider rabbinic tradition, which, especially in the form of midrash, also recontextualized the Hebrew Bible, often strikingly? Why, in short, is the Israelite past to be seen only in light of the early church, the Hebrew Bible only as an "Old Testament"? At times von Rad seemed to answer this in the same way Wellhausen and Eichrodt did, through the disparagement of Judaism, as when he wrote that:

> The end was reached at the point where the law became an absolute quantity, that is, when it ceased to be understood as the saving ordinance of a special racial group (the cultic community of Israel) linked to it by the facts of history, and when it stepped out of this function of service and became a dictate which imperiously called into being its own community.[46]

But, in general, he seems to have been oblivious to the question, perhaps because as a Christian theologian in the *judenrein* Germany of the post-Holocaust era, he had no one to raise it with him. Like Hegel, Wellhausen, and Eichrodt, he simply assumed the spiritual necrosis of Judaism after Jesus. After "the end was reached," why consider the Jews?

The finality that von Rad attributed to the New Testament is in contradiction to his resolute emphasis on the ongoing nature of tradition. Apparently, he expected us to respect the continuousness of history up to and perhaps including the experience of the apostolic church, but then to make a leap of faith that would deny the continuousness and ongoing nature of all subsequent history. All fulfillments before Jesus are to be seen as provisional. Jesus is to be seen as final and unsurpassable. But must not historical criticism point out that history also passed up Jesus, if, that is, we are to believe he really said what the New Testament evangelists attribute to him? His prediction that the kingdom would come within the generation (Mark 9:1), for example, proved false, forcing his later followers to devise extenuations and explanations, which are themselves recontextualizations.[47] In fact, the entire history of Christian theology can be seen as testimony to the provisional character of the New Testament and its putative "fulfillments." History continues, and for Christians who read their tradition in light of Nicea, Aquinas, Luther, Trent, or Vatican I and II, the New Testament has itself long been an "Old Testament," in need of reinterpretation and supplementation. *No* statement is final because, whatever apocalypticists may say, history continues. Indeed, if we are to assume the validity of recontextualization, why stop with Judaism and Christianity? Islam, after all, claims to have superseded the church in a way not altogether different from the way the church claims to have superseded the Jews: Jesus becomes a link in the chain of prophets that culminated in Muhammad (the supersessionists superseded!). Von Rad would probably claim, in rebuttal, that the ultimate fulfillment in Christ is known only through faith; the critical historian can never see it. But in that case, he would have conceded that a historical-critical examination of the religion of the Hebrew Bible does *not* point to Jesus Christ and that the unity of the Christian Bible cannot be demonstrated by tradition-history after all.

Von Rad, in sum, seems to have wanted to move from the Hebrew Bible to the New Testament by means of certain methods that, whether accurately applied or not, are fully in accord with historical criticism. Having done so, he then wishes to suspend those methods and to introduce an act of faith in the consummative finality of Jesus. It is this anticritical act of faith that distinguishes the "biblical theologian," in von Rad's terminology, from the "historian of the religion of Israel."[48] When the radical implications of historical criticism got close to home and began threatening the unity and sufficiency of the Christian Bible, von Rad reverted to a position formally indistinct from fundamentalism. He expected faith to stop Heraclitus's river.

At first glance, von Rad's emphasis upon tradition at the expense of canonical scripture seems strange in a Lutheran theologian. Was it not the Protestant Reformers who asserted that all church tradition must be scrutinized according to the norm *sola scriptura,* "by scripture alone"? At the point when scripture is shown to be the product of tradition, it surely becomes more difficult to assert the sovereignty of the scripture *over* the tradition, as the Reformation generally sought to do.[49] On the other hand, von Rad's assumption that traditions, as recovered by form criticism, are the fundamental units to be interpreted does serve one traditional Lutheran goal, the polarization of grace and law. In an early programmatic essay,[50] von Rad argued that beneath the earliest documents of the Hexateuch (Genesis to Joshua) lay two sets of traditions. One, connected with the Festival of Booths, centered on the experience at Sinai and the proclamation of cultic law. The other, connected with Pentecost, was the tradition of the settlement in the land, a tradition in which the exodus was of prime import. Thus, originally, one could narrate the story of descent into Egypt, enslavement, liberation, and the assumption of the land without any mention of the revelation at Sinai. Von Rad thought that texts such as Deut 26:5b–9, Josh 24:2–13, and 1 Sam 12:8, which omit all reference to the Sinaitic experience, bore out his claim. Of course, many texts witness to the merger of the two sets of traditions (e.g., Nehemiah 9 and Psalm 106). In von Rad's mind, that merger, that "incorporation of the Sinai tradition into the Settlement tradition should be attributed to the Yahwist" (J). "The blending of the two traditions," he concluded, "gives definition of the two fundamental propositions of the whole message of the Bible: Law and Gospel."[51] Thus, through a very different method from Wellhausen's, von Rad, like him, was able to reverse the canonical merger of "Law and Gospel" (assuming he was right that they were once separate) and thus to cast doubt upon the theology of those traditions in which they were not dichotomized or even differentiated. On the basis of this, von Rad could then replicate the classic Pauline subordination of norm to soteriology. Once again, a historical method — this time, form criticism — has been employed to decompose the received text and to reorder it according to the needs of Christian theology. This use of historical criticism has proven to be the most important in Old Testament theology, for it enables the theologian to find meanings in the book that the *textus receptus* does not suggest. The retrieved past (the Hebrew Bible) can thus be rapidly assimilated to the familiar present (the Old Testament). The man can repress the child within and go about his business as if nothing has changed.

The same *Tendenz* can be seen in von Rad's teacher, Albrecht Alt, a form critic for whom the problematics of contemporary theological affirmation were not a central concern. This makes it all the more revealing that Alt's historical reconstructions move in the direction of the same Christian theology that we have detected in the works of Wellhausen, Eichrodt, and von Rad. Alt found that biblical law separates into two broad categories, "casuistic" and "apodeictic." Casuistic law is case-law, characteristically phrased in the form: "if a man . . . then . . . "; it specifies crimes and punishments. Apodeictic law tends to be phrased in the imperative; it takes the form of a personal command and omits any mention of sanctions. Alt's discovery was that the distinction is not simply formal, but substantive as well. Casuistic law tends to be secular, whereas apodeictic law (e.g., the Decalogue) is sacral. Casuistic law is general in the ancient Near East (Alt thought it a borrowing from the Canaanites), whereas apodeictic law is native to Israel and reflects the unique character of YHWH. Ultimately, according to Alt, the apodeictic law expanded at the expense of the casuistic. It "pursues the Israelite out of the sanctuary of [YHWH] into his daily life, and inevitably clashed with the carefully itemized instances and exceptions of the casuistic law."[52] Essentially the same dichotomy appeared in America in the work of George E. Mendenhall, only under the rubrics of "law" and "covenant." Two decades ago, Mendenhall published an essay in which he argued that these two stand in a contrastive relationship.

Law, for example, "presupposes a social order," whereas covenant is based on "gratitude." Law is "binding upon each individual by virtue of his status . . . usually by birth," but covenant comes "by voluntary act in which each individual willingly accepts the obligations presented," and so on.[53]

A full critique of these theories of von Rad, Alt, and Mendenhall lies outside the purview of our discussion.[54] Each has been challenged or severely qualified. What is of interest here is that each comes to a position that is in profound harmony with a crucial point in the Pauline-Lutheran understanding of the Torah: one can inherit the promise to Abraham and the status of his lineage without "the Law." Von Rad is the most explicit and probably the most self-conscious: he openly uses the terms "Law and Gospel" and defines them as "the two most fundamental propositions of the whole . . . Bible." Obviously, the last word refers to the twofold Bible of Christianity. What von Rad attempted to show was that this Christian dichotomy, ostensibly so alien to the thought-world of the Hebrew Bible, is, in point of fact, basic to the evolution of that set of documents.[55] Alt, despite his less explicit involvement in theological tradition, makes essentially the same point. Is it coincidence that Jesus (so far as we know) spoke only apodeicticly and bequeathed no case-law? To one who stands in the Christian tradition, it is surely of use to argue that case-law was always foreign and secular — that is, religiously inessential: what Paul abolished was always dispensable, so much cultural baggage from the environment (actually, a point that Paul himself would not have accepted). Mendenhall's dichotomy of law and covenant makes the same point. "Law" here sounds very much like the same term in Paul, for whom it is an agent of death, now happily super-seded. Law, unlike covenant, for example, is usually a matter of birth for Mendenhall (cf. Rom 9:6–8). Christians, however, sought to retain the term "covenant," applying to themselves the prophecy of a "new covenant" (Jer 31:31), which they interpreted as anomian, a covenant without law (Heb 8:6–13). Thus, it is no surprise to find most Old Testament theologians as much in favor of covenant as they are against Torah or "law." This is credible only when law and covenant can be made into contrasts.[56]

The claim that there was a time, before the composition of the canonical Pentateuch (or Hexateuch), when Israel could tell its story without the intrusion of law is simply a form-critical analogue to Paul's argument in Galatians 3 that Abraham was justified through faith with-out the Law, which came fully 430 years later, in the generation of

Moses (v. 17). Aspects of the theory are older than Paul. Martin Hengel points out the Hellenistic writer Posidonius (ca. 135–50 B.C.E.) claimed "that the good and simple legislation of Moses had been falsified at a later period by superstitious and forceful priests who by separatist regulations had changed the simple and truthful worship of God intended by the founder into something quite different."[57] It has been suggested that this theory influenced the Jewish Hellenizers of Seleucid times and even that Paul may have been their heir.[58] If so, then this Hellenizing trend, with its eagerness to suspend the *mitsvot,* has been preserved for two millennia through the triumph of Pauline Christianity, and the process of its intellectual self-justification continues in the stepchild of the church, biblical criticism. The great vulnerability, however, of those who wish to pursue this line of self-justification through the study of the Hebrew Bible is that the hypothetical two themes — law and gospel, casuistic and apodeictic law, law and covenant — have been woven together so thoroughly that their separation can be effected only through the wholesale dismantling of the canonical literature. For nothing is more characteristic of the biblical law codes than the meshing of casuistic and apodeictic law. In fact, the Pentateuch endows *all* its laws with the status of personal commandments from God by reading them into the revelation through Moses on Mount Sinai: law and covenant are one. It is here that the techniques of von Rad, Alt, and Mendenhall become useful for Christian apologetics, for these techniques allow the scholar to penetrate back to a putative era that supports the Christian dichotomy, whereas the canonical shape of the literature only casts doubt upon it. Like Wellhausen, those scholars are really engaging in reconstructive surgery, whose purpose is to produce an "Old Testament" in place of the Hebrew Bible, to use *historical-critical methods* to validate the *literary context* that is the Christian Bible. Such surgery becomes all the more essential to the Christian historical critics when they discover that this characteristic interlacing of norm and narrative continues in the Talmud and Midrash, where halakhah and aggadah alternate uneventfully, a fact that raises the alarming possibility that the Jews are indeed rightful heirs to the Hebrew Bible and that the Christian tradition of supersessionism, as old as the New Testament itself, is inconsonant with the Hebrew Bible. It is no coincidence that the dispossession of the Jews has been an important motive force behind much of the study of "biblical theology."[59]

• VI •

I have argued that the essential challenge of historical criticism to book-religions lies in its development of a context of interpretation, the *historical* context, which is different from the *literary* (or *canonical*) contexts that underlie Judaism and Christianity, in their different ways. In one fashion or another, these religions presuppose the coherence and self-referentiality of their foundational book. These things are what make it possible to derive a coherent religion, *one* religion (one's own), from the Book. Historical critics who are uncompromisingly honest, by contrast, exploit the inconcinnities and the discontinuities as part of their effort to decompose the Book into its multiple strata in order to reconstruct the history that redaction has repressed. It is not surprising, to resume our psychoanalytic metaphor, that the recovery of repressed material should meet with "resistance," in this case, the angry salvos of fundamentalists. What is surprising, however, is that so many religious traditionalists who plight their troth to historical criticism insist that their work only *enriches* and never *undermines* their religious identity, as if the fundamentalists (who are, incidentally, far more numerous) are simply silly. What makes this optimism possible is the use of historical-critical methods in defense of only the traditional canon and its underlying theology. In the case of the five scholars discussed — Wellhausen, Eichrodt, von Rad, Alt, and Mendenhall — the Hebrew Bible is analyzed in ways that reinforce its status as the "Old Testament" (itself an ahistorical or anachronistic term) and that defuse the threat that historical criticism poses to Christian supersessionism.

If this is the case, then these historical studies play for their Christian authors much the same role that midrash played for the classical rabbis: like the midrashim that we examined in section 1, this kind of historical inquiry serves to harmonize discordant texts. This time the texts are not, as there, the differing Passover laws of Exodus 12 and Deuteronomy 16, but Leviticus and Galatians, for example, or Deuteronomy and Romans. For Christian Old Testament scholars who wish their work to be *Christian* and not simply historically accurate, the urge to harmonize arises, as it did for the rabbis, from the conviction that the sacred text is ultimately a unity, that all those seemingly diverse passages belong in the same book after all. The differences must be shown to be complementary or in dialectical tension; no outright contradictions may be allowed to stand. For if they do stand, then it will be apparent that Christianity attempts to keep the scriptures of at least two different religions in its bifurcated Bible, and the Christian Bible will cease to give a univocal endorsement to Christianity. The endurance and vigor of Judaism should always have cast doubt upon the claim of univocality, but, as we have seen, the dominant Christian theological tradition, practiced by ostensible historical critics no less than by fundamentalists, has, in the past, blindfolded itself to that vigor and clung religiously to the old defamations. The aspersions so often cast upon Judaism in the "Old Testament theologies" and related works are thus not incidental. They are indispensable to the larger hermeneutical purpose of neutralizing historical criticism from within.

Most Christians involved in the historical criticism of the Hebrew Bible today, however, seem to have ceased to want their work to be considered distinctively Christian. They do the essential philological, historical, and archaeological work without concern for the larger constructive issues or for the theological implications of their labors. They are Christians everywhere except in the classroom and at the writing table, where they are simply honest historians striving for an unbiased view of the past. Even in the world of Old Testament theology, however, there has grown over the last twenty years or so considerable awareness that the historical-critical enterprise is in tension with the demands of Christian proclamation. One thinks of Friedrich Baumgärtel's argument that "we cannot eliminate the fact, derived from the history of religion, that the Old Testament is a witness out of a non-Christian religion."[60] A. H. J. Gunneweg has drawn the hermeneutical implication: "But it is impossible to give a Christian interpretation of something that is not Christian; Christian interpretation of something that is not Christian is pseudo-interpretation."[61] With these two sentences, Gunneweg has pronounced judgment on two millennia of biblical studies in a distinctively Christian mode. He has fired a torpedo into the prediction-fulfillment schema of the Gospels; into Paul's allegories and all their patristic, medieval, and Reformation kin; into Wellhausen's historicism, Eichrodt's and Mendenhall's anomian covenantalism, and von Rad's salvation-history; and into much else. For all these efforts to make a Christian use of the Hebrew Bible commit the greatest sin known to the historical-critical method, the sin of anachronism. If they are to survive, they must find a defensible mode of reasoning other than historical-critical analysis.

The Jew who may be inclined to enjoy the thought that historical criticism may at long last be about to liberate the Hebrew Bible from the New Testament had best observe the admonition of Prov 24:17–18.

Indeed, the wrath of historical criticism has already fallen upon Judaism and not only upon the church. No critical scholar of the Hebrew Bible believes in its *historical* unity or in the *historical* unity even of the Pentateuch. If Leviticus and Galatians cannot be accommodated in one religion, then neither, perhaps, can Exodus and Deuteronomy, and certainly Isaiah and Qohelet cannot. Jews need their harmonistic midrash no less than Christians need theirs, for it is midrash that knits the tangled skein of passages into a religiously usable "text" (from Latin, *texo*, "to weave") and continues the redactional process beyond the point of the finalization of the text. The pulverizing effects of the historical-critical method do not respect the boundaries of religions: the method dismembers *all* midrashic systems, reversing tradition. Rigorous historical critics are no more likely to accept a rabbinic interpretation of literature that is not rabbinic or a Deuteronomic interpretation of literature that is not Deuteronomic than they are to accept a Christian interpretation of literature that is not Christian. All religious use of past literature is, to some extent, at cross-purposes with historical criticism, if only because the world of the contemporary religious person is not the world of the author. It is a world into which the author's work arrives only after it has been recontextualized through redaction, canonization, and other forms of tradition. Without these recontextualizations it is unavailable. The matrix in which the ancient text speaks to the contemporary community is this larger, anachronizing context. To be sure, historical-critical and traditional religious study are not always mutually exclusive. They may, in fact, cross-fertilize or check each other. But it is naive to expect the historical-critical study of the Book only to serve and never to undermine traditional religious purposes, whether the Jewish *mitsvah* of *talmûd tôrâ* (the central obligation of Torah study) or Christian kerygmatic proclamation. Both sacred and profane modes of study have value and meaning, but they must not be collapsed one into the other.

Two factors account for the remarkable endurance of the tendency to collapse or muddle contexts of interpretation. First, the motivation of most historical critics of the Hebrew Bible continues to be religious in character. It is a rare scholar in the field whose past does not include an intense Christian or Jewish commitment. That commitment brings scholars to the subject, but the character of the method with which they pursue it has less in common with the religious traditions than with the Enlightenment critique of them. The incongruity of the motivation and the methods is seldom acknowledged. It is more convenient to maintain an expectation that somehow the historical-critical method will, in the last analysis, *only* vindicate, purify, and enrich the original religious motivation.

The second factor is simply the institutional correlative of the first. It is that most of the critical scholarship in Hebrew Bible is still placed in Christian theological schools. Indeed, were it not for the religious connection, the field would be no more prominent in Christendom than are most other studies of ancient Western Asiatic cultures. But the religiousness of this location sets up a continuing expectation that, in principle, this nontraditional, nontheistic method will serve traditional theistic goals, such as Christian ministry. The dissonance caused by the placement of Hebrew Bible in Christian contexts is a profound inducement for the creation of a mediating myth that will mask the contradiction. Each of the five scholars whose work we have examined aided profoundly in this myth-making enterprise. Indeed, as I shall argue in chapter 2, the field known as "Old Testament theology," in which Eichrodt's and von Rad's works are classic, is marked by a profound ambivalence as to whether the endeavor is a branch of Christian theology or not. The nearly universal tendency is to have it both ways: Old Testament theology is to be both historical and Christian. Acknowledgment of the survival and vibrancy of Judaism would be difficult to harmonize with this belief in a *historically* responsible *Christian* exegesis of a non-Christian set of books, for, if nothing else, the Jewish presence would serve to relativize the Christian reading and to suggest that it is particularistic and confessional and not simply some self-evident "plain sense" that accords with the ancient Israelite author's intentions. The anxiety that this possibility produces accounts, in part, for the traditional eagerness of Old Testament theologians to negate postbiblical Judaism: out of sight, out of mind. The relativistic implications of the multicontextuality of its sacred book are difficult, and perhaps impossible, for any religion to accept.[62] In the case of Christianity, however, a long-standing tendency to conceive of itself as universal and of Judaism as particularistic makes the evidence for its own particularism more painful to embrace. The path of least resistance has been to suppose that the Christian context subsumes all others.

The emergence and increasing prominence in recent years of scholars and academic departments that are not committed to any religious perspective have inflicted grave damage upon the status of Christian theology as the ruling paradigm in biblical studies. The explosion in knowledge of the ancient Near East has shifted the focus of many advanced programs in Hebrew Bible from theology to philology and archaeology. As we saw in our discussion of Eichrodt, the hope that the new focus would only complement the old one bore little or no good fruit. In North America, the emergence of religion departments and Jewish studies programs and departments has further contributed to the dethronement of Christian theology, indeed *any* theology, as the organizing paradigm for the study of the Hebrew Bible. As a consequence, in the elite academic world, those for whom the term "Old Testament" is more than vestigial have been put into the unenviable position of an ex-emperor who now must learn how to be a good neighbor. As of yet, no new emperor has assumed the throne. Given the social mix and the methodological diversity that are both increasingly characteristic of the field, the throne is likely to be vacant for a long time. Whether the result will be liberty or anarchy remains to be seen.

Chapter 2

———— • ————

Why Jews Are Not Interested
in Biblical Theology

• I •

Soon after I began teaching I received a revealing phone call from a colleague in another institution. The caller was teaching "Introduction to the Old Testament," a course for both divinity school and liberal arts students. Among the latter was a Jew upset at what he perceived to be the Christian bias of the bibliography. Eager to be evenhanded, the professor called me to find out what Jewish scholar had written the best "biblical theology." My hesitation in answering was surely sufficient to call into doubt my colleague's confidence in my competence. Finally, I stammered out the names of a few serviceable works concerned with biblical concepts and authored by committed Jews, such as Yehezkel Kaufmann (*The Religion of Israel*) and Nahum Sarna (*Understanding Genesis*).[1] The caller thanked me, but I remember thinking as I hung up that he ought to feel disappointed, for what he was hoping to get from me was the title of the Jewish equivalent of Walther Eichrodt's *Theology of the Old Testament* or Gerhard von Rad's *Old Testament Theology*.[2] And for reasons that I shall explore in this essay, there is no Jewish equivalent.

I had occasion to recall this little incident several years later, as I sat in a Protestant seminary listening to a distinguished continental biblicist lecture on Old Testament theology. At the end of his talk, he remarked that in a year of research in Israel, he had been unable to find anyone interested in the subject. Finally, he had asked a member of the Bible

33

department at the Hebrew University of Jerusalem about this curious situation, and the latter, a man known for his keen theological interests, replied that he thought no one in Israel, presumably including himself, had any interest in the whole exercise. The lecturer was visibly perplexed as he told this story. Sophisticated Israeli biblicists uninterested in Old Testament theology? It made no sense. In the end, he shrugged his shoulders in a gesture of mingled disbelief and resignation.

The expectation of these Christian scholars was not unreasonable. Whereas for centuries the field of biblical studies was divided along religious and even denominational lines — with little respect and less communication between groups — today the field, at least in North America, boasts a vibrant ecumenicity. Collaboration in biblical work among Jews, Catholics, Protestants, and secularists no longer elicits surprise, except among the laity and the extreme right of each religious grouping. Among professional academics and well-informed clergy, the pluralism of the field is assumed. Indeed, it can be readily discerned from the diversity of backgrounds and institutional affiliations among contributors to the two most influential American commentary series, the Anchor Bible (Doubleday) and Hermeneia (Fortress). The old identities have faded and are now often vestigial. On this, my own situation speaks volumes, for, an observant Jew, I teach Hebrew Bible at a liberal Protestant divinity school in a university of Puritan origin, and I am a member of the Catholic Biblical Association and have contributed repeatedly to its journal.

If Jewish participation is plentiful in academic programs, professional societies and journals, excavations, and commentaries, one would expect it to be no less plentiful in studies of "biblical theology" or, at least, in research on its Old Testament side. Instead, we may question whether there is any identifiably Jewish participation in that aspect of biblical studies. To be sure, Jews have contributed studies of the theological themes in various texts of the Hebrew Bible. In his *Preface to Old Testament Theology,* Robert C. Dentan devotes one sentence to these Jewish thinkers, citing Martin Buber, Will Herberg, and Abraham J. Heschel as examples.[3] But whereas Christians have written scores of books and articles with "Old Testament Theology" or the like as their titles, I know of no book with that title or anything similar ("Theology of the Hebrew Bible," "Biblical Theology") written by a Jew. The best approximation is *The Philosophy of the Bible,* by David Neumark, professor of Jewish philosophy at the Hebrew Union College in Cincinnati early in the twentieth century.[4] This book dates from 1918, and even it is more a history of the religion of Israel than a biblical theology. The distinction, as we shall see, is essential.

The meaning of the term "biblical theology" is itself an issue much discussed in the discipline that goes by that name.[5] Dentan notes that the term "might *mean* either a biblical kind of *theology,* or the theological parts of *biblical* studies." Opting for the latter, he insists that "the only definition of biblical theology which does justice to the history of the discipline is that it is *the study of the religious ideas of the Bible in their historical context.*"[6] John Bright sets forth essentially the same dichotomy, although he notes a "third sense . . . , the attempt of certain theologians and preachers to expound the Bible in its unity as authoritative in the church." Bright's own preference is similar to Dentan's. For him, "biblical theology" is "the theology that is expressed in the Bible."[7] It is common in these discussions to date the birth of the discipline to its separation from dogmatics late in the eighteenth century. If biblical theology has a birthday, it is March 30, 1787, when Johann Philipp Gabler gave his inaugural address upon assuming the chair in theology at the University of Altdorf. "Biblical theology," Gabler insisted, "is historical in character and sets forth what the sacred writers thought about divine matters; dogmatic theology, on the contrary, is didactic in character, and teaches what a particular theologian philosophically and rationally decides about divine matters, in accordance with his character, time, age, place, sect or school, and other similar influences."[8] For Gabler, as for most Protestants, one of the most important of those influences was the Bible. But the distinction he so lucidly drew between biblical and dogmatic theology ultimately opened the door for the present pluralism in scholarship. If "biblical theology is historical in character," the affiliation of the biblical theologians is of no account for their work. As we shall see, this implication is one from which biblical theologians themselves often recoil. This recoiling is a major reason that this branch of biblical studies is less pluralistic than the others.

If the distinction from dogmatics is rather easily made, if not easily accepted, the distinction between biblical theology and the history of the religion of Israel is more problematic. Dentan contrasts the two thus: "One treats of the story of Israel's developments in its chronological sequence; the other describes the persistent and distinctive principles of Old Testament religion in some kind of logical or 'theological' order."[9] In other words, those principles are not examined in a historical vacuum but are assumed to have a stable identity through history, and it is this stable identity, rather than their growth and minor permutations, that interests Old Testament theologians. They focus not on the "long-cut" but on the "cross-cut" (*Querschnitt* is Eichrodt's term).[10] Bright is of essentially the same opinion, insisting that "the fact of diversity does not eliminate the possibility of an overarching unity, either in the biblical faith or any other."[11] If, however, there are "persistent . . . principles" or "an overarching unity," then it would seem that the historian of Israelite religion ought to be able to see them as well as can the Old Testament theologian. Bright, I think, would agree. His historical and his theological work present essentially the same picture, in which "covenant" and "promise" are the twin centerpieces. They "run through the whole of the Old Testament and inform all of its parts."[12] If this were true, it would surely simplify the biblical theologians' task. All they would need to do is to describe the religion of Israel as the Old Testament wants it to be, and the result would be both a history of the religion of Israel (with due note of Israel's backsliding) and an Old Testament theology. The fact is, however, that this cross-cut, indeed *any* cross-cut, is really a Procrustean bed that cannot accommodate major segments of the book or, to be more precise, cannot regard as major the segments of the book that it does not accommodate. Covenant and promise dominate the Pentateuch, but they are missing from Proverbs, Qohelet, and the Song of Songs. These books, especially Proverbs, make no attempt to situate themselves within Israel's foundational story; they are unconcerned with the exodus, the revelation at Sinai, and the promise and conquest of the land. Indeed, they demonstrate no awareness of these themes. Bright's claim that in Proverbs "the place of Israel as [YHWH's] people, bound to live under his law, is clearly taken for granted"[13] is specious and circular. One cannot even assume the Israelite origin of all the biblical proverbs.[14] In light of the themes that Bright regards as constitutive of the "overarching unity" of the Old Testament, one is hardly surprised to find that his book on *The Authority of the Old Testament* refers to Amos five times and to Proverbs only twice, and never to a specific verse, even though Amos is less than one-sixth the length of Proverbs. Some themes are more widespread than others, but a widespread theme does not make an "overarching unity." The sad truth is that Old Testament theologians have generally treated the themes that appeal to them as more pervasive in the Old Testament and the religion of Israel than is warranted. Historians of religion without theological commitment would, instead, be inclined to acknowledge the diversity and contradiction of biblical thought frankly. They would feel no need to concoct a spurious "unity."

Dentan insists that the theologian's "concern should be the norma-tive religion of the Old Testament,"[15] but, like Bright, he does not see that this criterion stands at odds with his commitment to the "historical context." The specifically historical context of the authors of Proverbs, for example, may not have included the pentateuchal traditions, and the historical context of the pentateuchal sources may not have included Proverbs. The juxtaposition of these various sorts of literature in the same book is a matter of *literary* context; it becomes a fact of *history* per se only very late in the period of the Second Temple — long after the original historical contexts of the pentateuchal literature and perhaps also the proverb collections had vanished. The construction of a reli-gion out of *all* the materials in the Hebrew Bible violates the historian's commitment to seeing the materials in their historical contexts. The re-sult will correspond to the religion of *no* historical community, except perhaps some parties very late in the period of the Second Temple. The argument that Old Testament theology can maintain both an uncom-promisingly historical character and its distinction from the history of Israelite religion is therefore not valid.[16]

If the distinction between the long-cut and the cross-cut is insuf-ficient to differentiate Old Testament theology from the history of Israelite religion, another differentiation must yet be considered. There is a tendency among Christians to insist that biblical theology requires a measure of faith in its practitioners. "We may assume," writes Dentan, "that the Old Testament theologian of today, at least, will be a man of faith." "Faith," to quote the title of one of his subsections, "helps make such insight possible."[17] Gerhard Hasel is less restrained. "What needs to be emphatically stressed," he writes, "is that there is a transcendent or divine dimension in Biblical history which the historical critical method is unable to deal with."[18] Similarly, Moshe Goshen-Gottstein, a Jew, takes special note of the distance involved in the religio-historians' stance to-ward their material as against that in the theologians' stance of "faith, identification, acknowledgment of value and meaningfulness, of taking a personal stand in the present, which draws nourishment from the same spring from which the teachings (*tôrôt*) of the past flowed."[19] As a means to differentiate the two disciplines, this idea works far better than the long-cut/cross-cut distinction, which, as we saw, cannot do justice to the variety and changeability of history. Even if we do not subscribe to the naive positivism that claims the historian simply tells what really hap-pened (*wie es eigentlich gewesen ist*), we can still differentiate scholars who strive after a not fully realizable objectivity from those who openly acknowledge their transcendent commitments and approach their work in the vivid hope of deepening and advancing them. Here, however, biblical theology purchases its distinction from the history of religion at the price of its equally essential distinction from dogmatics. For if we shift the focus from the biblical writings to the contemporary theological use of them, even in a nontraditional mode, then we have substantially reconnected the umbilical cord that Gabler sought to sever two centuries ago. Our biblical theologian, like his dogmatician, will discuss "divine matters, in accordance with his character, time, age, place, sect or school, and other similar influences."[20] Even if one seeks, as Goshen-Gottstein does,[21] to maintain the autonomy of tradition, in his case normative rabbinic law (halakhah), one cannot gainsay that the "personal stand in the present" of any Jew or Christian includes postbiblical elements. Indeed, if it does not, then the theology in question will be neither Jewish nor Christian but only historical, and we are back to the dilemma discussed in the previous paragraph, and Goshen-Gottstein's plea for a specifically Jewish biblical theology will have failed. How can self-consciously *Jewish* biblical theologians take a personal stand on behalf of a text that they interpret against its rabbinic exegesis? The effect would be the neo-Karaism against which Goshen-Gottstein cautions.[22] This is not to say that serious theological study of the Hebrew Bible for a Jew must be restricted to an uncritical repetition of talmudic and medieval rabbinic interpretations. It is to say, however, that the "personal stance" of a faithful contemporary Jew does not allow for the *isolation* of the Jewish Bible (Tanakh) from the larger tradition. Such an isolation is possible on historical grounds, but not on personal, existential grounds. One can, of course, attempt constructive Jewish theology with special attention to the biblical sources — and I believe there is a great need for such studies. But this is closer to what Christian faculties call "dogmatics" or "systematics" than to "biblical theology."

If it be admitted that biblical theology presumes existential commitment and that the commitment will necessarily include other sources of truth (the Talmud, the New Testament, etc.), then it becomes clear that biblical theology is different in kind from the other branches of biblical studies and that, unlike them, it cannot so easily lend itself to ecumenical, pluralistic collaboration. One pursues either Jewish biblical theology or Christian biblical theology, but not both, for the term "biblical" has a different reference for the Jew and the Christian. The first sentence of Dentan's book says it all: " 'Old Testament theology' is one part of a greater discipline called 'biblical theology' and cannot be studied in isolation from the larger subject." This is because "Old Testament theology is *a Christian-theological discipline* and, as such, does not deal with the Old Testament in isolation, but always has some concern for its relation to the New." It is, in fact, "a preparatory exercise for the study of the New Testament."[23] Here, Dentan is typical of the discipline in wishing to have it both ways. Biblical theology must be both *"the study of the religious ideas of the Bible in their historical context"* and *"a Christian-theological discipline."*[24] But Christianity is not the historical context for a single religious idea in the Hebrew Bible, the latest of whose writings predates the earliest Christian material by a full two centuries. The Christian interpretation of non-Christian literature — or, for that matter, the rabbinic interpretation of nonrabbinic literature — may have great strength. It may be defensible, even persuasive. But it cannot be *historical.*[25]

If Old Testament theology is "a preparatory exercise for the study of the New Testament," then an Old Testament theology that did not demonstrate the compatibility of the theologies of the two Testaments would have to be judged a failure. Norman Porteous, after an exhaustive survey of the discipline, concludes that "a theology of the Old Testament, however, will not seek to obscure the fact that Christ did not merely decode the Old Testament but fulfilled it."[26] If this be a criterion for success in the field, then by definition no Jew could ever succeed in it, and the absence of Jewish interest is hardly mysterious. One could, in the spirit of a somewhat obsolescent ecumenism, expect Jews to make the same sort of connection with the Talmud and Midrash that the Christian makes with the New Testament. Neumark, in fact, tried to do something close to this,[27] and it is still surely the case that the continuity between rabbinic and older forms of Israelite religion is not sufficiently known or appreciated among scholars. Nonetheless, the Jew will feel far less compulsion to make such connections, not least because the Talmud and Midrash do not present themselves as the teleological consummation of the Tanakh but only as the rightful continuation and implementation of biblical teaching. Indeed, since rabbinic Judaism lacks the apocalyptic urgency of apostolic Christianity, the rabbis were not generally disposed to identify events or institutions from their own time as the definitive fulfillment of biblical texts. Their attitude toward the Hebrew Bible and theology in general was more relaxed and more pluriform. As a consequence, the endless discussion among biblical theologians as to the relationship between the Testaments has not found and is unlikely to find a parallel among Jewish scholars.[28]

• II •

One reason for the distance Jewish biblicists tend to keep from biblical theology is the intense anti-Semitism evident in many of the classic works in that field. Old Testament theology, in fact, often continues the ancient *adversus Iudaeos* tradition in which the New Testament writers and the church fathers excelled.[29] After the insistence on the compatibility of Old and New Testament theology, few points have been more de rigueur in the Old Testament theologies than deprecatory remarks about rabbinic Judaism. A small sample of this unhappy literature should suffice.[30] Eichrodt informed his readers early on that Judaism has only "a torso-like appearance ... in separation from Christianity,"[31] a point that does not speak well of the intelligence of the two millennia of Jews who have never noticed. "It was not," Eichrodt wrote, "until in later Judaism a religion of harsh observances had replaced the religion of the Old Testament that the Sabbath changed from a blessing to a burdensome duty."[32] What he did not tell his readers is why Jews into our own time have continued to speak of the Sabbath as a blessing and to feel that its ample duties are liberating and exhilarating rather than burdensome.[33] In the Mishnah, Eichrodt observed, the "real worship of God [was] stifled under the heaping up of detailed commands from which the spirit has fled."[34] He did not, however, discuss the tannaitic liturgy that those commands regulate, with its heavy dependence on the Tanakh in both idiom and theology. In Judaism, he remarked, "the living fellowship between God and man ... shrivelled up into a mere correct observance of the legal regulations," so that "the affirmation of the law as the revelation of God's personal will was lost."[35] Here it is apparent that Eichrodt, like most Christian theologians of his generation (and many today), has been misled by the Christian tendency to regard "Torah" as synonymous with "law" so that the whole aggadic dimension of Judaism is ignored. He altogether missed the theology that grounds the halakhah and is, in the last analysis, inextricable from it. He took the Pauline polemic against the commandments for historical fact, failing to see that it was only one perspective, and, at that, an external one, born in the heat of polemic and devised for the service of certain rhetorical needs. The truly remarkable aspect of Eichrodt's anti-Judaism, however, is his apparent failure to feel a need to argue his case, to delve deeply into Talmud and Midrash in order to demonstrate that they are what Christianity always said they were. In a historical scholar — Eichrodt was far from a fundamentalist — this is exceedingly odd. It is almost as though he thought faith exempted him from the obligation to respect historical reality and elemental fairness.

The other great exemplar of Old Testament theology in our century, Gerhard von Rad, was more gentle in spirit. Rather than flaying Judaism, he generally pretended that it did not exist. In fact, his theology was, to a certain degree, implicitly predicated on the disappearance of Old Testament tradition after the death of Jesus. "The way in which the Old Testament is absorbed in the New," he wrote, "is the logical end of a process initiated by the Old Testament itself," and the analysis that suggests this, he insisted, does not utilize any "mysterious hermeneutic device."[36] Israel's history of redemption (*Heilsgeschichte*) is fulfilled in Jesus, and the inconvenient facts that most Jews did not think so and that Jewish literature remained alive, vigorous, and growing, are simply ignored. Joseph Blenkinsopp is surely justified in rejecting "this curious idea of a *Heilsgeschichte* which comes to an end at a certain point or (even more curious) which stops and starts again."[37] On the one hand, it would, to be sure, be unfair to attack von Rad and Eichrodt for failing to exemplify the pluralistic attitude that now prevails in biblical studies in America (with the exception of biblical theology). For in their formative years, such an attitude was unknown and not in conformity with the intense anti-Semitism of German theology.[38] On the other hand, it is not unfair to hold a historian of literature to the standards of historical research, and by those standards, these two theologians were woefully inadequate. They were unable to make the elementary if disquieting distinction between faith and fact. In this, they are typical of Old Testament theologians. A Christian theologian like Bright, who openly and respectfully acknowledges that "Israel's history does continue in Judaism,"[39] is the exception. The exception is much more likely to be found in the Anglo-American world than in the Germanic world whence the seminal works in Old Testament theology have emanated. Even as I write, the most influential current in liberal Christian theological circles, liberation theology, is rife with ignorant stereotypical depictions of the Judaism of Jesus' time.[40] New life is being breathed into the old defamations.

The derogations of Judaism by biblical theologians in the twentieth century are essentially the same as those promulgated by the historians of Israel in the nineteenth, both being merely thin secularizations of calumnies that ultimately derive from the New Testament. The ideas of Julius Wellhausen (1844–1918), the greatest student of the Old Testament in the nineteenth century, are a case in point. Wellhausen made a sharp distinction between the religion of Israel and Judaism. *In nuce,* the latter is the former after it has died: "When it is recognized that the *canon* is what distinguishes Judaism from ancient Israel, it is recognized at the same time that what distinguishes Judaism from ancient Israel is *the written Torah.* The water which in old times rose from a spring, the Epigoni stored up in cisterns."[41] From the correct observation that the religion of late Second Temple times and beyond was book-centered in a way in which the earlier stages were not, Wellhausen moves to the questionable judgment that "Judaism" is cut off from its spring of vitality. "Yet it is a thing which is likely to occur, that a body of traditional practice should only be written down when it is threatening to die out," he wrote, "and that a book should be, as it were, the ghost of a life which is closed."[42] The spiritual death of the Jews is symbolized and perhaps caused by their severance from the land: "With the Babylonian captivity, the Jews lost their fixed seats, and so became a trading people."[43] If the term "trading people" seems to reflect the Jews of Wellhausen's Europe more than those of the Near East in biblical and rabbinic times, it must be remembered that he wrote the classic work in which these remarks appear, *Prolegomena to the History of Ancient Israel,* at a time of swelling Jew-hatred. As Blenkinsopp points out, in the year after it was published, "1879, . . . Adolf Stöcker, founder of the Christian Social Workers' Party, described Orthodox Judaism in one of his speeches as a 'form of religion which is dead at its very core' and in the same year Heinrich von Treitschke, professor of history at the University of Berlin, spoke of the Jews as Germany's misfortune (*'Die Juden sind unser Unglück'*)."[44] We must not allow Wellhausen's theological liberalism and his anticlericalism to distract us from the degree to which he participated in the anti-Semitic culture of his time and place and failed to challenge its theological underpinnings. That his was not a racial anti-Semitism of the kind that flowered in Nazism should not blind us to the fact that his work "made its modest contribution," in Blenkinsopp's words, "to the 'final solution' of the Jewish problem under the Third Reich,"[45] a generation after his death.[46]

If Jews needed a reason to suspect the study of the Hebrew Bible in universities, Wellhausen and others like him surely provided it. Healthy persons do not willingly put themselves into a situation in which they will hear themselves defamed, pronounced dead, or both. In 1903, the Jewish riposte came in its most pungent form in an address by Solomon Schechter, one of the greatest scholars of Judaica of the time and the guiding light of the Jewish Theological Seminary of America in its formative years. Schechter's address was entitled "Higher-Criticism — Higher Anti-Semitism." It is this "Higher Anti-semitism of the critical historians," he argued, "which burns the soul though it leaves the body unhurt." He continued: "The Bible is our sole *raison-d'être*, and it is just this which the Higher Anti-semitism is seeking to destroy, denying all our claims for the past, and leaving us without hope for the future."[47] For this affliction, Schechter did not prescribe a return to uncritical, ahistorical traditionalism or a severance from the larger academic world and a reentry into an intellectual ghetto. Instead, he urged that fire be fought with fire, only of a purer kind: "But this intellectual persecution can only be fought by intellectual weapons and unless we make an effort to recover our Bible and to think out our theology for ourselves, we are irrevocably lost from both worlds."[48]

The sour taste left by the anti-Semitism, however, did not die out so fast. Indeed, it remains potent today, and the theology for which Schechter called, one that would enable Jews to recover their Bible in an intellectually defensible way without shutting out either world, has yet to emerge. One reason is that the critical study of the Hebrew Bible is itself often seen by Jews as inherently anti-Semitic. The method and the uses to which it is put are not always adequately distinguished, and the fact that historical criticism has undermined Christianity no less than Judaism, as any Christian fundamentalist knows all too well, is too often ignored.[49] As a result, even non-Orthodox institutions have often shied away from critical study or "tiptoed through the tulips," studying some aspects of Jewish literature and history critically, and others traditionally. Thus, "Pentateuch criticism was avoided for most of the history of [Schechter's own] Jewish Theological Seminary."[50] When this is the case, theological work will be limited to a learned elucidation of the theology of the classic sources. This is no mean accomplishment, as one of Schechter's own works, *Aspects of Rabbinic Theology: Major Concepts of the Talmud*, nicely demonstrates.[51] But this is not what comes of the tense and parlous collision of tradition and modernity that generates among Christians the genre of "biblical theology."

It is worth noting that whereas Christian theological training usually involves work in both historical and constructive theology, training in Jewish philosophy ("theology" is a somewhat alien term) tends to be historical in focus and to lack a constructive dimension altogether. I have found that if students of Jewish philosophy are asked, for example, what Maimonides thought of revelation, they are comfortable in answering, but if asked what we ourselves are to think of revelation, they are often stopped short and regard the question as a bit insulting. The analogous situation does not, for the most part, obtain among students of Christian theology.

Another consequence of the anti-Semitic tendencies of biblical studies has been a certain defensive, even reactionary, posture among Jewish biblical scholars. One thinks, for example, of the *History of Israelite Religion* by perhaps the greatest Jewish biblicist of modern times, Yehezkel Kaufmann (1889–1963).[52] This eight-volume Hebrew work, some of which has appeared in English,[53] is surely one of the greatest syntheses of ancient Israelite experience, perhaps its last great synthesis. It is a work replete with novel insights and one that every student of the Hebrew Bible should own and consult frequently. This makes it all the sadder, however, that Kaufmann, whose magnum opus came out between 1937 and 1956, spent so much of his intellectual life shadowboxing with Wellhausen, who died in 1918. It is true that Wellhausen's ideas survived him and, for that matter, remain alive today among both Jews and Gentiles. But his evolutionary approach, with its great emphasis on written documents and inner-Israelite experience, had been in eclipse since the 1890s. In the index to Moshe Greenberg's English abridgment of Kaufmann,[54] one finds numerous references to Wellhausen but none to Eichrodt or von Rad or even Albrecht Alt, whose historical focus paralleled Kaufmann's own in many ways.[55] All three were his contemporaries, yet it is Wellhausen who was his sparring partner. Kaufmann's history is written in the spirit of "Know what answer you will give to the unbeliever," to quote the Mishnah (*Abot* 2:19). In this, Kaufmann found a goodly measure of success, although he had more in common with Wellhausen than he may have realized. The fact remains, however, that Kaufmann was acutely aware of being a latecomer to the scene of biblical studies in a critical mode and, consequently, of having to clear out space in which to work. The reverence in which Kaufmann continues to be held among most Jewish biblical scholars is owing not only to the magnitude of his intellectual achievement, but also to the endurance of that need to clear out a place for Jews in the field and to counter the anti-Jewish positions that took root early in its history and have never been completely dislodged. As Henry Kissinger once said of political liberals and intellectual discourse, Christian theologians have "preempted the categories" of biblical theology, and the Jews, like conservative intellectuals, can usually only sustain a holding action and occasionally get in a shot of their own. In other branches of biblical studies, the anti-Jewish impulse is much weaker and much less common. There, the legacy of the nineteenth century and of Christendom in general is more easily transcended, religious identities mean less, and the Jewish presence is correspondingly larger.

• III •

Historically, biblical theology has been not only non-Jewish, but actively Protestant. A full Roman Catholic embrace of the historical-critical method came about only in 1943 with the promulgation of the papal encyclical *Divino afflante spiritu.* In spite of their rapid ascent to the top ranks of most branches of biblical studies in the last four decades, Catholic scholars have not substantially changed the overwhelmingly Protestant complexion of biblical theology. This is as one would expect, given that the Christian Bible bears a greater weight in Protestantism than in Catholicism. Although the Bible has become more important in Catholicism in the decades since the Second Vatican Council, the Reformation doctrine of *sola scriptura* (by scripture alone), if it lives at all, lives only in Protestantism, and one cannot overestimate the connection of this doctrine with the study of biblical theology.

It is important to remember that most Protestant communions have historically tended to think of their Bible as a source of renewal, as the agent that enables the *ecclesia semper reformanda* (the church forever in need of reform) to slough off its accumulated distortions and to recover its pristine gospel, which is its exclusive authority. "How often must I scream at you thick, ignorant papists to come with Scripture?" asked Martin Luther, with characteristic self-restraint. "Scripture. Scripture. Scripture. Do you not hear, you deaf goat and dumb ass?" "Paul wrote, 'scrutinize all teaching, and retain that which is good.' " "If we would prove, as Paul says, what shall we take as a touchstone [*Probierstein*], other than the Scriptures?" "I will and must be subdued with Scripture," he wrote, "not with the uncertain life and doctrine of men, however holy they may be."[56] John Calvin laid down a comparable principle:

Let this, therefore, be a firm axiom [*axioma*]: nothing should be permitted in the church as the Word of God except what is, first, in the Law and Prophets, and, secondly, in the writings of the apostles; and that there is no correct mode of teaching except within the prescribed limits [*praescriptio*] and under the rule of this Word.[57]

In light of this polarization of scripture and tradition, the motivation to state the scriptural doctrines precisely and purely, without the admixture of other parts of tradition, becomes paramount. It is this inner-Protestant dynamic that is the mother of biblical theology in both of Dentan's senses, "a biblical kind of theology [and] the theological part of *biblical* studies."[58] In fact, the Protestant dynamic helps obscure that essential distinction, since it does not allow for much of a differentiation between one's own theology and that of one's Bible.

The unending Protestant quest for repristinization that spawns this great involvement in the Christian Bible finds scant parallel among the Jews. The motto of Anan ben David, founder of the Karaites, a Jewish sect that dates to the eighth century (C.E.) in Babylon, adumbrates the Reformation theology. *Ḥappēśû šappîr bĕ'ôraytā*, he admonished his followers in Aramaic: "search out the Torah thoroughly." For the Karaites, there is only one Torah, the Pentateuch, whereas for the rabbis (from whom they separated) Torah was twofold, written and oral, and it is this oral Torah that eventually found written expression in the Mishnah, the Talmuds, the midrashic collections, and their medieval and modern descendants. Karaism was not without its effects. It helped spur among Rabbanites the emergence of a mode of Jewish exegesis that pursued the "plain sense" of the Bible (*peshat*). Karaite commentators influenced the content of much Rabbanite exegesis. Nonetheless, Karaism itself has survived as only a tiny minority of that larger minority, the Jews. "Searching the scriptures" remains, at least in theory, a high priority of religious Jews, but not for the purpose of overthrowing rabbinic enactments. No rabbi has ever cited the biblical principle of "an eye for an eye," for example, in order to clear away the rabbinic law that corporal damages must be compensated monetarily and not in kind, as the *peshat* of scripture might be thought to suggest.[59] Instead, biblical study in Judaism falls under the category of *talmûd tôrâ* (the study of Torah), a sacred and central obligation (*mitsvah*) in the rabbinic universe, but a *mitsvah* that applies to Mishnah, Gemara, medieval rabbinic exegesis, and so on, as well. The traditional Jewish dynamic is quite the opposite of the Protestant, and, unlike the latter, it does not foster an effort to isolate a peculiarly *biblical* theology.

The nineteenth-century Jewish Reform movement and its rebellious offspring, Conservative Judaism, made it possible for Jews to think of themselves as actively religious without fulfilling many of the traditional commandments. The term "Reform" can be misleading to Christians in that it might suggest a denomination that adheres to a high doctrine of scripture such as that of the Reformed or Calvinist churches. To be sure, the Reform movement and its seminary, the Hebrew Union College — Jewish Institute of Religion, have historically tended to place more emphasis on Tanakh than on Talmud (unlike the Conservative movement and its Jewish Theological Seminary). Nonetheless, unlike the Reformed churches, Reform Judaism is not the offspring of the Renaissance with its slogan of *ad fontes* (back to the sources!), but of the Enlightenment with its rationalistic critique of *all* religion, including biblical religion. One sees this in the second and third planks of the famous "Pittsburgh Platform" (1885):

> 2. We recognize in the Bible the record of the consecration of the Jewish people to its mission as the priest of the one God, and value it as the most potent instrument of religious and moral instruction. We hold that the modern discoveries of scientific researches in the domain of nature and history are not antagonistic to the doctrines of Judaism, the Bible reflecting the primitive ideas of its own age, and at times clothing its conception of Divine Providence and Justice dealing with man in miraculous narratives.
>
> 3. We recognize in the Mosaic legislation a system of training the Jewish people for its mission during its national life in Palestine, and today we accept as binding only its moral laws, and maintain only such ceremonies as elevate and sanctify our lives, but reject all such as are not adapted to the views and habits of modern civilization.[60]

Here, it is clear that the *norma normans et non normata* — the ultimate, unconditioned norm — is not the Bible, but only its "moral laws" and "the views and habits of modern civilization," before which even Moses must bow the head and bend the knee. The Jewish reformers did not, by and large, appeal to the Bible to purge Judaism of Talmudicisms. They did not, for example, seek to change the liturgy back to one principally of animal sacrifice or to substitute the talion for monetary compensation. Instead, they appealed to reason in order to purge the tradition of anything, whether biblical or rabbinic, that they found incompatible with "modern civilization." The willingness of Reform Judaism to recognize historical development and to accept the principle of historical criticism made it more likely to become involved in modern biblical study, with less anachronistic infusion of rabbinic ideas. Neumark's *Philosophy of the Bible* is testimony to this.[61] But the great impulse to develop a distinctly biblical theology that the quest for repristinization gives Protestants, found no parallel in classic Reform Judaism. It also finds none in the Reform Judaism of today, which, in general, continues to prize progressivism over fidelity to the classical sources of the tradition.

One finds a better parallel to the Protestant dynamic in some forms of secular Zionism. Here, the urge to repristinize the Jewish people is intense. Two millennia of rootlessness, persecution, passivity, dependency, spiritualistic escapism, and over-intellectualization were to be undone by a return to the land, the language, and, to a certain extent, the mores of the Tanakh. The rhetoric of reenactment was in plentiful evidence in early Zionism, and, indeed, it can be heard to this day across most of the spectrum of Israeli politics — but especially at the extreme right, with its demand for biblical borders and its occasional and alarming tendency to equate Palestinian Arabs with the seven Canaanite nations of the Torah. But whereas nowadays the extreme political right includes within it a very substantial Orthodox component, in the late nineteenth century there was a stronger, although not universal, tendency among Zionists to equate Orthodoxy with those negative attributes that supposedly had defined two millennia of Diaspora. Thus, it was possible to invoke the Tanakh in anticlerical polemics. One thinks of a figure like Yehudah Leib Gordon (1830–1892), the greatest Hebrew poet of the Russian *Haskalah* (Enlightenment). Like most Hebrew poetry in every period, Gordon's was highly biblical in idiom. He chose biblical episodes for some of his most successful pieces. Yet he was also bitterly anticlerical, and his long poem *Beqotso shel Yud* ("For a Mere Detail," literally, "For the Hook on the Letter *Yud*") remains the finest satire on Orthodox Judaism ever written. Gordon's involvement in biblical themes and language and his polemical attitude toward the rabbinical establishment and the course of postbiblical Jewish history show some similarities to the tendencies of the Protestant Reformation. But it is inconceivable that Gordon would have written a biblical theology, if only because his biblicism was not an expression of any theological commitment but only of his recovered ethnicity, his militant sense of nationhood.

This profound involvement in the Tanakh on the part of secular — even militantly secular — people is a fixture of Israeli culture. One thinks of David ben Gurion, the first prime minister of the state, a confirmed secular socialist for whom biblical study was an avocation pursued with missionary passion, or of Moshe Dayan, the famous general and politician, who was an amateur archaeologist, or of Yigael Yadin, also a famous general and politician, who was a foremost archaeologist as well as a scholar of the Second Temple period and its aftermath. I have repeatedly had occasion to notice that young nonreligious Israelis often have a better command of the language and contents of the Hebrew Bible than devout senior Christian Old Testament scholars. But it is important to remember that the motivation is different. For better or for worse, in both Israel and the Diaspora most modern Jews are inclined to find their identity in Jewish history, not in Jewish theology. Even among observant Jews, the tendency is to focus on the sacred text and its behavioral implications, and not on the theology that might be abstracted from it. To overgeneralize only a bit, the Christian Old Testament scholars may know biblical *theology,* but the Israelis know the biblical *text.* For the Hebrew Bible is inseparable from their national tradition and basic to their cultural formation. It is the first and most influential classic of their native tongue.

The replacement of Judaism by Jewish history is not unique to secular Zionism. Yosef Yerushalmi points out that whereas in the Middle Ages "the most profound intellectual synthesis" between Jewish and Gentile cultures "took place in the realm of philosophy," and not at all "in the sphere of historiography . . . , in modern times we have, as it were, the reverse":

> There has been little genuine interpenetration between Jewish and general philosophy, but a deep and ubiquitous interaction with modern historicism. By this I mean simply that while there was a common realm of discourse and mutual influence among Jewish, Muslim, and Christian philosophy in the Middle Ages, this has not been true of Jewish and general philosophy in modern times. The primary intellectual encounter between Judaism and modern culture has lain precisely in a mutual preoccupation with the historicity of things.[62]

If we include the study of philology, its handmaiden, as a form of history, then we have in Yerushalmi's words a fine statement of the nature of the relationship between Jews and Christians in contemporary biblical scholarship. There is little Jewish involvement in theological investigation, and the Jews who are so involved tend to define their work as the history of Israelite religion rather than biblical theology. In contrast, in the realm of philological and historical study, a broad commonality of discourse obtains, and Jews and Christians can work together without difficulty. In a sense, this is precisely the situation one would expect in light of the tendency of religion in the modern world to become a private, confessional matter confined to subcultures that, on religious issues, lack much ability to communicate. In the public realm, the realm of the macroculture, naturalistic and even scientific thinking ("technocratic rationalism") prevails, and public communication is possible for anyone who accepts this kind of thinking or pretends to. It is in this naturalistic realm that modern historiography and philology fall. And so, the anomaly is that what unites Jews and Christians in biblical studies is a common commitment to a nonsupernaturalistic approach to the text. Partnership is possible only on terms that cast the truth claims of both traditions into doubt.

To Jews, for whom the history of Israel confers some identity in the present even without a religious affirmation, this historicization of biblical studies will usually seem less of a loss than to committed Christians. For Christians tend to see themselves grafted into the historic Israelite tree only by faith, and if they cannot elucidate the content of that faith, they cannot appropriate that history. For this reason, Christians tend to be more committed to keeping alive the theological dimension, whereas Jews are usually more inclined to rest content with history and philology. The study of biblical theology receives much of its energy from the fact that Christians read the Hebrew Bible through a logic of displacement. It is driven by the anxieties of the younger sibling eager to overcome the deficiencies with an affirmation of the supranatural.

Apart from the exigencies of public discourse in a pluralistic world, there are compelling internal motivations for the replacement of Judaism by Jewish history. Yerushalmi makes the following observation:

> The modern effort to reconstruct the Jewish past begins at a time that witnesses a sharp break in the continuity of Jewish living and hence also an ever-growing decay of Jewish group memory. In this sense, if for no other, history becomes what it had never been before — the faith of fallen Jews. For the first time, history, not a sacred text, becomes the arbiter of Judaism.[63]

The Jews to whom this observation applied were brought to historical reconstruction not because of faith but because of the lack of it. They approached the past — even the biblical past — in hopes not of defining a theology but of replacing it. The impulse to replace faith with history began to affect Christianity at about the same time. Well-hausen's historicism, in which biblical history replaces the (Christian) Bible and acquires its recently lost normativity, is an instance of the same process.[64] But as we have seen, the complex nature of the Christian relationship to the Israelite materials serves as a check on the anti-theological or antireligious impulse, a check that is not well paralleled among the Jews. This is one reason that historicism has survived longer in Jewry and why the antihistoricistic backlash of Protestant biblical the-ologians like Eichrodt and von Rad in the middle decades of the century found only small resonance in the Jewish community.

Change, however, would seem to be in the offing. Recent demo-graphic studies have strongly suggested that the old hope of maintaining Jewish identity in the Diaspora without Jewish observance is unrealis-tic.[65] There is, in turn, reason to believe that those Jews who survive the extreme pressure toward intermarriage and assimilation will be the ones who maintain an intense religious practice. What these changing demographics will mean for the Jewish involvement in biblical studies remains unclear. It is, however, most unlikely that the grip of historicism upon Jewish self-definition that Yerushalmi remarks will remain as tight as it has been through most of modern Jewish history. Ironically, the sec-ularization of the Jews upon which this romance with historicism has been based may itself prove to be a transient historical phenomenon.

• IV •

The effort to construct a systematic, harmonious theological statement out of the unsystematic and polydox materials in the Hebrew Bible fits Christianity better than Judaism because systematic theology in general is more prominent and more at home in the church than in the *bet midrash* (study house) and the synagogue. The impulse to systematize among Christians tends to find its outlet in theology. Augustine, Aqui-nas, Calvin, Tillich, and Rahner, to name only a few, have no really close parallels in Jewry — figures such as Maimonides and Hermann Cohen notwithstanding. Among Jews, the impulse to systematize finds its out-let in law. The Mishnah, the *Mishneh Torah*, the *Shulchan Aruch*, and the *Aruch Ha-Shulchan* have no good counterparts in the church, despite traditions of canon law and moral theology. The views each tradition holds of the other are instructive in this regard. Christians often have the impression of Judaism that its belief system is too amorphous and

ill-defined and that its legal system is excessively precise and overdeter-
mined. Jews often have the impression of Christianity that its ethical and
liturgical life is dangerously subjective, emotionalistic, and impression-
istic and that its theology is too rigid and too abstract. Joseph Kitagawa,
the eminent historian of religion, once put the contrast this way: if you
ask Asians to describe their religion, they will tell you about their practices; if you ask Christians, they will tell you about their beliefs. Judaism,
concluded Kitagawa, is in this respect more like an Asian religion than
like Christianity.[66]

Since the church early on concluded that the particular *practices*
of the Hebrew Bible are not incumbent upon Christians, it again follows that the *beliefs* in that book will bear proportionally more weight
among Christians than among Jews. Bright's discussion of the laws of
the Sabbatical and Jubilee Years in Leviticus 25 is revealing:

> The chapter can scarcely be called one of the high points of the
> Old Testament. Indeed, the regulations described therein are obvi-
> ously so little applicable to the modern situation that the preacher
> may be pardoned if he told himself that the passage contains no
> relevant message for his people whatever.... So let us say it: The
> Law, as law, is ancient, irrelevant, and without authority. But what
> of the theology of the law?... It seeks to tell us that the land is
> God's and that we live on this earth as aliens and sojourners,
> holding all that we have as it were on loan from him (vs. 23);
> that God narrowly superintends every business transaction and
> expects that we conduct our affairs in the fear of him (vss. 17, 36,
> 43), dealing graciously with the less fortunate brother in the rec-
> ollection that we have all been recipients of grace (vss. 38, 42).
> And that is normative ethics! It speaks with an eternal relevance
> to the Christian.... The law we cannot obey; but we are enjoined
> in all our dealings ever to strive to make the *theology* of the law
> actual.[67]

In Bright's words one feels poignantly the precarious situation of the
Old Testament theologian. A good Paulinist, Bright must steer clear of
the heresy of Judaizing. The implication that the laws must be obeyed,
whenever possible, cannot be accepted. But across the straits from the
Scylla of Judaizing sits the Charybdis of Marcionism, with its bold proclamation that the Jewish Scriptures are irrelevant to the Christian. This,
too, must be resisted. Only theology enables safe passage, for by con-
verting law into theology, specific practice into general belief, Bright

can grant Paul his doctrine of exemption from Torah without granting Marcion his idea that the Jewish God and the Christ are antithetical. The specifics fade, the laws wither, but Old Testament theology endures forever.

The theology that Bright abstracts from Leviticus 25 is fully in accord with rabbinic Judaism. The two part company, however, in that, traditionally, Jewish thinkers would not present the theology as a direct *alternative* to the specific legal institutions. Instead, they would have seen these two items as inextricable. Even when historical conditions have rendered a law unfulfillable, rabbinic tradition regards the law as still in effect and worthy of study in all its particularity. For example, in his *Mishneh Torah*, Maimonides codifies talmudic law about the Temple cultus that the Romans rendered inoperative in 70 C.E., early in the rabbinic period and more than a millennium before Maimonides himself. The stubborn rabbinic resistance to losing the particular in the general stands in stark contrast to the tendency of most Christian exegesis. In a discussion concerning the adaptation of Judaism to a Gentile audience in Christian tradition, principally by Paul, Erich Auerbach presented the contrast this way:

> The total content of the sacred writings was placed in an exegetic context which often removed the thing told very far from its sensory base, in that the reader or listener was forced to turn his attention away from the sensory occurrence and toward its meaning.... [This is] the antagonism which permeates the early, and indeed the whole, Christian view of reality.[68]

Susan Handelman contrasts the Christian inclination toward spiritualization, allegorization, and other forms of abstraction with rabbinic thought as follows:

> One of the most interesting aspects of Rabbinic thought is its development of a highly sophisticated system of interpretation based on uncovering and expanding the primary concrete meaning, and yet drawing a variety of logical inferences from the meaning without the abstracting, idealizing movement of Western thought.[69]

Although one hesitates to tar all of "Western thought" with one stroke of the brush, it must be granted that as a generalization about rabbinic and Christian interpretation of the Hebrew Bible, Handelman's judgment stands. As a result, the search for the one great idea that pervades and unifies the Hebrew Bible is unlikely to interest Jews. Instead, Jewish biblical theology is likely to be, as it always has been, a matter of piecemeal observations appended to the text and subordinate to its particularity. As Gershom Scholem put it, speaking of rabbinic Judaism: "[n]ot system but *commentary* is the legitimate form through which truth is approached."[70] I would amend his remark only so as to limit it to the aggadic dimension of Judaism. In the case of halakhah, Judaism does offer impressive architectonic structures in the form of law codes. But the aggadic and the halakhic dimensions of Judaism are complementary and not antithetical, and when halakhah is the basis for aggadah, the former is not transmuted into the latter by theological alchemy. Rather, the particularities of the law remain alive and in force in and alongside the larger theological and ethical message.

The search for the one idea into which the Hebrew Bible is to be subsumed, for the "center (*Mitte*) of Old Testament theology," as the issue is known in the field, has produced a bewildering array of candidates — for example, covenant (Eichrodt), the holiness of God (Ernst Sellin), God as the lord (Ludwig Köhler), Israel's election as the people of God (Hans Wildberger), the rule of God together with his communion with humankind (Georg Fohrer),[71] God's acts in history (G. Ernest Wright),[72] communion alone (Th. C. Vriezen),[73] the book of Deuteronomy (Siegfried Herrmann),[74] and the presence of God (Samuel Terrien).[75] It is interesting to note some rather obvious candidates that do not appear in this list and have received little attention in the theologies. One is humankind's duties, a theme that occupies most of the biblical materials, legal, prophetic, and sapiential alike. "What does YHWH require of you?" (Deut 10:12; cf. Micah 6:8) is a theme that cuts across a number of these aspiring centers and covers much of books like Proverbs, as covenant, holiness, rulership, acts of God, and presence, for instance, cannot. I am, for reasons that will become evident, skeptical of the entire pursuit of a center. My point is that with its devaluation of the deed ("works"), the Pauline theology of these Protestant Old Testament scholars has made it unlikely for them to propose a theme like these as the center of Old Testament theology, lest they suggest the Marcionite notion of the antithetical relationship of the Jewish and the Christian Gods. It is instructive to compare their approach with that of John L. McKenzie, a Roman Catholic scholar who explicitly set out to write "the theology of the Old Testament as if the New Testament did not exist."[76] McKenzie put the discussion of "cult" first in his book (whereas Eichrodt, for instance, put "covenant" first) and devoted only twenty-five pages out of 341 to "the message of the prophets" (whereas von Rad, for example, devoted well over a third of his second volume to the same theme). It is difficult to resist the suggestion that the theologians' own personal faith is the determinative factor in their positing a center for the Old Testament. In fact, it is not unusual for the authors to claim that the New Testament, *mirabile dictu,* has the very same center. Given the normative role that biblical theologians, especially the Protestants, tend to ascribe to their discipline, this is not surprising. What is surprising, however, is that the method by which this all-encompassing systemic unity is uncovered is itself seen as compatible with the historian's sensitivity to change, development, contradiction, and difference.

The assumption of the theologians who quest after the center or overarching unity of the Hebrew Bible is that all the books and pericopes therein announce essentially the same message. This has, in fact, a rough parallel in rabbinic thought. "Forty-eight male and seven female prophets prophesied to Israel," reports an anonymous baraita, "and they neither took away from nor added to that which is written in the Torah, with the exception of the reading of the Scroll [of Esther on Purim]" (*b. Meg.* 14a). Here, the assumption is that the first of the three sections of the Tanakh, the Torah (Pentateuch), is prior and normative; the prophets only applied it and did not innovate. It is hard to see how a biblical theology that did not respect the doctrine of the priority and normativity of the Pentateuch could be authentic to the Jewish tradition. The ubiquitous assumption of the biblical theologians that one might learn the biblical message better from a book in another section of the canon and then utilize that book to correct or counterbalance the Torah (e.g., Jeremiah against Leviticus) derives from the modern Christian idea that the unit to be interpreted is the *testament,* an idea foreign to Judaism and in contradiction to the Jewish prioritization of the Torah over the rest of the Tanakh. Like the different conceptions of scripture held by the two traditions, the different organization of the Tanakh and the Old Testament ensures that a biblical theology common to Jews and Christians is impossible.[77]

In section 1, we saw that this notion that all the literature of the Hebrew Bible, which was composed over a millennium, has one message presents grave historical problems. Needless to say, the idea of the antiquity of the entire Pentateuch does this also. Neither the Jewish nor the Christian assumption is in accord with historical criticism. The message that the Hebrew Bible conveys to any community is necessarily in large measure a function of the tradition in which it is contextualized. In their historical contexts, the numerous passages in the Hebrew Bible represented a multitude of differing and conflicting messages. The continuing lack of consensus as to the center of Old Testament theology offers ironic evidence for the diversity of theologies in that book and the error of attempting to construct a systematic theology directly from it.

I suspect that Judaism is somewhat better situated to deal with the polydoxy of biblical theology than is Christianity. Whereas in the church the sacred text tends to be seen as a *word* (the singular is telling) demanding to be proclaimed magisterially, in Judaism it tends to be seen as a *problem* with many facets, each of which deserves attention and debate. The way midrash collections introduce a new comment is revealing — *dābār 'aḥēr* (another interpretation). The rabbinic Bible (*Miqra'ot Gedolot*), too, surrounds the text with a plurality of commentaries that very often take issue with each other explicitly. And most of the Talmud is a debate, with both majority and minority positions preserved and often unmarked. This is very different from most of the theological literature of Christianity. A tradition whose sacred texts are internally argumentative will have a far higher tolerance for theological polydoxy (within limits) and far less motivation to flatten the polyphony of the sources into a monotony. It is not only that Jews have less motivation than Christians to find a unity or center in their Bible: if they did find one, they would have trouble integrating it with their most traditional modes of textual reasoning. What Christians may perceive as a gain, Jews may perceive as a loss.

• V •

The context in terms of which a unit of literature is to be interpreted is never self-evident. In the case of the Hebrew Bible, the candidates are legion. They include the work of the author who composed the unit, the redacted pericope in which it is now embedded, the biblical book in which it appears, the subsection of the Jewish canon that contains this book (Pentateuch, Prophets, or Writings), the entire Hebrew Bible treated as a synchronic reality, the Christian Bible (Old Testament and New Testament), and the exegetical traditions of the church or the rabbis. Each of these locations — and there are more — defines a context; it is disingenuous and shortsighted to accuse proponents of any one of them of "taking the passage out of context." Rather, the success of an interpretation is relative to the declared objectives of the interpreter. The great flaws of the biblical theologians are their lack of self-awareness on the issue of context and their habit, in the main, of acting as though the change of context makes no hermeneutical difference. In point of fact, it makes all the difference in the world.

I can illustrate the difference that context makes by analyzing an elegant little study of Gen 15:6 by von Rad, "Faith Reckoned as Righteousness" (1951). Von Rad prefixed the text as follows:

> He believed YHWH; and he reckoned it to him as righteousness.
>
> [Von Rad's question about it is:] . . . [H]ow precisely ought we to understand what we have referred to as the "theological" element here? Is it conceivable that the statement that faith is reckoned as righteousness arose wholly and solely from the reflections of a theologian? What is the derivation of the terms employed in this notable statement?[78]

In answer, von Rad traces the use of the verb *ḥāšab* (to reckon) back to the pronouncement of a priest as he passes "a kind of cultic judgment" on a worshiper: "If any of the flesh of his sacrifice of well-being [*zĕbaḥ haššĕlāmîm*] is eaten on the third day, it shall not be acceptable; it shall not be reckoned [*lōʾ yēḥāšēb*] to him. It is an abomination" (Lev 7:18). Similarly, if one slaughters an animal "and does not bring it to the entrance of the Tent of Meeting to present it as an offering to YHWH before YHWH's Tabernacle, bloodguilt shall be reckoned [*yēḥāšēb*] to him" (Lev 17:4).[79] Since elsewhere we read of the priest's pronouncing an oral judgment announcing the will of God in the matter (e.g., Lev 13:8), it seems likely that in the case of these offerings, the priest also announced whether YHWH "reckoned" the sacrifice to the worshiper, that is, whether it has been accepted or not.[80] Von Rad found a similar declaratory formula in passages like Ezek 18:9, which tells of a man who has done all the right things that "he is righteous; he shall live — (*ṣaddîq hûʾ ḥāyōh yiḥyeh*) — oracle of the Lord God." Von Rad saw this as "a relic of the liturgical usage" and connected it with the judgment on the fitness of worshipers that one finds in the "temple-gate liturgies," such as Pss 15:2–5; 24:5; and Isa 33:15–16.[81] In light of this cultic background, we see the remarkable transformation that the author of Gen 15:6 has brought about. There we find that

> [t]he process of "reckoning" is now transferred to the sphere of a free and wholly personal relationship between God and Abraham.

There is no cultic intermediary, no priest to speak as the mouth-piece of YHWH.... In a solemn statement concerning the divine purpose, it is laid down that it is *faith* which sets men on a right footing with God.... He says that only faith, which is the whole-hearted acceptance of YHWH's promise, brings man into a right relationship — that YHWH "reckons" it to him.[82]

As a consequence, von Rad concluded "that our author lived at a time and place in which ideas and terminology which were formerly tied to the cultus had come to be used more or less unconsciously in such spiritualized contexts."[83]

It is remarkable that von Rad nowhere in this essay refers to the New Testament, for Gen 15:6 was a crucial text in the early church. Paul, combating the insistence of the Jerusalem church that the Mosaic Law obliged Gentile Christians, pointed to Abraham in support of the idea that faith provides an exemption from the commandments:

> [5]I ask then: when God gives you the Spirit and works miracles among you, why is this? Is it because you keep the Law, or is it because you have faith in the gospel message? [6]Look at Abra-ham: he put his faith in God, and that faith was counted to him as righteousness. (Gal 3:5–6)[84]

Later, he made essentially the same point in his letter to the Roman church:

> [1]What, then, are we to say about Abraham, our ancestor in the natural line? [2]If Abraham was justified by anything he had done, then he has a ground for pride. But he has no such ground before God; [3]for what does Scripture say? "Abraham put his faith in God, and that faith was counted to him as righteousness." [4]Now if a man does a piece of work, his wages are not "counted" as a favor; they are paid as debt. [5]But if without any work to his credit he simply puts his faith in him who acquits the guilty, then his faith is indeed "counted as righteousness." (Rom 4:1–5)

For Paul, Abraham served as proof that faith (*pistis*) could be detached from deeds and reckoned as self-sufficient. If so, then those who had faith in Christ had nothing to gain by accepting the obligations of the Torah. Von Rad's exegesis of Gen 15:6 supports this line of thought beautifully. Faith spiritualized the cult, nullifying both it and the priest-hood in the process. It is now "only faith" that "brings man into a right relationship with God."[85]

It is instructive to compare Paul's handling of Gen 15:6 with that of a Jew of the previous generation, Philo of Alexandria. Philo, too, makes much of Abraham's faith, specifically cites Gen 15:6, and introduces in this connection many ideas unattested in Genesis.[86] But soon thereafter he notes, "This man carried out the divine law and all the divine commandments,"[87] evidently an allusion to Gen 26:5, which grounds the promise to Isaac in the fact that "Abraham observed my charge, my commandments, my laws, and my instructions." Needless to say, this verse, with its possible implication that Abraham already knew the total body of revelation and scrupulously observed it, is not one cited by Paul. And so, we have two types of interpretations of Gen 15:6, a Pauline type, which takes the verse in isolation and insists on the autonomy of faith, and a Philonic type, in which faith and the observance of commandments are each predicated of Abraham on the basis of texts in Genesis. It is worthy of note that another New Testament document, the epistle of James, takes, in essence, the Philonic position (James 2:21–24), citing Gen 15:6 but warning as well that "a man is justified by deeds and not by faith in itself" (v. 24).[88]

One of the great rallying cries of the Protestant Reformers was *sola fide:* humanity is justified (or saved) by grace through faith alone, and not through the church or the sacraments administered by its priests. It was this doctrine that turned Luther against the epistle of James, which was one of four books he printed "separately at the back of his German translation of the New Testament."[89] Paul, in contrast, he much admired, and it is Paul's reading of Gen 15:6 that he explicitly endorsed in his own commentary:

Accordingly, lest my discussions obscure what the best interpreter says, I shall speak rather briefly here. Read Paul, and read him attentively. Then you will see that from this passage he constructs the foremost article of our faith — the article that is intolerable to the world and to Satan — namely, that faith alone justifies.[90]

Luther goes on to attack "the rabbis of the Jews [who at the instigation of Satan] reveal their folly and the wrath which they harbor against Christ" by interpreting the verse to mean "that Abraham believed the Lord and through that God was just."[91] Here, Luther surely overgeneralizes. Most of the rabbinic commentators interpret the subject of *wayyaḥšěbehā* ("and he reckoned it") as YHWH. But Nachmanides (1195–1270) had argued that it was in fact Abraham who reckoned God as righteous. "A man who had enough faith to slaughter his only beloved son and [to endure] all the other trials — why shouldn't he have faith in good news?" asked Nachmanides. Instead, he argued, the verse shows that Abraham's faith followed from his conviction that God is a God of righteousness. He cited as proof Isa 45:23, "By myself have I sworn — oracle of the Lord — righteousness has gone out of my mouth, and the word will not turn back."[92] Luther's utter contempt for this interpretation originates in his Pauline theology, for, on purely grammatical considerations, either specification of the implied subject is defensible.

This brief sketch of the premodern exegesis of Gen 15:6 enables us to locate von Rad's reading within the Pauline-Lutheran line of interpretation. His assumption that "only faith . . . brings man into a right relationship" implies an exclusion that is not to be found in the Hebrew Bible and certainly not in the J document, the pentateuchal source responsible for this verse as well as for Gen 26:5, which notes the reservoir of merit established by Abraham's observance of law. The facts that cult and priesthood were not spiritualized away in the Hebrew Bible and that righteousness could be imputed not only for faith, but also for observance (e.g., Deut 6:25 and Ps 106:31), are ignored. Von Rad also neglected completely the possibility that it is Abraham who is doing the reckoning and God who is being reckoned righteous. In part, this is owing to the mistaken assumption that he shared with most modern Christian Old Testament scholars that one can be well-equipped for exegesis without knowledge of the medieval Jewish commentaries. In this, Luther, for all his anti-Judaism, was more advanced. Given von Rad's penchant for finding liturgical and cultic origins for things, he should have been attracted to Nachmanides's reasoning. After all, the affirmation of God's righteousness was a common liturgical act in ancient Israel (e.g., Lam 1:18; Pss 119:137; 145:17).[93] What prevented von Rad from even considering the possibility seems to have been an eagerness to endorse the Pauline-Lutheran reading.

The context in which von Rad's interpretation situates Gen 15:6 is one defined first by the verse itself, in isolation from the rest of the Abraham material in the Hebrew Bible and indeed from the Hebrew Bible itself. The understanding of righteousness as derivable from faith alone is a second aspect of context — one that derives from Pauline materials in the New Testament, especially as these materials have been understood in Lutheran tradition and without regard for the Jacobean-Catholic trajectory in Christian tradition. Ultimately, the only context in which von Rad's essay can be considered successful is Reformation theology. He has ignored the historical context of ancient Israel and defied the various literary contexts defined by the J source, by the book of Genesis, by the Pentateuch, by the Hebrew Bible in its entirety, by the Philonic-rabbinic traditions, and by the Jacobean-Catholic dimension of Christian theology. Within the limited context of theological interpretation informed by historical criticism — the context von Rad intended — his essay must be judged unsuccessful. Within another limited context, however — the confessional elucidation of scripture for purposes of Lutheran reaffirmation — it is an impressive success.

It is precisely the failure of the biblical theologians to recognize the limitation of the context of their enterprise that makes some of them surprised that Jews are not interested in it.

Chapter 3

—— • ——

The Eighth Principle of Judaism
and the Literary Simultaneity
of Scripture

• I •

Although in modern times it is often said that Judaism has no dogmas, Jewish life being a matter of "deeds, not creeds," the fact remains that in many circles a dogmatic formulation continues to serve as the principal obstacle to the critical study of the Hebrew Bible. Any Jew who recites the traditional liturgy will encounter this dogma daily in two forms. The first is in the hymn known after its first word as "Yigdal," generally thought to have been authored by Daniel ben Judah, rabbinical judge in Rome early in the fourteenth century C.E.:

> There has never arisen in Israel another prophet like Moses,
> Who beheld God's very image.
> God gave his people a true Torah
> Through his prophet, the most faithful of his household.[1]

In this formulation, the dogma results from an artful interweaving of the two affirmations of the uniqueness and insurpassability of Mosaic revelation in Deut 34:10 and Num 12:7–8. The former states that "there has never again arisen in Israel a prophet like Moses whom YHWH knew face to face," whereas the latter differentiates Moses' revelation from that of other prophets, whose messages come in visions, dreams, or parables, and affirms that Moses is "the most faithful of my household

... and he beholds the image of YHWH." In this case, the commendation of Moses serves to parry the derogation of him that Miriam and Aaron utter in support of their own claims to political authority. In Deut 34:10, too, the affirmation of Mosaic incompatibility serves a polemical function by subordinating all other prophecy to the traditions associated with Moses. In its present literary location, the verse brings about a sharp axiological demarcation between the Pentateuch and the rest of the Hebrew Bible. Indeed, it can justly be said that it is the theology of Deut 34:10 that is the mother of the very idea of a Pentateuch, that is, the idea that a sharp qualitative division lies between Deuteronomy and its continuation in Joshua. Although the point of the verse is to exalt Moses at the expense of later prophets, within the literary reality of the Hebrew Bible it can be taken to mean that the block Genesis–Deuteronomy constitutes the "Torah of Moses," whereas Joshua begins the "Prophets," a later and inferior corpus of revelation. This is, in fact, how rabbinic tradition has always conceived the issue.

The other instance of this dogma in the traditional daily liturgy appears in "'Ani Ma'amin," a set of thirteen principles of Judaism of late medieval origin and unknown authorship. The eighth of these reads: "I believe with perfect faith that the entire Torah presently in our possession is the one given to Moses our master (may he rest in peace)."[2] Like "Yigdal," " 'Ani Ma'amin" is a paraphrase of the thirteen principles of Maimonides (1138–1204), which first appeared in his commentary on the Mishnah, specifically in preface to the mishnah in tractate *Sanhedrin* that lists those categories of Jews that "have no portion in the world-to-come" (*M. Sanh.* 10:1). Maimonides's own statement of the relevant portion of his eighth principle is as follows:

That the Torah is from heaven [i.e., God], that is: that we believe that the entire Torah presently in our possession is the one given to Moses our master (may he rest in peace), that it is all from the mouth of God, that is, that it was all given to him from the Lord (may he be blessed) in the manner that is metaphorically called "speaking." It is not known how it came, except by Moses (may he rest in peace), to whom it came. Moses was like a scribe writing from dictation all the events, narratives, and commandments. For this reason he was termed a "copyist." And there is no difference between verses like, "And the sons of Ham were Cush and Egypt" [Gen 10:6], or "And his wife's name was Mehetabel" [Gen 36:39] or "Timna was a concubine" [Gen 36:12] and verses like "I am the

Lord your God" [Exod 20:2] and "Hear, O Israel" [Deut 6:4]. For
all of them come from the mouth of God.[3]

The wording indicates that the issue that exercised Maimonides was
not whether it was Moses or someone else to whom the Torah was first
made known — like most medievals Maimonides simply *assumed* Mosaic authorship — but, rather, whether the Torah in its present form is of
divine or human origin. This is as we should expect, since the mishnah
that called forth this particular creedal formulation of Maimonides never
mentions Moses but does exclude from the future world one who says,
"The Torah is not from heaven." The heresy that generates this enduring
orthodoxy, in other words, denies not that Moses wrote the Torah but
that God dictated it. By choosing Num 16:28 as his proof text — "And
Moses said, 'By this you shall know that the Lord sent me to do all these
things, for they are not of my own devising' " — Maimonides shows
that it is divine origin rather than Mosaic authorship that is at point or,
in Shalom Rosenberg's formulation, "Torah from heaven" rather than
"Torah from Sinai."[4] Indeed, a baraita in the talmudic discussion of the
heresy that holds that "the Torah is not from Heaven" assumes that its
problem is not that it denies Mosaic authorship but that it asserts it too
exclusively: "even if he says the whole Torah is from heaven, except for
a particular verse, which was not uttered by the Holy One (blessed be
he), but by Moses himself, to him, too, applies the verse 'Because he
has despised the word of the Lord and broken his commandment, that
person shall be cut off: he must bear his guilt' " (*b. Sanh.* 99a).[5] In his
law code Maimonides labels this particular heretic one who "denies (or,
disbelieves) the Torah" (*Mishneh Torah, Hilkhot Teshuvah* 3:8).

Like most orthodoxies, Maimonides's eighth principle suffers the
embarrassment of contradiction from within the normative sources.
One may note, for example, the talmudic comment that the covenant
curses in Leviticus 26 differ from those in Deuteronomy 28 in that
"Moses uttered the former from the mouth of God, [whereas] the latter
he uttered on his own" (*b. Meg.* 31b).[6] The Hebrew here is strikingly
close to that of the baraita cited above. Apparently, within the rabbinic
tradition the absolute and uncompromising insistence on "Torah from
heaven" did not enjoy the consensus that the tannaitic teacher in that
baraita so devoutly desired. The status of Torah could even adhere to
texts that a prophet had originally "uttered on his own" and not heard
"from the mouth of God." God becomes, as it were, the author-redactor,
rather than the sole author, of the Torah.

In the case of Maimonides's adaptation of the baraita, however, the danger to be fended off would seem to have come not from internal dissent about the divine origin of all the Torah but from the external threat of Muslim claims that Jewish authorities had maliciously tampered with the text, so that the Torah presently in our possession is not the one God gave. It has often been pointed out that Maimonides most likely intended his eighth principle against this Islamic teaching and his ninth — that the Torah will not change — against the Christian idea that the coming of the Christian messiah voids the normativity of the Torah.[7] According to Rosenberg, this explains why Maimonides, who generally had more esteem for Islam than for Christianity, permits Torah to be taught to Christians but not to Muslims: the former at least accept the text, whereas the latter claim it is partly a Jewish forgery.[8] Presumably, the Christian teaching that God's Torah has been abrogated in the present aeon is less dangerous than the Muslim charge that what the Jews have is not now and never was God's Torah. The church at least recognized the unity and divinity of the Torah, as Islam did not, and it is the unity and divinity of the Torah that Maimonides's eighth principle and its tannaitic antecedents sought to protect. The chief objective of this essay is to argue that although in historical-critical discourse the notion of Mosaic authorship of the Pentateuch is indefensible, the underlying and antecedent ideas of the unity and divinity of the Torah must remain relevant considerations for Jewish theologians, and whether these are affirmed or denied makes a larger difference than most of their Christian colleagues wish to concede. In that difference lie the enduring importance of the eighth principle of Judaism, properly understood, and an essential constraint on traditional Jewish biblicists that not all their Christian counterparts will feel.

· **II** ·

If the interpretation of Maimonides's eighth principle outlined above is taken to its logical extreme, the effect is to separate the question of the legitimacy and authority of the Torah from that of its historical origin. No longer are the circumstances of its composition the factors that determine its transcendent status. What is most important is not the empirical issue of how the several parts of the Torah came to assume their present shape but, rather, the affirmation in faith that they now form an indissoluble unity and a revelation from God. The corollary is that the faithful Jew may conduct historical inquiry freely, without the need to allow old dogmatic formulations to predetermine the results. In this model, historical research thus poses no threat to the religious life so long as it restricts itself to the reconstruction of the past and avoids prescribing present practice. In Rosenberg's words, biblical criticism would exceed its legitimate role "only if there would be built upon the 'scientific' theory a theology that, by relying on this theory, would justify the nullification of the commandments [*mitsvot*] or changes in religious law [halakhah]."[9] If critical study refrains from endorsing those two agendas (represented typologically by Christianity and Islam), Rosenberg suggests, it should elicit no quarrel among traditional religious Jews.

Since this interpretation allows both for freedom of inquiry and uncompromising intellectual honesty, on the one hand, as well as for the preservation of a traditional, theocentric Jewish life, on the other, it is not remarkable that it has won adherents across a wide spectrum of Jewish thinkers, from Reform through Orthodoxy.[10] Closely related to it is a strategy that attempts to argue that deviation from belief in Mosaic authorship is not merely religiously defensible but, in fact, traditional. Here the explicit conclusion is that the modern study of the Hebrew Bible is an *evolution* out of medieval rabbinic exegesis and not a *revolution* against it, as the right wing of Orthodox Judaism and others would have it.

The outstanding standard-bearer of this second strategy of legitimation is Nahum M. Sarna, and his principal data are the Torah commentary of Abraham ibn Ezra (ca. 1092–1167) and a traditional supercommentary on it. In support of the notion that, like the moderns, this medieval exegete was not constrained by the doctrine of Mosaic authorship, Sarna draws attention to ibn Ezra's celebrated comment in Gen 12:6:

> "And the Canaanite was then in the land."
>
> It is possible that Canaan seized the land from someone else. And if it is not so, it has a great secret, and the person who understands will keep quiet.[11]

The verse asserts that when Abraham first entered the Promised Land, the Canaanites were there. The word "then" (*'āz*) implies that this was not the case in the narrator's own time — in other words, that the narrator lived after the time when Joshua, Moses' successor, is supposed to have annihilated the Canaanites. The alternative is the position that ibn

Ezra offers first: that *'āz* here means not "then," but "already," so that by telling us that the Canaanites had already arrived, the verse simply lets us know that they were not indigenous but had appeared there some time before Abraham. Sarna points out that Gen 12:6 appears again in ibn Ezra's extensive comment on Deut 1:2, which lists several other verses that are difficult to square with Mosaic authorship.[12] "He who recognizes the secret [of these verses]," remarked the rabbi coyly, "will recognize the truth."[13]

Sarna points out that the truth in question was clearly recognized by Joseph Bonfils (Hebraized as Tov Elem), a rabbi of the mid–fourteenth century who wrote a supercommentary on ibn Ezra entitled *Tsaphenat Pa'aneah*. Here is Bonfils's conclusion about ibn Ezra's enigmatic comment upon Gen 12:6:

> It stands to reason that the word *'āz* was written in a time when the Canaanite was not in the land, and we know that the Canaanite did not leave until after Moses' death, when Joshua conquered it. Accordingly, it appears that Moses did not write this word here; rather, Joshua or another of the prophets wrote it, just as we find in the Book of Proverbs [25:1], "These two are the words of Solomon, which the men of Hezekiah, king of Judah, transmitted." Since Solomon composed the book, why was Hezekiah, who was born several generations later, mentioned? Only because they had an oral tradition going all the way back to Solomon and thus they wrote it but it was reckoned as if Solomon had written it. Similarly in this case, Israel had a tradition that in the days of Abraham the Canaanite was in the land, and one of the prophets wrote it down here. And since we are to have trust in the words of tradition and the prophets, what should I care whether it was Moses or another prophet who wrote it, since the words of all of them are true and inspired?[14]

Sarna further notes that this willingness to deny Mosaic authorship when the data so demand was not unique to ibn Ezra and Bonfils, but appeared in a number of other premodern commentators, including even Rabbi Judah the Pious of Regensburg (ca. 1150–1217), revered mystic, theologian, and halakhic authority.[15] This rationalism on matters of authorship was thus not an idiosyncrasy of Abraham ibn Ezra; it was widely diffused among medieval Jewish exegetes, despite its apparent contradiction of traditional dogma. One might say that whereas in the Middle Ages the dogma of Mosaic authorship diffused into the Jewish folk-mind through its incorporation in various forms into the liturgy, the opposite idea, the willingness to entertain doubts on the issue, diffused (though less widely) through the incorporation of commentators like ibn Ezra into the traditional rabbinic Bible. The tension between these two opposite tendencies remains to this day.

The conclusion that Sarna draws from his impressive compilation of examples is a bit ambiguous. On the one hand, he avers that the medieval rabbinic concept of *peshat* (plain sense) "cannot be stretched to encompass the types of 'higher' and 'lower' criticism that have developed during the last two centuries." On the other hand, he does "wish to put forward the proposition that modern biblical scholarship does not actually constitute a discontinuity with tradition, but the forging of another link in an unbroken chain of Jewish exegesis," and he opposes the assumption that "had these [medieval] authorities had access to modern knowledge and scientific methodology, they would have rejected present-day solutions."[16] In sum, Sarna's position seems to be that although medieval exegesis is not the same as modern biblical study, it does lead to it naturally, so that the two forms of inquiry stand within a single continuum.

On matters of what used to be called "lower criticism," this is undoubtedly true. A medieval exegete willing to propound a novel understanding of a Hebrew word based on a Greek, Aramaic, or Arabic etymology would surely not have objected to the use of Akkadian or Ugaritic for the same purpose. On the larger matters of "higher criticism," however, it is precisely Sarna's "present-day solutions" that are conspicuous by their absence in the medieval commentaries. It is, to be sure, beyond dispute that ibn Ezra doubted the doctrine that Moses wrote each and every word of the Torah. But it cannot be gainsaid that even he included only a handful of verses among those of other authorship, and even in these cases, he, unlike Bonfils, only hints, if none too subtly, at his heterodox opinion. Why should "the person who understands . . . keep quiet" if intellectual honesty overrides traditional belief? Was it only a matter of fear of retaliation by the religious Babbitts of the day? It would seem more likely that ibn Ezra regarded the truth he had come upon as dangerous and therefore to be restricted to those of sufficient spiritual and intellectual maturity not to be shaken by it.[17] In spite of some historical connections, this position is surely not to be put on the same continuum with the modern scholars who every year announce the inadequacy of Mosaic authorship of the Pentateuch to a room full of unfamiliar adolescents in the first meeting of "Bible 101" and who publish their findings, however heterodox, as widely as the editors' acceptances will permit.

This most unmodern concept of spiritually dangerous truth — no less true for being dangerous, but no less dangerous for being true — also explains why ibn Ezra never answers the question, in Moshe Greenberg's words, "[I]f so, who did write these expressions?"[18] Whereas the modern biblical critic deems the determination of authorship, at least within broad chronological limits, a sine qua non for responsible interpretation, ibn Ezra, Bonfils, and the other more daring exegetes of the Middle Ages do not really care who, other than Moses, had a hand in the composition of the sacred text. And the reason for this highly unmodern attitude is to be found in Bonfils's supercommentary on Gen 12:6: "What should I care whether it was Moses or another prophet who wrote it?" That is, if the real author is God, it is of no account which human vessel he inspired with any given verse. As in the case of the interpretation of Maimonides's eighth principle outlined above, so here what is essential is not the *authorship* of the Torah but its *divinity* and its *unity*. In this case, these are of such moment that they override not only the dogma of Mosaic authorship, but *all* questions of authorship as well. The exegetical heterodoxy of these medieval rabbis stemmed not from theological skepticism but from its opposite, a profound and secure faith in the divine origin of Judaism. The difference between their endeavor and that of modern historical-critical study, with its passion for determining date and author, is both theoretical and practical.

The fatal weakness in Sarna's strategy to provide traditional legitimation for modern biblical study is that he allows his fundamentalist opponents to define the issue as belief in the Mosaic authorship of the Pentateuch. By drawing attention to the traditional dissents from this dogma, all he has done is to show the narrowness of the fundamentalists' image of the tradition. He has not confronted the distinctively untraditional component in modern biblical criticism. Menahem Haran defines the essential difference between the premodern approaches (which he terms "exegesis") and modern biblical criticism in these terms:

> The exegete observes only the verse as it lies before him.... Problems of authenticity or historical background of the text, for instance, never actually concerned the exegete.... The postulate of exegesis is that Scripture, being the word of God and not subject to change, is not bound to time and place, whereas the critical

method regards Scripture as a human manifestation (to be sure, a most brilliant one) of a culture confined to its own bounds of time and space — the culture of the ancient Near East.[19]

It must, of course, be readily conceded that Haran's view of scripture as only a brilliant artifact of human culture reflects the role of the Hebrew Bible among secular Israelis better than it does the conception of the book among critical biblical scholars of our time, for whom the terms "revelation" and "inspiration" may still have meaning (though not operational relevance). And it must also be conceded that traditional exegesis, Jewish and Christian, did leave some room for fallible human beings in the production and transmission of the divine book: it was not *only* "the word of God." This granted, the fact remains that Haran has correctly identified the salient distinction when he points to the divine character of the text in pre-Enlightenment exegesis and its human, culture-bound character in the distinctively modern aspects of biblical criticism. The implications of this change in attitude are indeed grave, for if we shift the focus from the divine to the human author, then modern variations of both the Muslim and Christian typological heresies will again find an opening. If the Torah is a human artifact, could it be that some of it lacks divine authorization after all, being the product not necessarily of malicious rabbis, but at least of human beings limited, like all human beings, by their cultural horizons and their self-interest? And if the Torah, however brilliant in its own time, is assumed to be the legacy only of a culture now vanished, could it be that its laws are, in fact, abrogated — not because of a change in aeon, as Pauline Christianity would have it, but because of the ordinary evolution of human history?

James Barr, in his fusillade against Brevard S. Childs's "canonical method" of biblical interpretation, has recently been at pains to argue against the view that "under biblical criticism the science of history and its methods were given control over the Bible." "On the contrary," Barr insists, "the criterion for biblical criticism is, and always has been, *what the Bible itself actually says.*"[20] There is something to this, but it must still be noted that when the Bible is perceived in the modern categories, the simultaneity of all parts of the Bible with all the others is undone — the Bible is, if you will, "decomposed" — and the unity of *"what the Bible itself actually [said]"* to the premodern exegete is fractured into a historical succession of messages, all from the past and without a clear, internal signal as to which is normative now. The application of a historical, or diachronic, perspective — even when it is denied a controlling role — severely undermines the principle that the Bible is a unity. It is precisely in opposition to this decomposition, this undoing of the traditional simultaneity of biblical literature, this fracturing of the message, that Childs devised his controversial hermeneutics.[21] The science of history need not *control* biblical study — it need only *influence* it — for the availability of the *whole* scripture (however delimited) to the traditional religious life to be seriously diminished. And when biblical theologians build their theology on a text that is perceived exclusively in diachronic terms — exclusively, that is, in its historical context — what results will, as I shall soon show, inevitably undermine the halakhic life that all the medieval rabbis discussed were at pains to protect. It is here that Rosenberg's insistence becomes relevant — historical study must not be used to nullify commandments and change religious law.

· III ·

A nice example of the way in which historical study has been used to suspend or otherwise invalidate large parts of the Bible can be seen in Paul D. Hanson's stimulating study of "The Theological Significance of Contradiction Within the Book of the Covenant."[22] In that collection (Exod 20:22–23:33), Hanson finds a glaring contrast between what he deems to be humane and inhumane ordinances. The humane ordinances include the prohibitions upon oppressing alien, widow, and orphan, exacting interest, denying justice to the poor, and working the land in the seventh year. The inhumane norms include the provision, in Hanson's words, that "slaves are property of their masters" and "women are property of their fathers and later, if they marry, of their husbands," and the expectation that "in the three cultic festivals, only males are to appear before [the Lord]."[23] A historian could argue — indeed, I think *should* argue — that there is no real contradiction here because norms of these two sorts coexist in many societies. In fact, the very perception that there are *two* sorts of norms here is external to the Book of the Covenant itself. It seems to derive, instead, from a thoroughly modern sensibility.

Hanson, however, is not interested in harmonizing his two sets of norms, either exegetically or historically. Instead, he seeks to retain the relevance and applicability of the biblical text without having to endorse aspects of it that he finds offensive. As a Christian, he could have said simply that all this Old Testament law belongs to a superseded dispensation anyway, except this would have driven him parlously close to Marcionism, and he still would have had to confront the same sort of "contradictions" in Paul, for example.[24] Instead, Hanson's strategy is to develop a scenario in which old tribal institutions are increasingly drawn into the cultic "confession of the one true God who delivered an enslaved people from oppression to communal life in covenant with him." In the process, we see "a lively dialectic within which a living confession acts upon legal materials drawn toward it." The final shape of the Book of the Covenant represents neither the total victory of the confession of the liberating God nor the unimpeded continuation of the oppressive old Near Eastern norms. Instead, we find here testimony "to the character of biblical legal traditions as a dynamic process — underway, pressing on, but never coming to rest and fulfillment."[25]

In the last paragraph of his study, Hanson asks a critical question: "Does this view of the theological significance of certain contradictions within biblical material undermine biblical authority?" His answer is that his approach "does not undermine the notion of authority, but redefines it."[26] It is telling that the adjective "biblical" has dropped out of this retort, for, in fact, in Hanson's redefinition of authority, much of the biblical material forfeits its positive character and is metamorphosed into a kind of antiscripture, the negative raw materials on which the positive side of scripture worked its liberating magic. The material that Hanson deems inhumane has become only the ugly canvas over which a beautiful picture is being painted. In fact, what Hanson calls the "dynamic process" going on behind scripture enables him to pronounce obsolescent any biblical text that he finds unpalatable. As in Islam, so in Hanson's theology not all of the Jewish Torah corresponds, even indirectly or germinally, to the will of God. Some of it is simply a deplorable human invention, except that Hanson, unlike the Muslim thinkers, sees some redeeming value in the latter category in that it serves as a foil for the liberationist deity with whom he wishes to identify the God of Israel. This theology compels Hanson to neglect the all-important fact that whatever the *historical process* was, the *text* presents the putative negative category, too, as the will of God and not as the fruit of human inadequacy. If this is not a problem for Hanson, it is only because, in his theology, the *process* countermands the *text*. The diachronic approach to the literature here produces a convenient means of voiding the currently unpalatable aspects of scripture. The price paid is the dismemberment — the decomposition — of the synchronic literary reality that was the Bible and the displacement of authority from the text as a whole onto those aspects of it with which the interpreter is already in sympathy. The authoritative statement can be found in the Bible, but it is no longer authoritative simply because it is biblical. The Bible is not normative but illustrative — and then only at its best. What it illustrates is a dynamic movement away from ancient inhumanity toward liberal humanitarianism.

Before we assess the relevance or irrelevance to Judaism of Hanson's principle of *sola liberatione,* it is important to notice the precedent for it in certain forms of Christianity. In his critique of Childs, John Barton points out that in most forms of Lutheranism (Hanson's own communion) "the only criterion of canonicity [is] the extent to which a given text [bears] witness to Christ," so that it is essential "to read each book of the Old or New Testament on its own terms *without regard* to its canonical context, and to decide whether its 'plain sense' is compatible with the Christian gospel."[27] The boldest statement of this theology is Luther's own remark in derogation of the epistle of James: "What does not teach Christ is not apostolic, even though St. Peter or Paul taught it: again, what preaches Christ would be apostolic, even though Judas, Annas, Pilate and Herod did it."[28] Now what Luther meant by "Christ" is surely distant from Hanson's "dynamic process" of sociopolitical liberation, but the hermeneutical point is that Hanson follows Luther in assessing scripture according to a feature that is not assumed to permeate every verse or even every book. Luther's variety of *sola scriptura* opposes the Roman Catholic notion of tradition as an independent source of revelation; it does not vest scripture uniformly with divine authority, and, in this, for all the differences with regard to political theology, it does smooth the way for Hanson's liberationism.

It is not only the Lutheran stream of Christianity to which Hanson's method bears typological resemblance. His view that the situation in the Book of the Covenant is essentially "a lively dialectic within which a living confession acts upon legal materials drawn toward it" replicates a classic movement of Pauline theology. Note that the law yields to the confession but not vice versa. In spite of his use of the term "dialectic," Hanson does not concede to the legal materials any right to restrict the scope of the confession of the delivering God.[29] On the contrary, the theological legitimacy of the legal materials is in direct proportion to their implementation of the cultic confession (and the fraction of them that meets this criterion is none too high). In this we see not only a reflection of Luther's belief that scripture is normative only to the extent that it teaches Christ but also a reflection of Paul's use of Torah narratives (aggadah, in rabbinic parlance) in support of his argument for the suspension of Torah law (halakhah) (e.g., Gal 4:21–5:1; Romans 4). At the basis of both Paul's and Hanson's hermeneutical strategies — again, different as they are in sociopolitical outlook — lie three crucial assumptions, all of them markedly at odds with the rabbinic tradition: that the Torah is not a systemic integer, that its confessional and its legal dimensions can be in serious contradiction, and that it is the confession rather than the law that must be ceded preeminence. In each case, the law is retained in scripture only as a sort of dead letter that shows Christians what the delivering God has delivered them from.[30]

Given the deeply Pauline structure of Hanson's theology and its indebtedness to Luther's spiritualistic concept of biblical authority, it might be thought to have no parallel in Judaism at all. It must be conceded, however, that the idea that a law is not to be practiced does have some realization in Judaism as well, although the differences with Hanson are very revealing. In rabbinic jurisprudence, a number of laws are deemed to be out of force because of uncontrollable conditions. For example, the law of the Hebrew slave in the Book of the Covenant applies, according to a baraita, only when the Jubilee Year is in force, since all Hebrew slaves are to be manumitted in the Jubilee, willy-nilly (Lev 25:39–46). The Jubilee Year, however, applies only when the whole people of Israel dwells in the land of Israel, that is, in the biblical past and the messianic future (*b. Git.* 65a and parallels). The effect of this legal reasoning is to make slavery within the covenant people obsolete in the present epoch. It is essential to remember, however, that this kind of reasoning does not proceed by *invalidating* one scriptural text in the name of another, nor by transferring the authority from the text to the historical process behind it, but by assuming that Torah law is to be inferred only from its *totality* and that discrepancies are to be harmonized rather than exploited for theological purposes. In other words, the invalidation of the law of the Hebrew slave is based on intratextual warrants, and for this reason it can never be so definitive as the invalidation based on Paul's or Hanson's extratextual warrants, Christ and liberation from oppression, respectively. Thus, in rabbinic theology (and law), the norms that are presently out of force are still treasured and revered. They are to be read liturgically, studied and taught daily, and refined dialectically. They are, in short, still authoritative — their divine origin unimpugned — and the Jew is to expect and pray for their eschatological reinstitution. In *practice,* the course of history countermanded the law, but in *theory,* the law is eternal and not a mere handmaiden of history. De facto, the oral Torah introduced changes; de jure, the authority of the written Torah remains supreme, and all its laws in effect. Where the historian perceives change, the legist insists on changelessness, stoutly refusing to allow history the regulative role. The enactments by which Judaism invalidated obsolescent practices were, in one sense, more authoritative than the written Torah — but in sanctity and theological meaning they could never approach it.

With the emergence of Reform Judaism early in the nineteenth century, this situation was reversed, as appeal to the concepts of modernity and progress came to serve as the normative criterion for determining the value of Torah law. In the words of the third plank of the Pittsburgh Platform (1885): "We recognize in the Mosaic legislation a system of training the Jewish people for its mission during its national life in Palestine, and today we accept as binding only its moral laws, and maintain only such ceremonies as elevate and sanctify our lives, but reject all such as are not adapted to the views and habits of modern civilization."[31] This statement of Reform Judaism in the nineteenth century demonstrates that the medieval rabbinic resistance to pursuing matters of human authorship was not unfounded. Subsequent history has shown that the traditional halakhic life is indeed endangered if the diachronic character of the Torah is openly and actively developed without any countervailing force. Concentration on the human authors could and, in this case, did detract from belief in the divine origin of the book. When a scripture comes to be seen as a product of culture, one that comes into existence through a long, variegated historical process, then the unity of the scripture — the simultaneity, self-referentiality, and mutual implication of *all* its parts — is thrown into doubt. As in the case of the third plank of the Pittsburgh Platform, the result is often a justification for the nonperformance of scriptural norms, in this instance, offensive or inconvenient Torah commandments (*mitsvot*). R. J. Zwi Werblowsky points out that "Liberal and Reform Judaism once welcomed Biblical criticism precisely [because] they found in criticism a welcome ally in their struggle to get rid of the Law and to substitute for it a purely ethical (and so-called 'prophetic') Judaism."[32] In fairness, however, it must also be noted that the perception of the Torah as an artifact of human culture that, like all others, reflects its own period led the liberals, in turn, to suspect that the totality of its norms could no longer be applied in the vastly different historical situation of modern Western Europe and America. As a contingent product of history, the Torah — or at least its superseded aspects — had to yield to the contingencies of history. To avoid the putative fossilization of the community, liberalism elected to fossilize large parts of the Torah, using historical methods to show that they are a dead letter. The theological liberals could do this only because they had shifted the locus of normativity from the text and the tradition onto the historical process, the dictates of autonomous reason, the conscience of the individual, and the like.

• IV •

All these efforts to define some verses of the Torah as divine and others as only human, or divine in origin but abrogated in the present, involve a denial of Maimonides's eighth principle, even according to the view that its point is not Mosaic authorship. For to Maimonides and his tannaitic sources, the doctrine that the Torah is from heaven requires that divine status be accorded *every* verse: "And his wife's name was Mehetabel" (Gen 36:39) no less than "I am the Lord your God" (Exod 20:2). For the observant Jew, this is not an abstract point of theology. Indeed, the very structure of Jewish law presupposes not only the equal authority of all parts but even their simultaneous reality as well. Disengage the parts, assign them to different periods or social groups, as responsible historical criticism cannot but do, and the halakhah falls apart.

The law of the Hebrew slave, to which reference has been made, is an instructive and not atypical case in point. In the Book of the Covenant, the manumission of male slaves takes place after six years, unless the man declines, in which case he remains a slave forever (Exod 21:20–6). This law is not contiguous with that of the Sabbatical Year in the same code (Exod 23:10–11), and from the wording ("When you acquire a Hebrew slave, he shall serve six years"), it would appear that all slaves are not to be released in the same year. The law of manumission, in short, seems unrelated to the Sabbatical in the Book of the Covenant.

In Deuteronomy, three changes have been introduced into the law of the Hebrew slave over against the Book of the Covenant: the provision for manumission now appears together with the law of the Sabbatical, perhaps suggesting that all slaves were to be released in the same year; the female slave is explicitly included; and the owner is required to send the slave away with a gift (Deut 15:1–18). But like the Book of the Covenant, Deuteronomy allows for perpetual servitude for the slave who declines freedom after six years, and it knows nothing of a Jubilee Year after seven Sabbaticals.

According to the section of Leviticus known to modern scholars as the "Holiness Code" (Leviticus 17–26), it is in this Jubilee that manumission takes place (Lev 25:8–17, 29–34). The Holiness Code knows nothing of a release after six years of service and no possibility of perpetual servitude for a slave who declines freedom.

The majority of historical-critical scholars is inclined to see in these related but differing sets of provisions a development from the rudimentary requirements of the Book of the Covenant to the complex and sophisticated system of the Holiness Code, with Deuteronomy occupying an intermediary position. Indeed, a compelling historical argument can be made that not only in the law of the Hebrew slave but also more generally, the Deuteronomic Code was intended to *replace* and not simply to augment or clarify the Book of the Covenant.[33] In recent years, biblical scholarship has been moving perceptibly away from this model of uniform historical succession toward one of social differentiation to explain such contradictions. This shift does not, however, reverse the "decomposing" character of modern critical study. Only the solvent is different — sociology rather than history. The effect on the manifest text remains as devastating as ever.

Rabbinic exegesis, on which traditional Jewish practice rests and which, in turn, reflects traditional practice, makes a radically different assumption — that the different provisions must be seen as synchronous and applicable to one group, the whole House of Israel. Thus, the provision for perpetual servitude in the Book of the Covenant and Deuteronomy must be understood as references to the Jubilee, which is known only from Leviticus:

> "You shall return" [Lev 25:10] and "forever" [Exod 21:6; Deut 15:17] both had to be written. For if the Merciful One had written [only] "forever," I would have thought it really meant forever. Therefore the Merciful One wrote "You shall return." (*b. Qidd.* 15a)[34]

It is important to note that by reading these differing bodies of literature as if they are one simultaneous reality — as indeed they are in the Torah — the rabbis produce a law for which *no* one passage in the Torah provides evidence. Exod 21:6 and Deut 15:17 know of no Jubilee Year; Lev 25:10 knows of no emancipation in the seventh year. The rabbis, depending only on the Pentateuch as their source of law, have enunciated a law unknown in the Pentateuch. "Where a law exists in different forms in Leviticus and Deuteronomy," argues Barr against

Childs's canonical method, "the canon as such does not tell us which should be taken as the dominant."[35] Quite so, but at least in the sense of the classical Jewish conception of the Mosaic corpus, the canon tells us that *neither* should be taken as the dominant. The idea of the uniform authority of the Torah requires its interpreters to recognize at least in the last stage of their work (but not necessarily before then) the present literary simultaneity of texts that once stood in historical succession or in a comparable relationship of mutual exclusion.

In a celebrated essay that sounded a clarion call for the emerging historical-critical approach to the Bible, Benjamin Jowett (1817–93) wrote "that Scripture has one meaning — the meaning which it had to the mind of the Prophet or Evangelist who first uttered or wrote, to the hearers or readers who first received it."[36] This works fairly well with this or that code in the Pentateuch, for example, but who wrote the whole thing and who first received it? If appeal is made to the redactors, shall we treat these murky figures as authors and privilege their intentions over those of their several sources? Perhaps so, but it is also quite possible that the redactors of the Pentateuch worked more like anthologizers unaware of the problems their labors posed, law being for them a matter of customary practice unrelated to current exegesis. Perhaps, instead, they wanted us to pick one code over the others in the smorgasbord of law that they provided, or perhaps they thought of Deuteronomy as the final and therefore normative statement. We shall never know, and partly because we shall never know, we must be skeptical of the efforts of Barr and others to equate the *signal* that the canon (in whatever form) sends with the *intention* of the canonizers.[37] However problematic the concept of authors' intentions has become, the analogous concept of redactors' intention is thus even more nettlesome. Rather than basing our interpretations on something so unavailable, we should be better advised to concede with Barton that "the text has meanings that no one ever meant."[38]

But how can the classic historical-critical method, with its concentration on "one meaning" (the author's), do justice to a text that, as it stands, has no author, so that its meanings are ones "that no one ever meant"? How can a method that distinguishes itself by its insistence on locating the text historically (and now sociologically) ever do justice to literature that conflates concrete situations and thus repels all efforts to define it temporally, locally, and socially? It is in this respect that the authorless text presupposed by a synchronic, or holistic, mode of analysis has certain affinities with the divinely authored text of premodern Jewish tradition. The affinities are operational rather than theological; they become clear when the modes of interpretation of the two are seen in contrast with the author-centered interpretation championed by modern biblical criticism. A method of interpretation that took cognizance of the authorlessness of the received text and the inclusion in it of "meanings that no one ever meant" would, like Maimonides's eighth principle, work to preserve the entirety of the textual unity (in Maimonides's case, the Pentateuch), rejecting the kind of eclecticism that fails to reckon with the systemic character of the text. But unlike fundamentalism, it would not seek to deny the processes of change and development that have yielded the text "presently in our possession," to use the older language. Instead of denying historical investigation, the kind of interpretation I have in mind would relativize it. It would recognize that the cost of restoring textual units to their *historical* context can only be some loss of their *literary* context, and, faithful to what I take to be the real meaning of the eighth principle, it would hold that the foundation for the edifice that is rabbinic Judaism is not the several sources of the Torah in their respective historical settings but the Torah "presently in our possession" in its integral, systemic wholeness. The efforts to take the text apart would not cease; they are informative and, as we shall soon see, not without precedent in the premodern tradition of biblical interpretation. They would, however, be dialectically checked by a continual awareness of the need to put the text back together in a way that makes it available in the present and in its entirety — not merely in the past and in the form of historically contextualized fragments.

• V •

The form of biblical scholarship that would incorporate these reflections is one like that of Brevard Childs, which, in the words of James L. Mays, "holds a series of moments [in the history of the biblical text] in perspective, primarily the original situation, the final literary setting, and the context of the canon."[39] In this form of scholarship, traditional doctrines have no authority over historical reconstruction or the exegesis of passages in their more limited contexts, and the historical-critical method must be allowed free rein. For this there is an interesting precedent in the bolder forms of medieval *pashtanut,* or plain-sense exegesis. Rabbi Samuel ben Meir (Rashbam), the great *pashtan* of Northern France in the twelfth century, provides an instructive example. A

Talmudist of great erudition and prodigious industry, Rashbam's commitment to the halakhic system is beyond doubt. Yet in his commentary on the Torah he was prepared to deny that the exegesis on which the rabbis of the Talmud based a halakhah was valid as the plain sense (*peshat*). To return to our example of the law of the Hebrew slave for illustration, Rashbam held that when Exod 21:6 tells us that the slave who refuses emancipation in the seventh year must serve "forever," it means exactly that — "all the days of his life"[40] — and not "until the Jubilee," as a traditional harmonistic exegesis would require. The Jewish Bible is now no longer limited to the Bible of the talmudic rabbis. For Rashbam *pashtanut* means the pursuit of the meaning of a text within its most limited context, the minimal sense unit. The larger, rabbinic context, which is based on the written Torah as an indissoluble whole (as well as on the oral Torah), remains normative for behavior, but it is not permitted to silence or marginalize the more limited context of the *peshat*.[41] The authority of the Torah does not require faithful exegetes to deny the contradictions within it, but the frank recognition of the contradictions does not allow them to base religious life and practice on something less than the whole. I argue that if either of the two halves of this paradox is omitted, something essential in the heritage of medieval Jewish biblical study will be lost.

On this pursuit of the historical and literal senses of scripture,[42] Jews, Christians, and others can work in tandem, and the broad ecumenical character of critical biblical scholarship can and should continue. Of these more limited literary and historical contexts of a passage, there can be no privileged interpretation, no uniquely Jewish or uniquely Christian form of biblical scholarship. Just as in medieval Europe there could be interreligious agreement on the *sensus literalis*,[43] so in modern biblical criticism there will continue to be a broad base for agreement on the meaning of textual units in their most limited literary or historical settings. But when we come to "the final literary setting" and even more so to "the context of the canon," we must part company, for *there is no nonparticularistic access to these larger contexts,* and no decision on these issues, even when made for secular purposes, can be neutral between Judaism and Christianity.[44] Jews and Christians can, of course, study each other's Bible and even identify analogically or empathetically with the interpretations that the other's traditional context warrants, growing in discernment and self-understanding as a consequence. For the normative theological task, however, a choice must be made: Does the canonical context of the Abraham story, for example, include the Abraham material in Galatians and Romans or not?[45] For Christians it must; for Jews it must not. May commentators rest from their labors without having correlated the written text with its classical and medieval rabbinic expositions? Christians may and almost always do; Jews may not. It will do no good to plead that the object of interpretation is the *final* form of the text, for *when* the text has reached finality, *when* it is closed and nothing more may be added to the page or to the collection is exactly the point at issue. In short, Judaism and Christianity differ from each other not only over "what it means" as opposed to "what it meant";[46] they also differ over the antecedent of "it," and this difference, crucial to the shape and identity of those communities, can never be resolved by historical criticism.

The largest unit, the "canon" in Childs's rather Protestant formulation, is itself a category that derives from postbiblical tradition, however one defines the "Bible."[47] The Pentateuch, on which Maimonides and his talmudic antecedents rest so much weight, is itself a postbiblical construct, despite the biblical attribution of the highest prophetic gifts to Moses alone.[48] The idea of five books is unknown in the Hebrew Bible itself, and deference to Moses is not widespread therein and did not prevent the school of Ezekiel, for example, from propounding a law code in blatant contradiction to those in the Pentateuch.[49] Chronologically and literarily, the analysis of biblical texts through the lenses of these larger units, the canon, the Torah of Moses, or whatever, is no longer biblical studies proper but the study of postbiblical Judaism. For the traditional Jew, however, this postbiblical lens has its own normative character and may not be disregarded simply because it distorts the *peshat*. What I believe I have here demonstrated is that no Jewish theology consonant with the classical rabbinic tradition can be built on a perception of the biblical text that denies the unity of the Torah of Moses as a current reality, whatever the long, complex, and thoroughly historical process through which that Torah came into being. In insisting that the supreme document of revelation is the whole Pentateuch and that the whole Pentateuch must ultimately (but not immediately or always) be correlated with the oral Torah of the rabbis, Jewish thinkers will separate themselves not only from those who absolutize the historical-critical perspective but also from their Christian colleagues in the field of "biblical theology." Only within the limited area of the smaller literary and historical contexts is an ecumenical biblical theology possible, and only as awareness grows of the difference that context makes shall we understand where agreement is possible and where it is not, and why.

Chapter 4

———— • ————

Theological Consensus
or Historicist Evasion?
Jews and Christians in Biblical Studies

· I ·

A few years ago I was asked to speak at a conference on the question of whether there can be a joint Jewish and Christian reading of the Hebrew Bible or whether we must choose between the Tanakh and the Old Testament. My thoughts turned immediately to the title of a collection that had appeared several years earlier. The book is entitled *Biblical Studies: Meeting Ground of Jews and Christians*.[1] The idea that Jews and Christians might meet to discuss the Bible is, of course, hardly surprising. Consider, for example, the Great Disputation between Rabbi Moses ben Nachman (Nachmanides) and the convert Pablo Christiani in Barcelona in 1263. The difference, of course, is that the meeting that the editors intend is not marked by disputation but by its opposite, collaboration and cooperation. What has made this new situation possible is not only the phenomenon of ecumenical dialogue as it has developed over the past three decades, but also a change within biblical studies themselves, one that Lawrence Boadt, a Catholic priest, is at pains to point out in his introduction:

> The tremendous gains in the study of Scripture itself in this century... [mostly] stem from our vastly enlarged knowledge of ancient history and civilization. This in turn has led to a deepened understanding of the manner of expression and the literary out-

put of the semitic world, and has created a scientific passion for capturing the original setting and sense of the biblical books.[2]

What this historical approach shows, according to Boadt, is that "the relationship of the Hebrew Scriptures to the New Testament . . . must begin with the premise that each speaks from its own complete integrity."[3] Pablo Christiani, call your office!

The idea that the historical study of the Bible has replaced Jewish-Christian disputation with ecumenical collaboration has not historically been one with a resounding resonance among Jews. Solomon Schechter, the great rabbinicist who was the guiding spirit of the Jewish Theological Seminary of America in its formative period, described "Higher Criticism" as "Higher Anti-Semitism" and defined its goal as the destruction of the raison d'être of the Jewish people, "denying all our claims for the past and leaving us without hope for the future."[4] And if this polemic from the turn of the century now seems out of date, consider a scene from Chaim Potok's novel, *In the Beginning.* David Lurie, a yeshivah student on the verge of ordination, has just informed his father, Max, of his application to a biblical studies program in a university:

> "Tell me what it means to study Bible in a university. Your teachers will be *goyim?*"
> "And Jews."
> "The Jews are observers of the commandments?"
> "I don't know. They may be. I'm not certain."
> "It is unimportant to you that they may not be observers of the commandments? . . . You will study Torah with *goyim* and with Jews who are like *goyim?* What do they know of the Torah?"[5]

It is easy to dismiss Max Lurie's words as the product of mere social prejudice, as tenacious as it is primitive, and simple fairness requires me to concede that such prejudice does indeed exist. I can attest from experience that in the minds of many Jews, perhaps most, and even many scholars of Judaica, it is better to study Bible with a Jew hostile to Jewish practice than with a Gentile deeply respectful of it. Such irrationality, however, does not characterize David's father, for his concern is not that his son study simply with Jews, but with *observant* Jews and not, as he indelicately puts it, "with Jews who are like *goyim.*" I find it fascinating that Father Boadt's introduction to the collection of essays never raises Max Lurie's question: In what way and to what degree are the Jews who meet Christians in biblical studies Jewish? Nor, I might add, does it raise the equally pressing converse of his question: What is Christian about the premise that the Hebrew Scripture "speaks from its own complete integrity" over against the New Testament? If I may state in advance the conclusion of this chapter, it is simply this: to the extent that Jews and Christians bracket their religious commitments in the pursuit of biblical studies, they meet not as Jews and Christians, but as something else, something not available in the days of Nachmanides and Pablo Christiani. The ground that the historical methods mentioned by Boadt have opened up can indeed be *common* to Jews and Christians, but more often it is actually *neutral* between them — a difference that has drawn insufficient attention. Though Jews mindful of Barcelona in 1263 or of Schechter's "Higher Anti-Semitism" will be grateful for the small favor of neutral ground, neither they nor Christians should overlook the costs and the limits of religious neutrality. Nor should a method that studiously pursues *neutrality* be mistaken for the key to a genuine and profound *dialogue* between these two great religious communities.

• II •

Even this lesser claim that the modern study of the Bible takes place on ground neutral between Jews and Christians has been challenged. James L. Kugel, for instance, has recently argued "that from its inception, this scholarly discipline was fundamentally a Protestant undertaking, one might even say, a form of Protestant piety" and one that "has, in ways great and small, still retained much of its particularly Protestant character." In support of his assertion, Kugel develops two types of arguments. The first is an argument from certain points often made by historical critics, "tantalizing particulars," as he puts it. The second and more profound argument involves the very stance of the modern critic, a stance that seeks "to establish as direct and unmediated a link as possible between the modern reader/interpreter and the biblical author at the moment of his speaking his words." Kugel connects this stance with the Protestant belief in a "flush encounter between man and God, unmediated by Church hierarchy and functionaries, by saints and human interveners."[6]

In his first type of argument, the "tantalizing particulars," Kugel offers what I regard as undeniable proof of a certain sort of Protestant bias in the putatively critical assessment of aspects of biblical history and thought. In the large amount of scholarly sympathy for the secession of the Northern Kingdom in the tenth century B.C.E., for example, Kugel, like myself,[7] sees a retrojection of the Protestant Reformation itself. Jeroboam's "rejection of entrenched power (including a religious hierarchy)" and his establishment of relatively "decentralized worship" (with two royal chapels rather than one) is not, as the Deuteronomistic history would have it (e.g., 1 Kgs 13:1–5), a sin of the highest order, but rather "a return to an older, truer . . . form of worship." Similarly, the relative lack of interest in the cult and the postexilic books bespeaks the classical Protestant preference for prophet over priest, for the word over the sacrament, and for the spirit over institutional structures, especially those that suggest the putative degeneration of Israelite religion into Judaism, that is, the religion that Jesus is believed to have sought either to cleanse or to overthrow. Or again, Kugel notes that "among Semitic languages, there is one that has consistently been given the cold shoulder in Christian seminaries and secular universities: mishnaic Hebrew," and he points out that the requirements of many Christian seminaries that New Testament students demonstrate knowledge of biblical Hebrew but not mishnaic is odd, since it is the later dialect that is most relevant to their work.[8] These curricular decisions are obviously owing to a religious stance that is anything but neutral, as Kugel suggests. I might add that more than a few scholars who think, whether they acknowledge it or not, that rabbinic Hebrew and Aramaic are too distant to be relevant to the Hebrew of the Bible, still apply themselves vigorously to the study of a form of Arabic that is half a millennium or more younger than these rabbinic tongues. And though no small amount of scholarly literature relevant to both Testaments of the Christian Bible is written in modern Hebrew, the number of scholars in this supposedly neutral field who can read modern Hebrew is exiguous. Only some form of residual Christian supersessionism can explain these strange, though all too familiar, data.[9]

Before considering Kugel's deeper argument, that the stance of critical scholars is essentially Protestant whatever their actual affiliation, I should like to add one particular of my own. This is the very definition of the field of biblical studies, even when the adjective refers only to the Hebrew Bible. The unspoken assumption of this definition is that the definitive break lies between the last of the biblical books (most likely, Daniel) and the next period, that of Qumran, Diaspora, and pretannaitic Judaism, as well as of the nascent church. I can imagine other ways of dividing the pie, though I cannot think of a long-standing program that actually does so. Consider, for example, the tendency to speak of

"Israelite religion" until the exile but "Judaism" afterward. Though the distinction has traditionally been made in disparagement of the later period, a strong argument could be made that Ezra (fifth century B.C.E.), for example, has more in common with Rabbi Judah the Patriarch (late second–early third century C.E.) than either has with Isaiah of Jerusalem, the great prophet of the eighth century B.C.E. As the Jewish authorities in the land of Israel acting under commissions from Gentile emperors, Ezra and Judah faced similar challenges, challenges that were unknown to Isaiah, and they strove for similar goals, namely, the standardization of religious practice within a society whose penchant for tearing itself apart was potentially suicidal. Indeed, one might go further and draw a kind of typological parallel between the messianic fervor in Jerusalem two generations before Ezra (Haggai, Zechariah) and that in the same locale two generations before Judah (Simon bar Kosiba [=bar Kokhba]). Having done so, one could go on to explore the legal activism of these two figures in light of this larger sociopolitical analogy between them.

My point is that the reason such studies are not common is that they are interdisciplinary, and this, in turn, is because the disciplinary boundaries have been drawn on grounds that are more confessional than historical. Every periodization makes a normative claim, though the claim is rarely explicit. The claim implicit in the setting of a disciplinary boundary between Ezra and Judah (but not between Isaiah and Ezra) is that a major revolution in the history of Judaism happened about the time of Jesus, so that biblical and rabbinic Judaism (admittedly different) cannot even be put on a continuum. In this connection, it is revealing to see how many studies entitled *History of Israel* end not with the last book of the Hebrew Bible, but two or three centuries later, in the time of the early church. A particularly curious and chilling example is Martin Noth's *History of Israel,* which ends after the defeat of the bar Kosiba rebellion in 135 C.E. Noth's last sentence is this: "Thus ended the ghastly epilogue of Israel's history."[10] What is curious is that Noth had already conceded in his introduction that national sovereignty was not essential to his definition of Israel.[11] To be sure, he did regard the existence of a homeland and the "chance of united historical action," especially participation in a common cult, to be essential to "Israel."[12] The problem is twofold. First, the Jews continued to live in their Palestinian homeland in large numbers for several centuries after 135 C.E., and, second, the Diaspora had by that date already attained venerable antiquity anyway. Furthermore, the rabbinic focus on the study and practice of Torah came to provide much of the sense of centrality and common experience that the Temple had offered in an earlier historical situation. Thus, Noth could just as easily have ended his history centuries earlier than 135 C.E., or, for that matter, centuries later. He also could have affirmed, like John Bright, J. Alberto Soggin, and some other Christian historians of Israel, that the history of Israel has never ended and perdures to this day in the form of Jewish historical experience.[13]

So much for what is curious in Noth's conclusion. What is chilling in it is that only half a decade after the Holocaust, a German professor at the University of Bonn could write that "the ghastly epilogue of Israel's history" had actually happened eighteen hundred years before those horrific events. Obviously, Noth knew that the Jews continued to exist after the Hadrianic rebellion and were even establishing a state named Israel as he was writing his history.[14] His choice to terminate the history of Israel in 135 C.E. — though clothed in the garb of historical analysis — was actually motivated by theology: Jewry forfeited its status as Israel about the time that the last New Testament documents were being composed. This, in turn, doubtless reflects, at least indirectly, the long history of Christian supersessionist thinking, which perhaps began with the insistence of Paul, or at least the early Paul, that it is Christians through faith rather than Jews through birth who inherit the status of Isaac, the son by the promise (Gal 4:28–5:1). Noth's choice of an ending also reflects the hoary Christian idea that the destruction of the Temple and the dispersion of Jewry (which were not historically contemporaneous) were a punishment for the rejection of the claims made on behalf of Jesus. Here we must not fail to draw attention to Noth's remark that the failed rebellions against Rome culminated a "process of inner and outer dissolution." Presumably, the rabbinic religion that Jews have struggled for two millennia to uphold is a prime symptom of that putative process of dissolution. If we bear in mind that Noth and others like him sincerely presented themselves as critical historians rather than as theologians, is it any wonder that so many Jews consider historical criticism of their Bible to be not only *goyish* but anti-Jewish as well?

Kugel's second type of argument for the Protestant character of biblical scholarship involves not such "tantalizing particulars" as these, but rather the basic stance of the modern critic, a stance in which, in his words, "nothing was to intervene between the open page of the Bible and its interpreter."[15] It must not be missed that one can concede every one of the "tantalizing particulars" of Protestant or other Christian bias that Kugel and I (among others) have developed without conceding the larger and more profound point that the stance of devout Protestants and critical historians toward the text need be the same. The truth of a method must be logically distinguished from the uses to which it is put. At the end of the little essay of Kugel's from which I have been quoting, he does recognize this when he writes that "intellectual honesty compels [Jewish biblicists] to immerse ourselves in the disciplines of biblical scholarship and its conclusions (albeit... somewhat more on our own terms)." I take the assumption here to be that "the disciplines of biblical scholarship and its conclusions"[16] are not "in [their] very essence, Protestant"[17] after all — that is, that the Protestant conclusions are no more necessary to the discipline of biblical studies than the conclusions of Nazi eugenics, let us say, are necessary to the discipline of genetics. The burden of the next part of my argument is that the Protestant biases are not only unnecessary to the historical-critical method, but, in fact, contradict its assumptions. We begin by turning to the origins of historical consciousness in the modern West.

· III ·

In *The Renaissance Sense of the Past,* Peter Burke speaks of three elements that make up the "sense of history": "the sense of anachronism," "the awareness of evidence" (that is, a willingness to evaluate putative evidence), and "the interest in causation." Lest his readers think that the first element has always dominated the study of the past, Burke points out that "medieval men lacked a sense of the past being different in quality from the present."[18] As for the Bible, "Since it was the word of God, who was eternal, there was no point in asking when the different parts of it were written down. It was treated not as a historical document but as an oracle; that is, what it had meant was subordinated to what it could mean."[19]

The lack of interest in authorship and literary chronology to which Burke points is nicely exemplified by those medieval Jewish exegetes who, like modern critics, doubted the inherited doctrine of Moses' authorship of the entire Pentateuch, yet, quite unlike modern critics, failed to consider the questions of by whom and when the non-Mosaic passages were written.[20] The very medieval and very unmodern reason is nicely stated by Joseph Bonfils (Hebrew), a fourteenth-century rabbi who wrote a supercommentary to Abraham ibn Ezra's Torah commentary: "What should I care whether it was Moses or another prophet who wrote it, since the words of all of them are true and inspired?"[21] Some

Jewish traditionalists, eager to show that modern biblical criticism is kosher, find in the heterodoxy of ibn Ezra, Bonfils, and the like, the certificate of kashrut they are seeking,[22] but the last thing I can imagine modern biblical critics saying is that they could not care less who wrote a given passage. Indeed, nothing has been more characteristic of the modern study of the Bible than a passion for questions of authorship and dating, and this passion is the outgrowth of a certain very unmedieval skepticism about the divinity, eternity, and immutability of the biblical message. I might add that the central figures of the Protestant Reformation are not to be numbered among those infected with this skepticism.

It is in the time of Petrarch (1304–74) that Burke sees the beginnings of the change from the medieval to the Renaissance sense of the past. He points out that the great Italian poet "explored Roman ruins" in hopes of "reconstruct[ing] the past from its physical remains." Petrarch was, moreover, "interested in inscriptions," and "he collected Roman coins and used them as historical evidence."[23] Most important, whereas medieval lawyers "thought of law as something outside time," Petrarch insisted that law be seen in its historical context.[24] We need only remind ourselves that Petrarch and Bonfils were contemporaries to realize the difference between Renaissance and medieval thinking on this point and to become aware that the terms refer more to mentalities than to periods.

Petrarch's sense of anachronism led him easily to the second of Burke's three elements that make up the sense of history, "the awareness of evidence." Burke points out that arguing on both formal and substantive grounds, Petrarch was able to prove that a document purporting to exempt Austria from the domain of Emperor Charles IV was not written by Julius Caesar at all.[25] This foreshadowed a whole series of exposés of forgeries in the Renaissance, which, as I shall soon argue, is not unconnected to the emergence of modern biblical criticism. Burke points out that in the century after Petrarch, Nicholas of Cusa, Reginald Pecock, and Lorenzo Valla all independently exposed the *Donation of Constantine*, a document in which the emperor was supposed to have given temporal power over Italy to the popes.[26] This discrediting of an ecclesiastical charter in order to assist in the birth of a new political order also foreshadows the emergence of the historical-critical attitude to the Bible two centuries later, as we shall see.

Burke also takes note of Valla's *Annotations on the New Testament*, in which he thinks "of the Bible as a historical document, written in particular historical circumstances," and not an inalterable document either, as Valla's willingness to suggest textual emendations shows. Burke connects this with the work of John Colet (ca. 1467–1519), a friend of Erasmus who "compared [the New Testament] with other sources for ancient history," such as Suetonius's life of Claudius. But most relevant to the birth of biblical criticism is Nicholas of Cusa's *The Sieving of the Qur'an* (1460), in which three components are distinguished — in Burke's words, "Nestorian Christianity, a Jewish adviser of Muhammad, and the corruptions introduced by Jewish 'correctors' after Muhammad's death." "This was," as Burke notes, "to treat the Koran as a historical document, and to write the history of its leading ideas."[27] It would be two centuries until men like Benedict Spinoza and Richard Simon would approach the Bible in the same way, but the connections of the nascent historical criticism of the Bible with the Renaissance sense of the past are undeniable.

Every one of the figures I have named in this connection — Petrarch, Nicholas, Pecock, Valla, and Colet — lived before the Protestant Reformation. It is not the Reformation that originated the acute and potentially explosive awareness of the difference between primary and secondary meanings, between primary sources and their secondary elaboration or distortion. What the Reformation did was to recast this awareness in highly charged theological language (*sola fide, sola gratia, sola scriptura*) and, in some instances, to change the relative preference for original meanings, already rapidly growing less relative, into something more like an absolute norm. "The Scripture hath but one sense," proclaimed William Tyndale (ca. 1492–1536), "which is the literal sense."[28] It must not be missed, however, that the tendency to set aside all senses but the basic (*peshat* in medieval Hebrew parlance) had been going on for over four centuries when the Reformation began. Moshe Greenberg points out that from the eleventh century on, Jewish exegesis is marked by "ever-increasing skill in, and preference for, ascertaining the plain sense . . . , an awareness of the invalidity of midrashic interpretations as an exegetical resource," and "a growing interest in the historical context of prophecies," as witnessed, for example, in the work of David Qimchi (1160–1235).[29] It does not strike me as coincidental that the great age of midrash compilation was coming to an end just as this preference for scripture's plain sense (*peshat*) over its homiletical meaning (*derash*) was coming into its own. My point is that the awareness of the difference between primary and secondary meanings and the preference for the former for purposes of exegesis are not unique to Protestantism or even to Christianity; nor do they originate with the Renaissance sense of the past and its embarrassment at anachronism. It did not take the Reformation to teach Jews that the study of midrash is not the study of Tanakh. What Protestantism introduced was a certain contempt for everything that was not biblical and a conviction that tradition that was not faithful to scripture was illegitimate (though Protestantism here had a Jewish antecedent in Karaism). To the extent that those engaged in modern biblical studies take those positions, they are indeed indebted to certain forms of Protestantism, but the history of biblical studies among Jews and Catholics abundantly demonstrates that the modern methods hardly require those classical Reformation attitudes. Indeed, those attitudes now seem quite quaint to a large number of historical-critical scholars with Protestant allegiances.

• IV •

As I remarked above, Spinoza's work on the Bible, though it came in the middle of the seventeenth century, is best placed within the tradition of the new sense of the past of the Renaissance humanists. To be sure, at times Spinoza sounds Protestant and thus appears to lend credence to the claim that biblical criticism, of which all concede he was a pioneer, must follow a Protestant agenda. When, for example, Spinoza tells us that "our knowledge of Scripture must then be looked for in Scripture only,"[30] he echoes the Reformation claim that the Bible is its own interpreter (*interpres sui ipsius*) and requires no ecclesiastical or other traditionary mediation. And when he concludes that the "authority of the Hebrew high-priests [is not a] confirmation of the authority of the Roman pontiffs to interpret religion, [but] rather tend[s] to establish universal freedom of judgment,"[31] he echoes a Protestant note that goes well beyond the humanistic critiques of the fifteenth century. This same penchant for breaking with traditional authority rather than simply protesting its misuse can be seen in Spinoza's treatment of Judaism. Excommunicated for obscure reasons from the Sephardic congregation of Amsterdam in 1656, Spinoza turned against the Jewish tradition and even against the Jews themselves with fury. "Now the Hebrew nation has lost all its grace and beauty," he wrote.[32] The Jews' preservation is owing largely to "gentile hatred,"[33] their religion having already in the Second Commonwealth sunk "into a degrading superstition, while the true meaning and interpretation of the laws became corrupted."[34] Spinoza's anti-Judaism both recapitulates classical Christian supersessionism and adumbrates an important theme among scholars of Israelite history, and of Old Testament theology, into our own day. In fact, few scholarly models have been more enduring in any field than the degenerative model of ancient Israelite history in biblical studies, with its ideal early period being progressively corrupted by Jewish priests and legists. The content of the ideal may change — most recently, it has become social and sexual egalitarianism[35] — but the underlying model has proven phenomenally durable, and this is undoubtedly to be connected with the fact that a principal *bête noire* is somehow always halakhic Judaism.[36]

In spite of these patent debts to Protestant and generally Christian positions, however, Spinoza's biblical criticism is actually, at the level of fundamental method, profoundly at odds with the Christian legacy and especially with its Reformation component. To take the essential point first, Spinoza denied supernatural revelation altogether. In contrast to the Protestant doctrine of the Bible as the unique and unparalleled word of God, Spinoza held that since "our mind subjectively contains in itself and partakes of the nature of God ... it follows that we may rightly assert the nature of the human mind ... to be a primary cause of Divine revelation."[37] Spinoza writes here of "the human mind" and not the inspired mind because in his view revelation (if we may still use the old term to denote the new entity) was universally available and the prophets differed from the masses only by virtue of their "unusually vivid imaginations"; they had no special knowledge.[38] Now if Spinoza's position looks like an escalation of Luther's notion of the priesthood of the individual believer (as it may in part be), consider that the claim of special authority that Spinoza sought to discredit was not simply that of the church but that of the Bible itself. His dagger is aimed at the very heart of the Protestant concept of authority, that is, the pneumatic experience that was thought to have produced the Bible and, through it, to animate the special life of Christians. When Spinoza concluded that "the rule for [biblical] interpretation should be nothing but the natural light of reason which is common to all — not any supernatural light nor any external authority,"[39] he was protesting Luther and Calvin no less than the Roman church. Earlier we saw that the humanist slogan "back to the sources" (*ad fontes*) set the stage for the Reformation doctrine of exclusive scriptural authority (*sola scriptura*). Now we see the movement come full circle, as Spinoza grants to the Bible no more reverence than the humanists granted the *Donation of Constantine* or than Nicholas granted the Qur'an. As Michael L.

Morgan puts it, "Spinoza's hidden assumption is that the Bible is like any other book."[40] It is this humanistic, rationalistic assumption (for it is never really argued, but only presupposed) that separates Spinoza from the classical Jewish and Christian traditions. Though the assumption is one that may have caused him a certain social isolation in seventeenth-century Holland, it is also one with a vast resonance in the subsequent history of biblical criticism. One need only consider that the idea of reading the Bible "like any other book" played a central role in the great manifesto for biblical criticism of Benjamin Jowett, "On the Interpretation of Scripture," published in 1860.[41] An assumption external to both Judaism and Christianity was put forth as the regulative principle for reading their respective foundational literatures.

Given Spinoza's naturalism, it follows that the meaning of a scriptural passage is the author's meaning alone, not God's, or, as he put it, "[W]e are at work not on the truth of passages, but solely on their meaning."[42] In order to find that out, we must engage in the activity that, as we saw, was so marginal to the medieval Jewish commentators, even those who doubted the traditional attributions: we must determine "the life, the conduct, and the studies of the author of each book, who he was, what was the occasion, and the epoch of his writing, whom did he write for, and in what language."[43] It is in Spinoza's program for biblical scholarship in chapter 7 of the *Tractatus Theologico-Politicus* that we see the origin of the preoccupation with dating and authorship that dominated the distinctly modern study of the Bible until this generation and continues to flourish. One effect has been the dismemberment of the Bible, as its components are disengaged from the larger whole and assigned to different periods, schools, and social sectors. The equivalent of the Christian sin against the Holy Spirit for this author-centered hermeneutic is "taking a passage out of context," the last word referring not to the *literary* context that is the larger Bible, Jewish, Catholic, or Protestant, but to the *historical* context of the original author, who was, of course, neither a rabbinic Jew, nor a Roman Catholic, nor a Protestant. The effect, whether intended or not (I believe Spinoza intended it), is to deny the Bible to traditional religion on biblical grounds, or as Morgan nicely puts it, to "proceed on the basis of the Bible to transcend the Bible."[44] If, as Schechter thought, higher criticism sought to destroy the raison d'être of the Jewish people, it must also be pointed out that if the critics had followed the program of Spinoza's great *Tractatus*, as in large measure they have, then the raison d'être of the church would also be

undermined, and on grounds that the churches could hardly reject —
the message of the Bible itself!

Richard H. Popkin points out that Spinoza fits into a tradition of
skepticism fueled in no small measure by the Reformation itself, which
having denied "the fundamental criterion" of Christian authority, willy-
nilly unleashed a great criteriological problem: "How does one tell
which of the alternative possibilities ought to be accepted?"[45] But, as
Popkin also notes, Spinoza's skepticism on religious matters did not
extend to mathematics and metaphysics.[46] I would add that one result of this displacement of authority from religion to philosophy (with
which scripture was no longer to be harmonized) was a theoretical relativization of Judaism and Christianity. Leo Strauss hinted at this when
he observed that for Spinoza, the two Testaments were equal, so that
the characteristic features of each (such as Torah and commandments
[*mitsvot*] or the cross) are dispensable because they cancel each other
out.[47] Indeed, the reason, according to Spinoza, that critical investiga-
tions are essential is "that we may not confound precepts which are
eternal with those which served only a temporary purpose."[48] What is
left after these operations have been completed is a few vague moral
imperatives, namely, the practice of justice and charity and obedience
to the state.[49] These are the substance of the universal and immutable
philosophical religion with which Spinoza hoped to replace Judaism
and Christianity and thus to end the political turmoil and insane blood-
letting that Christian sectarianism had inflicted upon his country and
the rest of Europe.

In order to put religious divisions behind him without attacking
the Bible head-on, Spinoza had to show that the divisions in humanity that its law mandates — the divisions between Jew and Gentile and
between Christian and non-Christian — are now simply obsolete. Thus,
he argues that the law revealed by God to Moses was merely the law
of the ancient Hebrew state; therefore "it was binding on none but
Hebrews, and not even on Hebrews after the downfall of their nation."[50] If this idea that the Torah once obligated only the Jews and
now not even them looks like Pauline supersessionism, look again, for
Spinoza argues not from dispensationalism, but from history: he sees
no change of aeons, but only a new political situation. His assumption is that these putatively spiritual systems are really only political.
Whereas Maimonides, for example, had seen the Mosaic polity as the
correlative within politics of God's characteristic actions,[51] for Spinoza
the issue was exclusively one of social control. (In this, he antici-

pated the ideology critique now so fashionable among liberationist exegetes and deconstructionist critics.)[52] History supplied Spinoza with the coffin into which he placed the Torah. Again, an analogy with the Renaissance humanists and their discrediting of documents like the *Donation of Constantine* readily suggests itself. Today it is too easily forgotten that the context in which pioneers of biblical criticism like Spinoza and Thomas Hobbes[53] presented their heterodox findings was one of political debate in which the authors' goal was to free the political order from subservience to religion. The easiest way to accomplish this goal was to attach the religious documents inextricably to a vanished political order. Allow them to survive that past order and they might re-create it, as the Puritans were, in fact, seeking to do.

A contemporary described Spinoza as "a very poor Jew and not a better Christian";[54] a scholar of our day has connected Spinoza's relativization of Judaism and Christianity with his family's Marrano past. The Marranos, it will be recalled, were Iberian Jews who chose baptism into Roman Catholicism over the alternative of expulsion, yet continued secretly to practice some Jewish rites. "The clandestine character of worship, Catholic education, the lack of Jewish education, a mental mixture of both faiths, and isolation from the living Jewish communities outside Iberia," writes Yirmiyahu Yovel, "created with time a special phenomenon in the history and sociology of religion, a form of faith which is neither Christian nor actually Jewish."[55] The effect of this compounded marginality was often an unbearable sense of dissonance, one that could be most easily resolved only through transcending *both* traditions. Indeed, listed among the Marrano patterns that Yovel finds in Spinoza are "heterodoxy and the transcendence of revealed religion" and "a skill for equivocation and dual language."[56] The first is nicely illustrated by Spinoza's disqualification of the characteristic features of each Testament — the chosenness of Israel, the Torah, and the commandments (*mitsvot*) in the Old, and the incarnation of God and the redemptive death and resurrection of Jesus in the New. The second, the equivocal language, is also in plentiful evidence in the *Tractatus*, as when Spinoza defines "theocracy" as a regime with separation of powers, using a slogan of the Calvinist party in a sense that no Calvinist would have accepted[57] — that is, if he or she were careful and not hoodwinked by Spinoza's clever manipulation of traditional language for very untraditional purposes.

A more portentous example of this pattern of dissembling can be seen in Spinoza's account of why the Hebrew Commonwealth fell. Among the causes for this, according to him, were the priestly institutions (especially the tithes), prophecy (which is associated with fanaticism and subversion), and kingship (which is equated, at least in this tractate, with tyranny).[58] Now any student of the Hebrew Bible knows that priests, prophets, and kings all take it on the chin quite a bit in that book, and the very worth of all three institutions was questioned at times. But what Spinoza does not respect is the claim of the text itself that each of them was divinely ordained and the fact that, on balance, the Bible is positive about them all. Spinoza, to be sure, was not the first person to read the Bible selectively or to twist its sense to meet his needs. What he did pioneer, however, was the systematic transference of the normativity of the Bible from its *manifest text* to its *underlying history* (at least as he reconstructed it). In part, this, too, is a continuation of Renaissance humanism. Chapters 17 and 18 of the *Tractatus Theologico-Politicus* resemble nothing so much as Machiavelli's accounts of how ancient kings and contemporary princes had lost their powers[59] — though, of course, Spinoza's substantive advice is very different from Machiavelli's. The Bible in Spinoza's naturalistic theology becomes another political text, and its real meaning lies not in its textuality, but in its historical message, of which its own authors may have been unaware. The *meaning* of the Bible belongs to the original author; the *message* of the Bible belongs to the contemporary moralizing historian. And when the message is derived from the underlying history and not from the manifest text that it often contradicts, then we are very much in the world of modern historical criticism and far indeed from the world of traditional religion, including the world of the Protestant Reformers.

The brunt of my argument to this point is that the results of the historical-critical study of the Hebrew Bible have rather generally been at odds with the underlying method. The *method* is historical and therefore privileges the period of composition at the expense of all later recontextualizations. The *results* have been skewed toward one of those recontextualizations, the Christian church, as Christian categories, preferences, and priorities have been restated and even occasionally reenergized by historical-critical study. The method derives from the Renaissance sense of the past as this is transformed through Enlightenment rationalism and then Romantic hermeneutics, with its emphasis on self-expression and authorial intention. The results are more than occasionally biased toward the Christian faith in the broad forms in which it already existed before the Renaissance, the Enlightenment, or Romanticism.

One cause of this anomalous situation is to be found in the placement of biblical studies in church-sponsored institutions or in departments whose central concern is the study of Christianity: the method and its institutional location are at odds. At times, this has been recognized, as when the great historical critic Julius Wellhausen resigned his professorship in Greifswald on April 5, 1882. "I became a theologian because the scientific treatment of the Bible interested me," wrote Wellhausen in his letter of resignation:

> Only gradually did I come to understand that a professor of theology also has the practical task of preparing the students for service in the Protestant Church, and that I am not adequate to this practical task, but that instead despite all caution on my own part I make my hearers unfit for their office. Since then my theological professorship has been weighing heavily on my conscience.[60]

Usually, however, the problem is covered over through compartmentalization. What the Bible *means now* and what it *meant in its own time* are sharply distinguished, as exegetes happily pass the former off to theologians (whom they nonetheless are not generally hesitant to accuse of taking the Bible out of context) or even deny that one can talk meaningfully about the Bible in any tense other than the past.[61] We confront here the two-sidedness of historical inquiry with special intensity. On the one hand, historical investigation can drive a wedge between the present and the past by showing how different they are. On the other hand, historical investigation can help retrieve the past for the present by reconstructing the missing context and thus adding essential resonance and verisimilitude. Historical criticism itself is neutral between these two opposing movements. It can help to heal — though not to reverse — the rupture caused by historical consciousness, or it can aggravate the rupture and help in dismantling tradition. To the extent that historical critics restrict themselves to descriptive history and avoid the thorny questions of contemporary appropriation, they contribute, even if inadvertently, to the dismantling of tradition rather than to the healing of the rupture. For historical criticism so restricted subtly fosters an image of the Bible as having once meant a great deal but now meaning little or nothing. It tells us that the current meaning of the text is better discovered by people only minimally involved in the historical investigation of its composition.

It has not, to my knowledge, been pointed out that this image corresponds to the biographical pattern of a large number of contemporary
biblical critics. These are people whose early lives were dominated
by an intense religious commitment, in many cases fundamentalism,
but whose adulthood is marked by quiet acculturation to the secular
liberalism of the academic world and often by a slow but steady dis-
affection from all religious institutions. Among biblical scholars, even
some of the most outspoken and effective debunkers of traditional
religious views are — though you would never guess it — ex-clerics
or graduates of theology departments.[62] Of course, the field is not
lacking in scholars with active religious lives and congregational affiliations: not every Catholic in biblical studies is lapsed, not every Jew
is nonobservant, and not every liberal Protestant values the adjective
more than the noun. But even among those who practice, it is the
past-tense sense of scripture that still predominates. The remarkable
pluralism of the field rests on a foundation of historicism, and the
cooperation of diverse groups is purchased at the cost of the tacit agreement on the part of all that the diversity matters so little that it can
safely be privatized and thus excluded from academic discourse. It is in
the historical-critical study of the Hebrew Bible that what Yovel calls
the "Marrano pattern[s]" achieve their most striking victory. Judaism
and Christianity have become historical contingencies, relativized by
historicism and replaced as indications of absolute truth not by philosophy but by the amorphous secular liberalism that dominates the
academic world.

This brings me back to Father Boadt, and to Max Lurie in Potok's
novel. Boadt tells us that one major reason that biblical studies have become a "meeting ground for Jews and Christians" is a new atmosphere
of "scientific passion for capturing the original setting and sense of the
biblical books." But Max Lurie asks whether the Jews who engage in this
quest are observant or, as he puts it, "like *goyim.*"[63] I would explicate
his question by posing this one: *Is the price of this restoration of the
past to the Bible not the relegation of the Bible to the past, so that the
scholar's own practice or lack of it is of no relevance?* Is the ability of
Jews and Christians to meet as equals in biblical studies owing to an
unspoken agreement to treat the scriptures of each community only according to the canons of historical relativism? If so, then the designation
of those who so meet as "Jews" or as "Christians" is really only vestigial. If the Jewish scholars are "like *goyim*" and the Christian scholars
are more scholarly than Christian, then the adherents of each commu-

nity will wonder with Max Lurie whether this historical approach to the Bible is a net gain.

I repeat that I am convinced that the restoration of historical context to the Bible can help bring it alive and add vast depth and meaning to our study of it. The problem to which I am pointing is that much biblical scholarship is not pursuing its historical-critical work as part of any such hermeneutic of retrieval. Instead, its operative technique is too often a trivializing antiquarianism, in which the bath water has become more important than the baby, and the enormous historical and philological labors are not justified by reference to any larger structure of meaning. This antiquarianism is parasitical in that its place in the curriculum depends on a supracurricular commitment that it refuses to nourish and occasionally even belittles.[64] In theory, of course, it should be possible to affirm the meaningfulness of the Bible on secular grounds, and, in some ways, this is what the new literary criticism of the Bible is doing. As we are about to see, however, the new agenda is itself more indebted to traditional theological positions than it cares to admit, and, in this, it carries on some of the worst defects of the antiquarianism that it so sternly opposes.

• V •

The subsequent history of biblical criticism has largely followed Spinoza's program of ascertaining "the life, the conduct, and the studies of the author of each book, who he was, what was the occasion, and the epoch of his writing, whom did he write for, and in what language [and] the fate of each book."[65] The birth of source criticism in the century after Spinoza and the efflorescence of Romanticism and the rediscovery of the ancient Near East in the next century brought about a focus on authorship that dwarfed Spinoza's own. Benjamin Jowett, in his controversial essay "On the Interpretation of Scripture" (1860), came to insist that "Scripture has one meaning — the meaning which it had to the mind of the Prophet or Evangelist who first uttered or wrote, to the hearers or readers who first received it."[66] Today, when so many scholars, especially in literature departments, are attacking biblical criticism for atomizing the Bible, it is salutary to recall the underlying purpose of source criticism — to restore passages to their historical context, to avoid anachronistic interpretation, and to recover the sense of the growth and dynamism of the biblical tradition that redaction and canonization have suppressed. That Jowett's essay was published only one year after Charles Darwin's *On the Origin of Species* (1859) and in the same country suggests a fruitful analogy: the contiguity in the Bible of two passages from very different periods is as profoundly misleading as the presence in the same pit of the bones of both dinosaurs and humans. The dismemberment of the Bible and the reassignment of its parts to more original documents or life settings are necessary implications of historical thinking. To fail to do these things would be to fail to reckon adequately with the historical context.

The problem is that by making the *historical* context sovereign and regulative, historical criticism destroys the *literary* context that is the Bible (either Jewish or Christian) as a whole and often even the smaller literary context that is the book, the chapter, or whatever. Hans W. Frei points out that when the historical events began to be seen as more indicative of reality than the biblical narratives about them, one casualty was the venerable hermeneutical technique of typology (or figuration).[67] No longer could it be assumed that the various narratives form a coherent sequence, with "earlier and later stories becoming figures one of the other."[68] In truth, the problem extends beyond the question of narrative (which occupies less of the Bible than literary scholars usually think). It soon became impossible to assume that all the texts even belonged to the same religion or theology. To adapt Tertullian, what has Isaiah to do with Qohelet, or for that matter, the New Testament with the Old?

Frei points out that the closest successor to figural reading is the "enterprise called biblical theology, which sought to establish the unity of religious meaning across the gap of historical and cultural differences."[69] Thus, Walther Eichrodt in the methodological manifesto to his *Theology of the Old Testament* declared that "it is high time that the tyranny of historicism in Old Testament studies was broken." He defined the problem as "*how to understand the realm of Old Testament belief in its structural unity and how, by examining on the one hand its religious environment and on the other its essential coherence with the New Testament, to illuminate its profoundest meaning.*"[70] Eichrodt, it appears, wanted to eat his cake and have it too, to reckon with the diachronic perspective that historical consciousness necessitates and to continue to endorse the synchronic perspective that the Christian canon affirms. Unlike a medieval exegete, however, Eichrodt refused to differentiate these methods in terms of distinct senses of scripture. He thought history would bear out his claim that the Hebrew Bible stands in *"essential coherence"* with the New Testament. It is this notion that accounts for the anti-Judaism that pervades Eichrodt's *Theology,* as when he wrote of "the torso-like appearance of Judaism in separation from Christianity."[71] Strange, is it not, that the Jews have never noticed that their tradition is only a torso — especially since Christians have been telling them this for nearly two millennia?

The opposite position to Eichrodt's and that of the Old Testament theologians generally is nicely stated by Boadt, who, it will be recalled, wrote that "the relationship of the Hebrew Scriptures to the New Testament... must begin with the premise that each speaks from its own complete integrity."[72] On historicist, or diachronic, assumptions, this is, of course, true, but what about the literary, or synchronic, perspective? To say that the Hebrew Bible has complete integrity over against the New Testament is to cast grave doubt upon the unity of the Christian Bible. It is like saying one can read the first ten books of the *Aeneid* as if the last two did not exist, and this, in turn, is to say that the last two add nothing essential: the story can just as credibly end without Aeneas's slaying Turnus. Now for Christians to say that the New Testament adds nothing essential to the Hebrew Bible is on the order of Marxists' saying that they have no objection to leaving the means of production in the hands of private capitalists: the assertion belies the speakers' announced identity. The supersessionism of an Old Testament theologian like Eichrodt (and he is not atypical) is not adventitious. It is an inevitable corollary of his faith in the unity and integrity of the two-volume Bible of the church. An unabashedly diachronic approach suggests, as Eichrodt dimly recognized, that the Christian juxtaposition of the Hebrew Bible with the New Testament yields an incoherent book. It is no wonder that some theologians committed to finding meaning in their scriptures have been retreating from historicism over the past two decades.[73]

One energetic intellectual assault on the historicist approach to the Bible in recent years has come not from theologians, however, but from literary critics, whose methods are more familiar in English departments than in seminaries. Two books in this genre, both published in 1981, present a telling contrast. In *The Great Code,* Northrop Frye offers a modern, secular version of the classic Christian typological reading of the Bible, which for him can mean only the Christian Bible. "I know that Jewish and Islamic conceptions of the Bible are very different," Frye concedes, with disarming honesty, "but that is practically all that I do know about them, and it is the Christian Bible that is important for English literature and the Western cultural tradition."[74] In *The Art of Biblical Narrative,* Robert Alter similarly concedes that "there are of course certain literary as well as theological continuities between the Hebrew Bible and the New Testament," but he goes on to say that "the narratives of the latter were written in a different language, at a later time, and, by and large, according to different literary assumptions. It therefore does not seem to me that these two bodies of ancient literature can be comfortably set in the same critical framework."[75] Here I am tempted to invert my remark about Eichrodt and to ask why, if the two Testaments do not constitute a profound unity, Christians for thousands of years (including Northrop Frye in our time) have never noticed.

Though neither Frye nor Alter writes as a representative of a religious tradition, and though both seem impatient with theology, the truth is that the unit each chooses for his study is dictated by his heritage, Christianity for Frye, Judaism for Alter. I suppose each could come up with an *aesthetic* argument for the superiority of his own canon, but the chances of winning over the other would be about as great as the chance that Pablo Christiani or Nachmanides could have won over his opponent in Barcelona in 1263. Whereas historical criticism, with its relativizing and atomizing tendencies, creates a certain neutral ground between Jews and Christians, the new literary criticism, with its concern for typology (or, in Alter's term, "narrative analogy"),[76] raises anew the question, Whose Bible? — try though its practitioners do to put distance between themselves and this old theological hot potato.

A brief and simple example of the difference that context makes should be helpful here. When YHWH, the God of Israel, first makes his covenant with Abraham, the only stipulation is YHWH's self-imposed promise to give Abraham the land, "from the river of Egypt to . . . the river Euphrates" (Gen 15:17–20).[77] Two chapters later the pact is restated as "an everlasting covenant," symbolized by circumcision (Genesis 17), but again without conditions that the human party must meet for the covenant to endure. Moshe Weinfeld astutely relates this promissory or unconditional covenant to ancient Near Eastern grants, in which the greater king rewards the lesser for "loyalty and good deeds already performed." This "covenant of grant" he distinguishes from the more familiar "treaty," in which the suzerain offers his vassal "an inducement for future loyalty" and the keynote is one of stern conditionality.[78] Whether the next covenant of which we read, that of Sinai in the generation of Moses, was originally conceived along the lines of a treaty is hard to determine; certainly, most of the Torah does indeed so conceive it now. The dichotomy of treaty and grant, however, can obscure the important point that the Patriarchal grant is not parallel with the Mosaic treaty, but, instead, intersects with it, even at Sinai. In the incident of the golden calf, Israel violates the conditions of covenant just concluded and brings about a divine threat of annihilation (Exod 32:9–10). It is precisely the Patriarchal grant that Moses invokes to avert the evil decree: "Remember Your servants, Abraham, Isaac, and Jacob, how You swore to them by Your Self and said to them: I will make your offspring as numerous as the stars of heaven, and I will give to your offspring this whole land of which I spoke, to possess forever" (Exod 32:13; cf. Deut 9:27). Nothing is more typical of the treaty as opposed to the grant than long lists of blessings and curses, yet after the characteristic list in Leviticus 26, we again hear of the Patriarchal Covenant, that is, the grant. When, heartsick in exile, having grievously desecrated the stipulations of Sinai, Israel shall confess their iniquity and humble their proud heart, "then will I remember My covenant with Jacob; I will remember My covenant with Isaac, and also My covenant with Abraham; and I will remember the land" (Lev 26:39–42).

The result of the intersection on Sinai of these two types of covenants, the grant and the treaty, is a type of spiritual relationship between the people Israel and their God that is not reducible to either component. The perpetual land grant to the Patriarchs has come to serve as a platform upon which the shaky structure of the Mosaic Covenant can rest securely. Human fallibility, the lethal threat to any conditional relationship, is countered by a prior and irrevocable divine oath to the ancestors of the errant community. Both Israel's unqualified obligation to observe the *mitsvot* and God's indefeasible promise to Abraham remain in force. This interlacing of covenants is characteristic not only of the Hebrew Bible, but of rabbinic Judaism as well, where the grant to Abraham is transformed into the idea of the "merit of the Fathers" (*zĕkût 'ābôt*) that Israel's transgressions can never altogether nullify.

Such is the picture if we limit the unit to be interpreted to the Hebrew Bible. You will recall, however, that I have argued that though a certain sense of scripture requires this limitation, Christians must ultimately aim for another sense as well, one that upholds the idea that their two-volume Bible is a meaningful whole, lest their scripture decompose before their very eyes. If we include the New Testament in our interpretation of Abraham, we must reckon with Paul's belief that God's pre-Sinaitic commitment to Abraham shows the possibility of justification apart from the Torah, at least for Gentiles (Galatians 3;

Romans 4). Instead of Abraham's serving as a kind of platform upon which Torah and commandments can stand firmly despite the innate human impulse to evil, he serves Paul as a kind of circumferential highway that enables one to bypass Sinai altogether and still reach God, as one never could, in fact, through Sinai itself. On this reading, the emphasis shifts from the integration of grant and treaty on Sinai to their original separation.[79] Abraham no longer prefigures the hope of a contrite Israel in exile, but rather the justification of the Christian apart from the works of the Law and even from the people Israel. Of course, this extreme position of Paul's must be qualified by consideration of other New Testament documents, especially the epistle of James, for the author of which Abraham was justified by faith and deeds conjointly (James 2:14–26). The fact remains, however, that just as each piece on a chessboard changes the meaning and value of every other piece, so does each text in the Bible change our reading of all the others. The first ten books of the *Aeneid* will never be the same after the last two have been read.[80]

We can always choose, of course, to limit our investigation to a smaller corpus, for example, to any one of the passages just mentioned. This is what *peshat,* the medieval Jewish pursuit of the historical-grammatical — or literal — sense did. On this narrowest context, Jews and Christians can work together, just as they can on modern historical investigation. Indeed, these types of study are done best by those scholars who can bracket their religious commitments or have none to bracket, as the whole sorry history of religious bias in biblical studies amply demonstrates. In the realm of historical criticism, pleas for a "Jewish biblical scholarship" or a "Christian biblical scholarship" are senseless and reactionary. Practicing Jews and Christians will differ from uncompromising historicists, however, in affirming the meaningfulness and interpretive relevance of larger contexts that homogenize the literatures of different periods to one degree or another. Just as text has more than one context, and biblical studies more than one method, so scripture has more than one sense, as the medievals knew and Tyndale, Spinoza, Jowett, and most other moderns have forgotten. As the context gets larger, Jews and Christians can still work together, as each identifies imaginatively with the other's distinctive context. But imagined identities are only that, and if the Bible (under whatever definition) is to be seen as having coherence and theological integrity, there will come a moment in which Jewish-Christian consensus becomes existentially impossible.

• VI •

Historical criticism has indeed brought about a new situation in biblical studies. The principal novelty lies in the recovery of the Hebrew Bible as opposed to the Tanakh and the Old Testament affirmed by rabbinic Judaism and Christianity, respectively. Jews and Christians can, in fact, meet as equals in the study of this new/old book, but only because the Hebrew Bible is largely foreign to both traditions and precedes them. This meeting of Jews and Christians on neutral ground can have great value, for it helps to correct misconceptions each group has of the other and to prevent the grievous consequences of such misconceptions, such as anti-Semitic persecutions. It is also the case that some of the insights into the text that historical criticism generates will be appropriated by the Jews or the church themselves, and they can thereby convert history into tradition and add vitality to an exegetical practice that easily becomes stale and repetitive. But it is also the case that the historical-critical method compels its practitioners to bracket their traditional identities, and this renders its ability to enrich Judaism and Christianity problematic. There is, to be sure, plenty of room in each tradition for such bracketing. There are ample and long-standing precedents for Jews to pursue a plain sense at odds with rabbinic midrashim and even halakhah and for Christians to interpret the Old Testament in a non-Christocentric fashion. But unless historical criticism can learn to interact with other senses of scripture — senses peculiar to the individual traditions and not shared between them — it will either fade or prove to be not a meeting ground of Jews and Christians, but the burial ground of Judaism and Christianity, as each tradition vanishes into the past in which neither had as yet emerged. Western Christians are so used to being in the majority that the danger of vanishing is usually not real to them; after all, the post-Christian era will still be post-Christian, not post–something else. But Jewry, none too numerous before the Holocaust, has now become "a brand plucked from the fire" (Zech 3:2), and most Jews with an active commitment to their tradition will be suspicious of any allegedly common ground that requires them to suppress or shed their Jewishness.

Bracketing tradition has its value, but also its limitations. Though fundamentalists will not see the value, nor historicists the limitations, intellectual integrity and spiritual vitality in this new situation demand the careful affirmation of both.

Chapter 5

———— • ————

Historical Criticism and the Fate
of the Enlightenment Project

• I •

Ten years ago I had an experience that made me vividly aware of the two worlds with which the practitioner of the critical study of the Bible inevitably deals. Reading applications for the doctoral program whose faculty I had only recently joined, I was struck by the frequency on the autobiographical statements of a pattern that a form critic might call the "conversion narrative." Sometimes this came in a doubled form, first the conversion into a robust but uncritical Christian faith and then, usually in college or seminary, a second conversion marked by acceptance of the historical-critical method and an abandonment of doctrines of inerrancy and the like, though never of Christianity itself. At other times candidates narrated only a conversion of the first sort or otherwise gave an account of their lives that showed no awareness of the nature of the historical criticism of the Bible, the only approach that our doctoral program utilized. Worried about the suitability of such applicants for the program, I broached the issue to a senior colleague, who immediately sought to allay my anxieties. "Don't worry," he said. "A lot of our students start out like that, but they change after they have been here two weeks."

Eleven years earlier, the comparative religionist Wilfred Cantwell Smith had published a scathing attack upon the profession of biblical scholarship in the historical mode. Smith did not argue that the methods employed are in any way false; his critique was not predicated upon a confession of faith in the revealed or inspired character of the docu-ments. His point, rather, was that by concentrating on the period of their composition, critical scholars neglect the assembled Bible and its immeasurable significance in the history of culture. "The analysis of a thing is interesting, and can be highly significant, but only subsidiarily," Smith wrote; "strictly, the history of that thing *begins* once its parts are synthesized."[1] If he was right, then we must confront the salient paradox of historical-critical scholarship on the Bible: it ends precisely when the history of the Bible begins.

The causes of this paradoxical situation are many and complex. One is the tendency of some influential forms of Protestantism to understand scripture in sharp contradistinction to tradition, even the tradition of the Protestant use and interpretation of the Bible. Without attention to postbiblical tradition, scripture vanishes before our eyes, for the basis of religion in biblical times was not a Bible: the religion *in* the Book is not the religion *of* the Book. The prophets did not preach a book or show any awareness that God had revealed one to Moses on Mount Sinai, and when early Christian documents mention the "scriptures," they are referring not to the Gospels and Epistles but only to what Christians would later come to call the "Old Testament." That in which the earliest Christian communities put their faith was not a book, but a person. The Book remained the Jewish Scriptures, there being in what some Christians call "New Testament times" no New Testament.

Within the context of those Protestant communions that emphati-cally set scripture over tradition, therefore, Smith's prioritization would, I think, have to be reversed: the Bible itself requires that its analysis take priority over its history, that biblical history be understood only as the history *internal to* the Bible, not the history *of* the Bible once it has at long last been assembled and standardized in one form or another.

My colleague's effort to allay my anxieties suggests, however, that much more than a certain Protestant tradition of antitraditionalism un-derlies the equally paradoxical tendency of critical biblical scholars to neglect the history of the Bible. For in all cases the applicants about whom I was worried were more involved with the biblical documents themselves than with the role of the Bible in postbiblical tradition. In-deed, exactly like those whom Smith castigated, these students were thoroughly unconcerned with the history of biblical interpretation within religious communities, that is, with the history of *scriptural* in-terpretation. Those who had converted only once thought that their Bible could be approached directly, without the interposition of an

interpretive framework. Perhaps that is what they thought historical criticism was — a framework that is not interposed or interpretive. Those
with a double conversion story were either ignorant or dismissive of
traditional Jewish and Christian commentary in the same degree. Their
second conversion had convinced them that historical criticism alone
provides an interpretive framework that is valid. My colleague believed
that after only two weeks in the program, all of our doctoral students
would assent to this latter claim.

Smith's description of the way biblical studies are taught captures
nicely the nature of the change that those students with the single
conversion story would undergo in their first two weeks as advanced
students of the Bible. "The courses actually available, and the training
of men actually available to teach them," Smith wrote (in 1971), "are on
the whole calculated to turn a fundamentalist into a liberal." Instead of
fighting autonomous historical inquiry, especially the eminently disquieting inquiry into the dates and processes of composition of the biblical
books themselves, the fundamentalist born again as a liberal would be
able to place the biblical documents into the ancient New Eastern or
Greco-Roman worlds in which they originated and thus to recapture
what they meant to their original authors and audiences, authors and
audiences who lived before there was a Bible. Perhaps underestimat-
ing the vitality and tenacity of fundamentalism, Smith pronounced this
transformation of fundamentalists into liberals "hardly any more a relevant task." But he did have a more profound objection, and this is one
that is even more urgent now than when he wrote over two decades ago.
The scholars who graduate from such programs, Smith observed, "seem
on the whole little equipped to answer a question as to why one should
be especially interested in those particular times and places, rather than
in, let us say, classical India or medieval China or modern America."[2] In
other words, having replaced the study of the Bible with the study of
an exotic culture, those whom Smith termed "liberals" are at a loss to
explain why *this* exotic culture is to be preferred over others or, for that
matter, over our own familiar culture, whose need for attention seems
obvious. If this problem was apparent already in 1971, how much more
pressing it is today, when multiculturalism is in the air and the groups
challenging the traditional curriculum of historically Christian societies
are likely to pursue their demand for inclusion more forcefully than the
partisans of classical India or medieval China ever did.

The answer that Smith offered to his own question is not adequate,
I submit, to the challenge of multiculturalism that has arisen since he

wrote his essay. For he proposed to replace the study of the Bible in its prebiblical historical context with "an investigation into the history of the Bible over the past twenty centuries," that is, into "the Bible as Scripture"[3] rather than as a diverse and evolving set of documents that would be assembled into a closed anthology only later. The problem with this is that it only replaces one form of historicism with another, exchanging the study of early Jewish or Christian history for the study of later Jewish or Christian history. That the cultures of the Jews and of the Christians have been enormously influenced, indeed shaped, by the Bible for the past two millennia (more in the case of the Jews) cannot be gainsaid. But why should the history of those two very different but related cultures be privileged over the history of Indian, Chinese, or, for that matter, African-American culture? And why, a dean might justly ask (and some doubtless do), should we devote a second appointment to the history of the Bible as scripture when we lack even one appointment in the history of the scriptures and classics of most of the world's other religious traditions? To answer with the claim that the Bible is a foundational document of *our* culture is to imply more cultural homogeneity than many believe to be warranted. What is worse, it is to make a claim of normativity that is at odds with the historicistic methods that Smith, despite his shift of period, continued to endorse. To replace an authoritative book with an authoritative culture founded upon that book is still to make a claim that goes beyond the limits of historical description. Attention to a culture requires no less justification than attention to a book.

The failure of Smith's historicistic proposal to validate biblical studies brings us flush with the two-sidedness — and the pathos — of biblical scholarship in the historical-critical mode. On the one hand, the essential claim of this approach is that one may legitimately interpret scripture against one's own tradition and personal belief. Historical critics thus rightly insist that the tribunal before which interpretations are argued cannot be confessional or dogmatic: the arguments offered must be historically valid, able, that is, to compel the assent of *historians,* whatever their religion or lack thereof, whatever their backgrounds, spiritual experiences, or personal beliefs, and without privileging any claim of revelation. On the other hand, the very value-neutrality of this method of study puts its practitioners at a loss to defend the *value* of the enterprise itself. In a culture saturated with religious belief involving the Bible, this weakness was less apparent, for the defense was less called for. Now, however, after secularism has impugned the worth of the

Bible, and multiculturalism has begun to critique the cultural traditions at the base of which it stands, biblical scholars, including, I must stress, even the most antireligious among them, must face this paradoxical reality: the vitality of their rather untraditional discipline has historically depended upon the vitality of traditional religious communities, Jewish and Christian. Those whom Smith termed "liberals" — that is, the scholars who assiduously place the Bible in the ancient Near Eastern or Greco-Roman worlds — have depended for their livelihood upon those who not only rejoice that the Bible survived those worlds but who also insist that it deserved to survive because its message is transhistorical. When fundamentalists become liberals (in Smith's usage), the need for an affirmation that goes beyond mere historical description does not evaporate. Indeed, in the humanities today, every "canon," cultural as well as scriptural, is under intense suspicion, and every selection of subject matter is increasingly and correctly understood to involve a normative claim and not merely a description of value-neutral fact. In all cases, what scholars study and teach is partly a function of which practices and beliefs they wish to perpetuate.

• II •

The contextualization of biblical documents in the cultures in which they were written is not only the hallmark of historical criticism; it is also inevitable. In spite of what we often hear from some of our literary colleagues, there is no such thing as the text in and of itself or the text as a world unto itself, and no possibility of standing *before* the text without also, in some measure, getting *behind* it. The question is not whether we make historical judgments; the question can only be whether we do so poorly or well. As soon as you have treated the discolorations on the page as a language, you have made a historical judgment. Focusing on lexical issues, John Barton of Oxford makes a related point in quintessentially British fashion:

> Charles II, when he visited the new St Paul's during its construction, complimented the architect on producing "so awful and artificial" a building; it is essential for our belief that Charles II was a person of refined manners that we should *not* hold sequence of words to have fixed and determinate meanings in all ages and contexts.[4]

And what is true for words also holds for larger units of meaning, such as genre. There is no communication that is altogether outside culture (even if it mediates a universal truth), and no culture that is outside history (even if it mediates a timeless reality).

If fundamentalists — and indeed the mass of religious believers — are inclined to overlook the inevitability and the unorthodox implications of historical reconstruction, liberal scholars face their own particular temptations. One we have already examined — the tendency to dissolve text into culture and the Bible into the history that preceded its synthesis. Of this, there is a subcategory that is especially prominent in times like our own when issues of social location and the distribution of power are receiving much attention. This is the temptation to interpret the text as *ideology,* that is, as only a justification for political arrangements. It is a temptation to which historical critics are most vulnerable, for, as the literary theorist Tzvetan Todorov points out, "[i]t is at the moment of their creation that works are the most political,"[5] and a method of interpretation that is especially attentive to the cultural meaning of a text at its point of origin will be most inclined to highlight its political dimension. The danger for the integrity of biblical studies is that the text will again come to be seen as dispensable, that the Bible will once more recede from biblical studies, this time because it is conceived as only a series of ciphers for political power.

That this danger is not hypothetical is abundantly demonstrated in a recent introduction, *Power, Politics, and the Making of the Bible,* by Robert B. Coote and Mary P. Coote. Already by their third page, the authors have told us that the "Hebrew Scriptures consist mainly of the Scriptures of the temple cult" in Jerusalem, and that "[t]he purpose of this cult was to legitimate rulers in Jerusalem, and this is what the Scriptures are mostly about."[6] Their book is in essence a sustained effort to replace the manifest text of the Bible with the putative underlying social and political reality that it disguises. No sooner have the authors employed the term "the nation Israel," for example, than they note parenthetically that "[t]he concept of nation suggests a political consensus among subjects ruled by Jerusalem; this rarely if ever existed, but the scribes who wrote the Bible worked for rulers who said it did."[7] Instead, they write, "Israel was [originally] a name for power, the power of a tribe or confederation of tribes formed in the New Kingdom period in relation to Egyptian authority."[8] The earliest narrative document that critical scholars detect in the Pentateuch, the J (or Yahwistic) source, was composed to legitimate King David. It was "designed to appeal for the loyalty of tribal sheikhs in the Negeb and Sinai, David's buttress against Egypt in the south, by suggesting that Israel's early chiefs, the Patriarchs, were southern sheikhs like themselves."9 It was only because "Egypt . . . was the principal enemy of David's Israel [that it] became the villain of the history."10 (In this, J has much in common with Psalm 2, which the Cootes term "a raucous salute to the pretensions of Davidic imperialism.")11 The next pentateuchal document, the E (for "Elohistic") source, was written to legitimate another king, the northerner Jeroboam I, who went from exile in Egypt to dominion over his kinfolk. In the Cootes' mind, this is the key to the story of Joseph, whose dreams of domination God vindicates against his brothers' skepticism and resentment: Joseph is a cipher for Jeroboam.12 Recognizing that the "fear of God" is also a major theme in E, the Cootes are undeterred from their politicizing hermeneutic. "Like all privileged," they write, "Jeroboam feared himself in other men, and hence projected this fear, in the guise of cultic and judicial respect, or the 'fear of God,' as public policy."13 The fear of God in the Elohistic narrative is, in other words, only a nervous politician's effort to allay his insecurities.

The Cootes apply the same hermeneutic of suspicion to the New Testament. Of the early churchmen who promoted the new set of scriptures, they write: "Taking God's anointed king Jesus, shamed in death and restored in resurrection, as the standard for making the temple Scriptures still meaningful, the bishops' interpretation insisted on Roman law in the absence of temple law, until Jesus' return should inaugurate a new nontemple law."14 Political power even determines the order of the Gospels: "Matthew's version of Mark was eventually positioned ahead of Mark because it laid down the jurisdiction of Peter, regarded by then to have been the first bishop of Rome."15 Indeed, the content of the canon itself — the very existence of a Bible as the church has traditionally known it — is a function of Roman hegemony and the refusal of some Christians to challenge it: the *Shepherd of Hermas,* we are told, "typifies writings that placed the laws of the 'City of God' in clear opposition to the laws of the state; such works never made the canon."16 But the essentially political character of the theology of the church did not, according to the Cootes, end with the closure of the Christian canon: "The philosophical debate on the divinity of Christ [that came to a head at the Council of Nicea in 325 C.E.] . . . veiled a political debate over jurisdiction." The Cootes continue: "In the terms of the Arian controversy, Arius's view of Jesus implied the subordination of the Church to the state, as the human Jesus was subordinate to God, while the bishops' view made the church the equal of the state, as Jesus was equal to God."[17] What the Nicene Creed really confesses, in other words, is the ambition of bishops in an age of empire.

Some of the interpretations in *Power, Politics, and the Making of the Bible* are not original, and most are open to serious question even from within the canons of historical criticism. The guiding methodology, however, follows upon a long historical-critical tradition of treating religious affirmations as subordinate to political interest. The first great statement of this lies in Spinoza's *Tractatus Theologico-Politicus* (1670), in which the norms of the Torah, regarded by rabbinic tradition as eternally valid, are presented as nothing more than the laws of the vanished Hebrew Commonwealth, and therefore, as Spinoza put it, obligatory "not even on Hebrews after the downfall of their nation."[18] Out goes Torah; in comes politics. The interpretation of particular institutions and narratives as projections of political relationships easily survived the antitheocratic impulses that motivated Spinoza's hermeneutic. It has, in fact, become a staple of critical scholarship in the last century and a half. What books like the Cootes' do is to pursue the logic of political reading in a way that is more relentless, systematic, and reductionistic than most historical critics have traditionally believed to be warranted. Indeed, *Power, Politics, and the Making of the Bible* slams shut many of the portals to transcendence that religiously committed historical critics have, in a variety of ways, been struggling to keep open since the Enlightenment. Unfortunately, in insisting upon political power as the prime motive force behind biblical literature, the Cootes are, in the present academic and religious climate, far from idiosyncratic.

Part of the weakness of their introduction, and many others in the same mode, is the operative concept of power. Catherine Bell, in her stimulating recent book, *Ritual Theory, Ritual Practice,* assails the Hobbesian theory of power, which is modeled on sovereignty. The Hobbesian theory is "the simplistic misconception that power is the imposition of one person's or group's will on another through a threat of violence."[19] Against this, she argues for Foucault's view that "power is contingent, local, imprecise, relational, and organizational." "Foucault also sees the strategies of power used by kings and governments," Bell points out, "as embedded in and dependent upon the level of 'micro-relations' of power, the local interactions and petty calculations of daily life."[20] If Hobbes is wrong and Foucault right, then even when the Bible is seen as ideological literature, it is a capital mistake to interpret its narratives as devices by which the powerful few hoodwinked the marginalized many and kept them in submission. Rather, we should have to concede that the roots of even David's regime and Jeroboam's lay in those " 'microrelations' of power" that suffused the society and acquired an enduring literary testament in the Hebrew Bible. Having made the conceptual change that Bell proposes, modern critics can, of course, continue to pronounce those ancient power relations unjust, but they will have to do so in their own names. They can no longer assume that those arrangements endured because the mass of ancients had been duped by propaganda that they gullibly mistook for sacred literature. The irony is that this adjustment would require scholars of transparent democratic allegiance, like Robert B. and Mary P. Coote, to concentrate less on the elites and to show the masses more respect.

There are, in fact, even more serious difficulties in the interpretation of biblical literature as ideology. That scholars should place the documents, at least initially, within the social and political structures of the communities in which they originated is not problematic so long as the sociopolitical lens is presented as only one of many through which the material may be viewed. The difficulties mount, however, when that lens — indeed, *any* lens — is awarded a monopoly within the interpretive process, as when the Cootes characterize the complex and marvelously evocative poem that is Psalm 2 as "a raucous salute to the pretensions of Davidic imperialism." At the base of the problem here is the privilege that the modern interpreters assert for themselves not only against their own contemporaries, but also, and more revealingly, against the very material that they are seeking to understand. Leszek Kolakowski, in discussing the same issue with respect to the interpretation of myth, identifies the two guiding presuppositions of the whole procedure:

> First, it is assumed that myths, as they are explicitly told and believed, have a latent meaning behind the ostensible one and that this meaning not only is not in fact perceived by those sharing a given creed, but that of necessity it cannot be perceived. Secondly, it is implied that this latent meaning, which is accessible only to the outsider-anthropologist, is the meaning *par excellence,* whereas the ostensible one, i.e., the myth as it is understood by the believers, has the function of concealing the former; this ostensible meaning appears then as a product of inescapable self-deception, of an ideological mystification or simply of ignorance.

Kolakowski's conclusion is crucial:

These two premises are philosophical rather than anthropological in kind. . . . We need more than [the empirical material of the anthropologist] to assert that when people speak of God or the gods, of invisible forces purposely operating behind empirical facts, of the sacred qualities of things, they are *in fact,* and without knowing it, speaking of something entirely different.[21]

The interpreters whose work rests on those two presuppositions, I would argue, are actually asserting a secular analogy to religious revelation: they are claiming to have a definitive insight, not empirically derived, into the meaning of things, even things that they have never directly experienced and that are interpreted very differently by those who have. They assume that the observer's observation is truer than the practitioner's practice. The effect, almost never acknowledged, of such a claim is to do what the Cootes claim that biblical literature does — to set up a hierarchy. Only at the apex of *this* hierarchy stand not power-hungry kings and self-interested bishops, but (to borrow a term from Paul Mankowski) a "new clerisy" of academic theorists who, unlike those they study, know what they are doing.[22] Here Bell's insights about the modern study of ritual are eminently telling: "theoretical discourse about ritual," she writes, "is organized as a coherent whole by virtue of a logic based on the opposition of thought and action."[23] But the action is always someone else's; the thought is the modern scholar's:

As a consequence of this distinction, the particularity of any one local ritual is contrasted with the more embracing, abstract generalizations of the researcher. . . . [The] rites . . . [are] portrayed as enactments exhibited to *others* for evaluation and appropriation in terms of their more purely theoretical knowledge.[24]

It should not be overlooked that this identification of ritual as action in contradistinction to thought follows not only upon a certain Enlightenment critique of religion, but also upon a long-standing Christian critique of Judaism, a Protestant critique of Catholicism and Eastern Orthodoxy, and a modern Western self-legitimation over against tribal peoples. It is no coincidence that in this model, it is the person whose life is *not* ritualized who has the clarity of vision: only as we break off from ritual communities and transcend their specific performances can we come to perceive the truth. The model does not allow for even the possibility that detachment from ritual performances may decrease one's insight and obscure one's vision. It definitively and non-dialectically shifts the locus of truth from the practicing community to the nonpracticing and unaffiliated individual.

Many will recognize in these last remarks of mine an example of the exercise that Peter Berger has called "relativizing the relativizers."[25] In the context at hand, it would be more accurately termed "suspecting the hermeneuts of suspicion." By posing the question of the modern interpreters' own place in reality as they sketch it, I have challenged them to justify their claim, express or implied, of independence from the dynamics that they depict as ultimate. Might it be the case that the interpretation of religion as only a mystification of power arrangements, for example, is itself an item in a discourse of power in which a new group, supported by new social arrangements, asserts its hegemony? If so — if, that is, there can be no transcendence over the social relationships in which we are embedded — then the assertion that the old order *ought* to bow to the new is groundless. To his credit, Marx, who is the indirect source of much of the current reading of religion as ideology, recognized that the logic of his system required that his own thought be something other than an ideology. As the late Allan Bloom points out:

> In Marx, ideology meant the false system of thought elaborated by the ruling class to justify its rule in the eyes of the ruled, while hiding its real selfish motives. Ideology was sharply distinguished in Marx from science, which is what Marx's system is — i.e., the truth based on disinterested awareness of historical necessity.

In other words, the Marxist system requires the availability of an "absolute moment" that makes a conspectus of *all* history (including the eschatological future) possible. If Marxism itself is only another *ideology,* unable to assert a claim on truth, then, as Bloom puts, Marx becomes a "fossil," superseded by the very process of history that he thought he had definitively comprehended.[26]

Leo Strauss, Bloom's teacher (in some subjects but not all), makes the same point about historicism, as he defines it:

> Historicism asserts that all human thoughts or beliefs are historical, and hence deservedly destined to perish; but historicism itself is a human thought; hence historicism can be of only temporary validity, or it cannot be simply true. To assert the historicist thesis means to doubt it and thus to transcend it. . . . Historicism thrives on the fact that it inconsistently exempts itself from its own verdict about all human thought. . . . We cannot see the historical charac-

ter of "all" thought — that is, of all thought with the exception of the historicist insight and its implications — without transcending history, without grasping something trans-historical.[27]

Above, I observed that the belief that the real meaning of religious phenomena is available only to the outside observer is a secular analogue to religious revelation. If so, then a system of thought like historicism, which "exempts itself from its own verdict," is a secular equivalent to fundamentalism. For though it subjects all else to critique, it asserts axiomatically its own inviolability to critique. Demanding to be the norm by means of which truth and error are disclosed, this type of thinking, by definition, can never be in error.

• III •

It is no coincidence that the early pioneers of biblical criticism — Hobbes, Spinoza, Richard Simon — lived in the aftermath of the Thirty Years' War. Through the famous formula *cuius regio, eius religio* (whoever's realm, his religion), the Treaty of Westphalia (1648), which ended that war, established the superiority of the state over religion in fact and provided a hospitable climate for a theory to the same effect. By the end of the next century, a process of delegitimization of religious structures could be detected beneath many changes in both the Old World and the New. Churches were disestablished, the structures of Jewish communal autonomy abolished, and citizenship increasingly, if unevenly, defined in express disregard of the structures that had traditionally mediated between the individual and the state. "One must refuse everything to the Jews as a nation," the French revolutionary Stanislas de Clermont-Tonnerre proclaimed in a memorable formulation, "but one must give them everything as individuals; they must become citizens."[28] Put positively, changes of this sort established the precious principles of civic equality and freedom of (and from) religion. Put negatively, they demoted traditional structures that claimed to be noncontingent and metahistorical — the people Israel, the church — to the status of mere voluntary associations. In theory, one's public role would now be determined apart from rather than through these mediating structures. To combine the positive and the negative formulations: the liberty and equality of the individual free male adult would be secured by granting the state a monopoly on coercive power. All ritual communities would be reconceived as optional arrangements, and the decision whether to participate in their performances or remain detached would be the individual's alone. It bears mention that the burden of the new arrangement fell more heavily upon those traditions, especially Judaism and Catholicism, that had not conceived of themselves as essentially individualistic and of their social bodies as only voluntary associations.[29]

In spite of its inequities, the great strength of the new arrangement that first emerged in the Enlightenment is that it allows for the maintenance of civility even in the presence of incompatible worldviews. By privatizing religion, restricting it to voluntary associations and the inner recesses of the individual heart, the new order permitted the emergence of a public space neither dominated nor even defined, at least in theory, by any of the clashing factors. The wars of religion would be no more. The new conflict would be between the liberal state and its absolutistic rivals.

Smith's use of the term "liberal" to designate historical-critical scholarship on the Bible is thus more than conventional: it is also profoundly appropriate. For historical criticism is the form of biblical studies that corresponds to the classical liberal political ideal. It is the realization of the Enlightenment project in the realm of biblical scholarship. Like citizens in the classical liberal state, scholars practicing historical criticism of the Bible are expected to eliminate or minimize their communal loyalties, to see them as legitimately operative only within associations that are private, nonscholarly, and altogether voluntary. Within the public space of the academy, scholars of every sort — Jewish, Catholic, Protestant, secular, or whatever — meet, again at least in theory, as equals. The academy must refuse everything to scholars as faithful members of religious communities, but it must give them everything as individuals; they must become critics. But here, too, the new arrangement exacts a price. For example, it tends subtly to restrict the questions studied and the methods employed to those that permit the minimization of religious difference with relative facility — Northwest Semitic linguistics, for example, or the material culture of ancient Palestine, as opposed to questions of theology, ethics, or the phenomenology of religion. Those unwilling to pay the price are unable to participate in this type of study. *Their* model of biblical scholarship too often corresponds to the older political situation typified at its worst by the wars of religion, with each group treating its own book and its own interpretive procedures as absolute and staunchly refusing to step out of its dogmatic or confessional assumptions — a model of fideisms at best ignoring each other and at worst colliding. The middle ground is becoming rarer, as the allied disciplines and their demanding sets of technical skills increasingly occlude vision of the larger religious and even humanistic issues.

Though some of its practitioners like to present it as philosophically and theologically neutral, historical criticism is not without assumptions of its own. These were set forth in a famous essay of Ernst Troeltsch in 1898 and nicely summarized in a recent article by a distinguished scholar of Hellenistic Judaism and biblical theology, John J. Collins:

> (1) The principle of criticism or methodological doubt: since any conclusion is subject to revision, historical inquiry can never attain absolute certainty but only relative degrees of probability. (2) The principle of analogy: historical knowledge is possible because all events are similar in principle. We must assume that the laws of nature in biblical times were the same as now. Troeltsch refers to this as "the almighty power of analogy." (3) The principle of correlation: the phenomena of history are inter-related and interdependent and no event can be isolated from the sequence of historical cause and effect. To these [Collins writes] should be added the principle of autonomy, which is indispensable for any critical study. Neither church nor state can prescribe for the scholar which conclusions should be reached.[30]

The historic confrontation between traditional religion and the new set of assumptions was, according to Collins, "a clash between two conflicting moralities, one of which celebrated faith and belief as virtues and regarded doubt as sin, whereas the other celebrated methodological skepticism and was distrustful of prior commitments."[31]

What is curious here is the unspoken assumption that the axioms of Troeltschian historicism are not "prior commitments" and themselves therefore a proper target for skepticism. (Here we are reminded of Strauss's observation about the tendency of historicism to "exempt[] itself from its own verdict about all human thought.")[32] This is even more curious in light of Collins's pregnant concession that historical criticism does not afford us uninterpreted facts, for "[i]t too is a tradition, with its own values and assumptions, derived in large part from the Enlightenment and western humanism."[33] This concession is vastly more devastating to Collins's argument than he seems to recognize, for the Enlightenment ethos to which he refers sought to *replace* tradition with reason and science and not simply to stand beside them as another option.[34] When the legacy of the Enlightenment becomes just another *tradition,* it inevitably suffers the same deflation that Marxism suffers when it becomes another ideology. We are left with the discomforting question: Why this tradition and not another? Why follow Troeltsch's three axioms, augmented by Collins's principle of autonomy, if they are not intrinsic to human rationality but themselves partake of historical and cultural particularity?

The question is especially acute for Collins, since there is another approach that his essay strives mightily to counter, an approach that does, in fact, relativize historical criticism. This is Brevard Childs's "canonical method," an agenda for biblical theology whose foundation, "the status of canonicity," is, in Childs's words, "not an objectively demonstrable claim but a statement of Christian belief"[35] and therefore a threat to John Collins's unqualified historicism. Collins writes: "Childs fails to give reasons why anyone should adopt this approach to the text unless they happen to share his view of Christian faith. The canonical approach then fails to provide a context for dialogue with anyone who does not accept it as a matter of faith."[36] Here, Collins is surely invoking a double standard, for he has not explained how the Troeltschian historicism that he endorses can provide a context for dialogue with anyone who does not accept *its* presuppositions. It, too, does not facilitate communication with those outside its boundaries: it requires fundamentalists, for example, to be born again as liberals — or to stay out of the conversation altogether. Collins thus fails in his claim that historical criticism is more inclusive than Childs's canonical method. Each approach corresponds to particular communities founded upon discreet assumptions, Troeltschian historicism for Collins, a certain variety of Christian faith for Childs. Neither set of assumptions is self-evident or free of cultural particularism. I note, however, that if inclusiveness could be gauged quantitatively, then Childs would win the match hands down, for far more people with biblical interests share Christian faith than a thoroughgoing historicism. Were we historical critics to be classed as a religious body, we should have to be judged a most minuscule sect indeed — and one with a pronounced difficulty relating to groups that do not accept our beliefs.

My point in noting this is that Collins's articulation of his "principle of autonomy, which is indispensable for any critical study," evades the crucial issue of the social character of knowledge. "Neither church nor state," he explains, "can prescribe for the scholar which conclusions should be reached." The implication seems to be that critical scholars are autonomous individuals pursuing the truth wherever it may take them, and thus committed to a principled unwillingness to defer to the judgments of a collectivity, religious or political. This implication is not without a substantial element of truth. The concept of academic freedom and the institution of tenure do provide academicians a measure of intellectual independence that is well-nigh unparalleled in human history or in nonacademic institutions of our own time. It is not at all the case, however, that the contemporary academy has found a way to dispense with all social processes for the validation of knowledge. On the contrary, various collectivities are endlessly passing on the value of what professors have taught or written, and when the judgments they render are negative, the professors' ability to continue teaching and publishing inevitably suffers. Not everyone is hired, promoted, or tenured. Not every manuscript is published, nor every project funded. The academy has its own equivalents of excommunication and the revocation of citizenship.

Instead of setting forth a sharp dichotomy between autonomy and submission to a collective body, therefore, we would be wiser to note the inevitable correlation between the character of a social body and the nature of the knowledge that it validates. In the past, most universities, to one degree or another, articulated the ideals and underlying assumptions of a society that was predominantly Christian. Thus, chapel could be required (even in state universities), and a curriculum that privileged Christianity and neglected, subordinated, or misrepresented other religious traditions held sway, though again in varying degrees. Even in the contemporary secular or minimally religious college or university, the remnants of this older pattern can sometimes be detected, as in Bible courses in which the canon is the Christian one and the rich literature of late Second Temple and rabbinic Judaism are overlooked or minimized. In general, however, it is now religion itself and not merely certain traditions that the academy tends to overlook or minimize, replacing one parochialism with another. The regnant presupposition is that religion is an exception to human rationality and thus tolerable only to the extent that it is privatized and thus denied a voice in the public conversation. The knowledge of religion that this new context validates tends therefore to conform to the perspective of outsiders, that is, of people who can survey various traditions in like manner because they either subscribe to none or keep their allegiances private.

It is this distancing that Childs's canonical method of biblical interpretation effectively and deliberately shatters. This does not, however, mean that his approach is less public than the historicist alternative, or even that it is of use only to his fellow Christians. In point of fact, those who do not subscribe to the Christian faith, or Childs's particular variety of it, can, in many cases, profitably draw analogies between his canonical method and the dynamics of scripture in their own traditions (including traditions whose scripture is a corpus of secular law or literature). In the case of the revised historicism Collins advocates, no such analogy is possible, for the method does not grant recognition to other traditions and cannot accept their textual procedures as valid analogies to its own. Indeed, even in this reformulation, historicism asserts itself in so totalistic a fashion that it cannot interact with other interpretive traditions, as Childs, for example, interacts positively with rabbinic and medieval Jewish exegesis in his commentary on Exodus.[37] Instead, the historicist position requires that scholars' loyalties to particular religious communities remain privatized and not be brought out into the open where dialogue takes place. Childs's revision of Calvinist scripturalism is therefore in some ways more pluralistic than Collins's revision of nineteenth-century historicism. Founded upon a historical particularity — the Protestant canon — Childs's method harbors a potential for respect for other historically particular traditions, a potential only begun to be realized in Childs's own work. By universalizing the claims of historical criticism, Collins denies himself the same potential for pluralism. Though he acknowledges that historical criticism is itself historically particular and a tradition, Collins continues to argue that all other traditions must yield to it.

There are good reasons that a method focused on canon should arouse the ire of uncompromisingly historicistic biblical scholars. One is that canons remind historicists of the community loyalties that their own tradition aspires at best to keep submerged and at worst to eradicate. For a biblical canon is always either Jewish or Samaritan or Eastern Orthodox or Roman Catholic or Protestant — but never generic, never universal. Its very existence reminds biblical scholars that the object of their study cannot, in the last analysis, be detached from specific religious communities and from traditions that are postbiblical. To the extent that they seek to invalidate those traditions — for example, by branding traditional interpretations as merely misinterpretations — they attack their own project. They cast considerable doubt upon the ongoing importance of the book to which they have devoted their life's work. They saw off the branch upon which they are sitting.

The fact of canon also challenges the most basic presupposition of historical criticism, that a book must be understood only within the context in which it was produced. The very existence of a canon testifies to the reality of *recontextualization:* an artifact may survive the circumstances that brought it into being, including the social and political circumstances to which so much attention is currently devoted.[38] Indeed, it can outlive the culture in which it was produced. Even when this happens, as in the case of the texts that came together in the Bible, as Barton points out,[39] that original culture continues to inform the text, nonetheless. Because the Bible can never be altogether disengaged from the culture of its authors, historical criticism is necessary (though not necessarily in accordance with Troeltsch's principles). But unless one holds that the Bible does not *deserve* to have survived its matrix — that the history of interpretation is only a history of misinterpretation — historical criticism alone cannot suffice. For were the meaning of the text *only* a function of the particular historical circumstances of its composition, recontextualization would never have occurred, and no Bible would have come into existence. If this be so, the tradition of historical criticism should not be abandoned within pluralistic settings, but only reconceived so as to recognize the challenge of pluralism. What must be abandoned are its totalistic claims. Room must be made for other senses of the text, developed by other traditions, and historical criticism must learn to interact more creatively with those other traditions, neither surrendering to them nor demanding that they surrender to historical criticism. Critical scholars must no longer pronounce other interpretations altogether erroneous simply because they take the texts out of their first historical context — simply because, that is, they permit the texts to survive the ancient civilizations in which they originated.

Historical criticism, in sum, will have to retreat from the severe philosophical historicism that can still often be detected in its applications. It will not only have to surrender the positivistic notion of critical autonomy and recognize itself as a *tradition,* as Collins rightly argues. It will also have to recognize that it corresponds to a *community of interpretation.* It is a very special kind, however, one dependent upon other communities of interpretation for the very object of its inquiry and, historically if not necessarily, for its motivation as well. Historical critics thus constitute a secondary community; they engage in second-order reflection upon the primary language of the religious communities they study. Like the liberal state at its best, biblical studies in nonconfessional settings must facilitate rather than impede dialogue and debate among the primary communities, religious and secular, within its compass. That compass will not be universal: fundamentalists who give historical criticism no quarter and historical critics who are fundamentalistic about their own methods will be unable to participate in the multisided discourse. But the new discourse will be more authentically pluralistic than the types that now dominate, especially the type that falsely claims to be pluralistic when it is only historicistic.

There are, to be sure, many philosophical issues here that are as nettlesome as they are pressing. What common conceptual framework will ground this new discourse once historicism has been relegated to another item within it? How can the pluralism of the new discourse avoid degenerating into relativism, as the senses of the text multiply uncontrollably and the common inquiry dies of fractionation? These points and others like them I all too happily leave to my colleagues in philosophical studies, except to note this: the idea that scripture has multiple senses — some available across community boundaries, others not — is not altogether unprecedented in the history of Jewish and Christian biblical interpretation. Rather, it has been obscured by a long-standing religious preference for the plain sense and by the disrespect that it has received from the hands of historical critics convinced that only they know what the Bible *really* means. It may be time to reexamine how different senses of the text once coexisted in minds that had not surrendered to the nihilistic notion of total semantic indeterminacy. The issue is not new. What is new is the urgency that it acquires in a setting of cultural pluralism. For pluralism makes demands not only upon traditionalists, but also upon critics, not only upon fundamentalists, but also upon liberals — in both the religious and the classical political senses of the word.

· IV ·

My point would be misunderstood if it were taken to be that only a religious affirmation can justify the presence of biblical studies in a curriculum and that the field cannot be open to secular practitioners. In point of fact, I have stressed both the necessity for historical criticism and its intrinsically secular character, which derives from its origins in Enlightenment rationalism. Given the long-standing tendency of historical-critical scholars to abuse the method for their own confessional purposes,[40] the presence of secular scholars is not only permissible, but desirable: they keep their religious colleagues honest. No small assignment!

I have also been misunderstood if I am thought to imply that the subjects that biblical scholars sometimes condescendingly term the "ancillary disciplines" (such as Syro-Palestinian archaeology and Northwest Semitic philology) cannot stand on their own, as some of their practitioners now indignantly insist they must.[41] My point is only that if they do stand on their own, they can no longer justify themselves on the grounds of their relevance to biblical interpretation. There may be a good *secular* reason for a dean to prefer to fund Ugaritic or Coptic (which no one speaks) over Hungarian or Tagalog (which millions speak), and those who want the so-called ancillary disciplines to stand alone must rely precisely on those secular reasons. If they rely, instead, on the residual momentum of religious belief, they are worse than ancillary: they are parasitic.

What I *have* argued is that the secularity of historical criticism represents not the suppression of commitment, but its relocation. Scholars with religious motivations are thus not out of order to challenge their secular colleagues to make public their own motivations to pursue biblical studies and to explain how the method realizes the motivation. In an era of multiculturalism and budgetary constraint, this inevitably entails explaining how the relocation of commitment from a traditional religious sphere can maintain a place of relative privilege for the study of the Bible. Should the answer substitute a cultural for a religious motivation and center on the importance of the Bible in Western civilization, then, in the current climate, a defense of the importance of the West, at least for American students, is imperative. This is, of course, ironic in light of the tendency of historical criticism to think of itself as transcending particularism and debunking claims of privilege. It is doubly ironic because historical critics have usually neglected the modes of biblical interpretation that preceded them, labeling them "precritical" and thus irrelevant to their own task.

Any secular defense of the study of the Bible will also need to account for the canon chosen. Will there be an "Old Testament" or a Tanakh?[42] If the former, then why, if christological claims are not credited? And if the latter, then why again, if Judaism is also disallowed? Should the response be the classic historicist point that the books should be examined within the limits of their dates of composition, one is compelled again to point out that when they were written, they were not yet biblical and that most do not presuppose a book-religion at all. In short, biblical studies inevitably (indeed, by definition) involves the affirmation of certain religious judgments — if not for the present, then at least as a legacy of the past with continuing *normative* effects. Secularity is no guarantee of religious neutrality.

• V •

Historical criticism has long posed a major challenge to people with biblical commitments, and for good reason. What I hope to have shown is that the reverse is also the case: the Bible poses a major challenge to people with historical-critical commitments. When those fundamentalist students with whom I began become liberals, they solve some of their problems, but they also open up new ones. And with *these* problems, the contemporary university, child of the Enlightenment and bastion of liberalism, is not well-equipped to help.

Chapter 6

———   •   ———

Exodus and Liberation

• I •

Nothing in the Bible so readily invites the term "liberation" as the exodus of the Israelites from Egypt. The essential question, however, has not been so readily asked: In exactly what sense ought the exodus to be seen as an instance of liberation, or, to pose the same question in other words, what is the character of the liberation typified by the exodus and how is this type of liberation to be distinguished from other phenomena to which the same term is presently applied?

For liberation theologians from Latin America, it has proven tempting to perceive the exodus from Egypt in the light of their own historical situation and political loyalties. This is not a temptation that many of them have resisted. Thus, according to J. Severino Croatto, it was through the exodus that "Israel grasped a liberating sense of God and an essential value in its own vocation, namely freedom." Now the challenge is to extend that freedom to the entire world: "We are enjoined to prolong the exodus event because it was not an event solely for the Hebrews but rather the manifestation of a liberative plan of God for all peoples . . . an unfinished historical project."[1] Surveying the literature of liberation theology as it stood in 1978, Robert McAfee Brown concluded that for the liberationists, the greatness of the exodus story is that it describes a "God who takes sides, intervening to free the poor and oppressed." And from whom does God free them? Who are the pharaohs of our time? "The rich and powerful from other nations," Brown informs us, "who keep national oligarchies in power, thereby becoming complicit in the ongoing exploitation of the poor."[2]

Brown's survey shows that this conception of the exodus as a socio-political revolution by and for the poor and oppressed has long been typical of liberation theology. It is in the more recent commentary by George (or Jorge) Pixley, a Baptist minister and biblical scholar born in Chicago but raised in Nicaragua, however, that the liberationist conception of the exodus receives its most thorough explication. Though Pixley is not to be numbered among the best-known and most influential of liberationists, he has accomplished something that the others, to my knowledge, have not. First, he has written a book-length commentary in support of the commonplaces about the exodus that one finds scattered throughout the works of other liberation theologians. Second, and more important, Pixley's commentary does not rest content with sporadic homiletical flourishes but continually and systematically engages critical scholarship on the book of Exodus. To assess whether that biblical book bears out its liberationist interpretation, we can therefore do no better than to concentrate on Pixley's commentary.

Pixley sees the exodus story as having undergone a four-stage evolution. The first stage corresponds to historical fact: "a heterogeneous group of peasants in Egypt, accompanied by a nucleus of immigrants from regions to the east," escaped from Egypt under the leadership of "the Levite Moses"; it was this heterogeneous underclass who were the original Levites, and the Levites, so understood, who actually came out of the house of bondage. In the second stage, these Levites joined an alliance of rebellious Canaanite peasants known as Israel, and the exodus "was then read as the experience of a struggle against exploitation at the hands of an illegitimate royal apparatus." In Pixley's third stage, when Israel had become a monarchy, the exodus was again recast, this time as "a national liberation struggle — no longer a class struggle [but] a struggle between two peoples: Israel and Egypt." Finally, in the Second Temple period, long after the monarchy had fallen, the exodus was converted into the foundation story for the depoliticized Jewish community — now solely religious in character — whose religious obligations then came to be seen as deriving from YHWH's rescue of his people in the exodus.[3]

As Pixley reconstructs the history of the exodus story, the overall movement is thus one from political religion to apolitical religion. The latter, however, is simply a cover for the maintenance of the political status quo and thus not really apolitical at all. For Pixley, texts that speak of God's unique initiative or credit an action exclusively to him are in the nature of "ideology, in the pejorative sense of camouflage and mystification." Their ideological function is to render the populace helpless, impotent, and dependent upon the "dominant class, monarchical or priestly."[4]

This ideologization of the exodus begins quite early, in Pixley's view, at least as early as the J (Yahwistic) source, for whom nation-state and monarchy were positive realities. For both the J and the P (Priestly) sources, "the account of the plagues serves to fill the vacuum left by the obliteration of the popular struggles against the Egyptian tyrant," a vacuum now filled by the "struggles between YHWH and the pharaoh."[5] In sum, Pixley sees the book of Exodus as an artful but ultimately unsuccessful attempt to disguise the reality of the exodus as a class struggle and social revolution.

Whatever the degree of probability of Pixley's reconstruction, his adopting it puts him in an unusual dilemma. We can best define the dilemma by examining the section of his introduction in which he explains what he means when he says that he intends his commentary to be "evangelical." On the one hand, as a Protestant, Pixley intends "evangelical" to signify those churches that "believe it is in the Bible that the highest authority for their faith is to be found." On the other hand, he also uses the term in what he deems "the more important sense," that is, the classical New Testament sense of "good news," and, given that the commentary is "dedicated to the heroic struggle of the Salvadoran people," it follows that Pixley would see this good news as inextricably associated with what he calls "the liberation of oppressed individuals and peoples."[6] But it is precisely here that a contradiction appears. For by Pixley's own account the Bible that is the "highest authority for...faith" has almost entirely suppressed the identity of the exodus-conquest as a popular insurrection and class struggle and replaced this with an *ideology* in the Marxist sense, that is, a system of belief that works to preserve the oppression and alienation of the masses and the privileges of the ruling class. Thus Pixley defines the P source, for which the ruling class is the postexilic priesthood, as "the ideological product of a class that seeks to have the people place religion at the center of its life," politics having become "secondary to religion."[7] But even the J source, which he dates to the early monarchy, supports, in his words, "an ideological indoctrination that would sustain the new national consensus, and counteract revolutionary or anti-monarchical tendencies"[8] — not exactly "good news" for "the heroic struggle of the Salvadoran people"!

The choice, then, is whether to expound the *counter-revolutionary*

Bible or the *hypothetical revolutionary history* that has been alleged to lie at the origin of the Israelite tradition. If the Bible is really "the highest authority," as Pixley avers in his first definition of "evangelical," then the answer is obvious and, if his own sociopolitical analysis is borne out, Pixley will have to become the theological equivalent of a *contra*, and, like the J source in his reconstruction, "counteract revolutionary . . . tendencies." This more Protestant side of the commentary does pop up from time to time, as when Pixley tells us, in another context, that "[o]ur task is to read the text, rather than to reconstruct the events that gave rise to the tradition it reflects."[9] But on the politically sensitive points, this text-centered approach tends to yield to the reconstructed revolution. The tenth plague, the slaying of the Egyptian firstborn, is a case in point.

Historical-critical commentaries have traditionally seen in this an aetiology for YHWH's traditional claim upon the firstborn of man and beast (e.g., Exod 22:28–29) and also for the special role of the clerical tribe Levi, whom YHWH takes for his own service in place of the firstborn males of the Israelites, whom he consecrated when he "smote every first-born in the land of Egypt" (Num 8:16–19).[10] According to Num 3:44–51, those firstborn for whom there are no Levites to be substituted must be redeemed through the payment of five shekels per head, payable to the priests of the line of Aaron. In short, one aetiological function of the tenth plague is to justify a system of priestly emoluments. Here the biblical *text* is once again an embarrassment to those animated by a vision of radical egalitarianism. But what about the underlying *history?* Many scholars would deny that there is any historical core at all to the legend of the death of the Egyptian firstborn; they would prefer to see ritual rather than history as the mother of the narrative — *Mythus* arising from *Ritus.* But Pixley takes a different tack. He suggests, with admirable tentativeness, that "[i]t may be that the massacre of the exodus night was a terrorist action — inspired by God."[11] The tentativeness is undoubtedly owing to Pixley's awareness of the absence of direct evidence to support his suggestion. The only "evidence" is the overall theory that the exodus was in the nature of an insurrection. What drives him to advance this idea is the advantage it offers to the liberationist perspective. By shifting the normative statement from the manifest *text* to the hypothetical *history,* one can convert a passage that upholds inequality and privilege (though both are subordinate to consecration and service) into a precedent for revolution.[12] Gospel as the putative good news of liberation scores a knockout against gospel as sacred text. One wonders, however, how many such knockouts the text can suffer before it must be retired from the ring altogether. If the Bible has authority only when it endorses liberation in the Marxist sense, why not dispense with the Bible altogether and devote oneself to collecting and expounding examples of this kind of liberation from the history of revolution throughout the world? For it could not be clearer that in this kind of hermeneutic, the authority of the utopian revolutionary ideal altogether supersedes that of the Bible — not exactly "good news" for Protestants who believe in the classical Reformation theology of *sola scriptura.*

From what I have said so far, it should not be difficult to figure out what type of revolution Pixley has in mind. "Perhaps we could understand Moses' special role," Pixley writes, in commenting upon Moses' lack of a successor, "by comparing it with the special role of revolutionary figures such as Lenin, Tito, Mao, Ho Chi Minh, and Castro."[13] Now, of course, Moses had his Joshua, whom some texts are at great pains to call his authorized successor (e.g., Num 27:15–23), and Lenin, to name only Pixley's first modern analogue, had his Stalin, though not a few Leninists have understandably wished the case were otherwise. What really joins the five revolutionaries that Pixley names is not their lack of a true successor, but rather their allegiance to some form of Marxism. This is also the feature that suggests the analogy with Moses, since Pixley thinks early Israel was "a classless society, a society of primitive communism."[14]

Given the importance of Marxist revolution in Pixley's view of the exodus, it is strange indeed that his bibliography does not include a book by the American muckraker Lincoln Steffens, *Moses in Red: The Revolt of Israel as a Typical Revolution,* published in 1926, before anyone ever heard of liberation theology and when almost all Christians and almost all Marxists saw the two perspectives as radically opposed. "Let Jehovah personify and speak for Nature," wrote Steffens; "think of Moses as the uncompromising Bolshevik; Aaron as the more political Menshevik; take Pharaoh as the ruler who stands for the Right (the conservative 'evolutionist'), and the Children of Israel as the people — any people; read the Books of Moses thus and they will appear as a revolutionary classic."[15] But just as ten out of twelve spies in Numbers 13–14 were afraid to enter the Promised Land, so writes Steffens, "minds as scientific as those of Bertrand Russell and H. G. Wells, and spirits as bold and revolutionary as Emma Goldman, reported against the Promised Land of Russia; they preferred England and the United States."[16] Now, having written only nine years after Lenin's revolution, Steffens can perhaps be forgiven for thinking of Russia as the Promised Land and England and the United States as analogous to pharaoh's Egypt. Perhaps Steffens would have reconsidered his adulation of the Soviet Union and his disparagement of England and the United States if he had lived to hear Jews shout Moses' demand "Let my people go!" not at Thatcher and Reagan, but at Brezhnev and Gorbachev, and to see death-defying rebels again escape across the perilous seas, only this time in crude boats launched from "liberated" Vietnam or from Castro's Cuba, boats crowded with people fleeing those promised lands in hopes of coming to the United States. For this, amazingly, is precisely what was happening as Pixley wrote his quasi-Marxist commentary on Exodus in the mid-1980s, just before Communism collapsed almost everywhere, even in Nicaragua. I suspect many of those Soviet Jewish emigrés, those Vietnamese boat people, and those Cuban refugees would indeed find their own experience in the book of Exodus, just as Pixley thinks — except that they would see in his Communist revolutionaries not Moses but pharaoh. The astonishing point is that Pixley, writing over half a century after Steffens, was not prompted by the bloody history of Communist regimes in our century to ask whether the Marxist-Leninist perspective advances true liberation (a question that in no way implies the exoneration of the *ancien régime* in Latin America). What is curious — but also depressing — is that the hermeneutic of suspicion that he applies to the biblical text — at least when it fails to endorse his social ideal — is never applied to the ideal itself and the modern political tradition that has tried the hardest to implement it.

Pixley's four-stage reconstruction of the exodus story reminds me of Mark Twain's description of a dinosaur he once saw in a museum: "three bones and ninety barrels plaster of Paris." To put it mildly, the evidence that those who escaped in the exodus were a racially and religiously heterogeneous underclass is slim.[17] The basis for the currently popular idea that Israel originated as a group of disenfranchised Canaanite peasants is only slightly more substantial.[18] This speculation about Israel's origins has recently been the target of substantial criticism from historians and archaeologists, especially Baruch Halpern and Israel Finkelstein.[19] Pixley's notion that early Israel was "a classless society, a society of primitive communism," is a similar case of historical projection. The oldest law code in the Torah, the Book of the Covenant (Exod 20:22–23:33), assumes property rights, knows of chiefs, freemen, and slaves, and differentiates sharply between men and women. Though it shows no knowledge of a priestly caste, it does require hefty offerings from the people for the sacrificial cults. None of this is to deny that the Book of the Covenant is, like the rest of the Hebrew Bible, especially concerned for the well-being of those who are vulnerable — the stranger, the poor, the widow, and the orphan — and goes to great lengths to construct protections for them.

This concern, which liberation theologians tend to call "the preferential option for the poor," is a central element of the Hebraic social ethic. But it does not in any way suggest classlessness or primitive communism as either a reality or an ideal. The condemnation of the oppression of the poor by the rich in the Hebrew Bible cannot be construed as a rejection of the very existence of the two classes. Such a construal projects Marxist and kindred egalitarian ideas into texts that had a very different view of the matter. In the Hebrew Bible, impoverishment can indeed be a symptom of oppression, but also of laziness, divine punishment, or simply bad luck. Conversely, wealth can signal exploitation, but also industry, merited blessing, or good luck. Into which category any given poor or wealthy person is to be placed depends on the circumstances. Even in its visions of a future age of redemption, marked by sufficiency of resources for all, the Hebrew Bible gives no indication that the abundance will be shared *equally,* and to the extent that its eschatological visions entail a reconstructed Temple and a restoration of the royal and priestly dynasties (e.g., Jer 33:14–18; Ezekiel 40–48), the scripture presupposes — and endorses — the eternity of inequality. The passionate demand for justice does indeed resound throughout the Hebrew Bible, but the identification of justice with equality is essentially a modern phenomenon and, in the hands of many modern exegetes, an impetus for gross anachronism.

If the Book of the Covenant were the code of a classless and primitive communistic society, its first piece of civil law would be passing strange:

> ²When you acquire a Hebrew slave, he shall serve six years; in the seventh year he shall go free, without payment. ³If he came single, he shall leave single; if he had a wife, his wife shall leave with him. ⁴If his master gave him a wife, and she has borne him children, the wife and her children shall belong to the master, and he shall leave alone. ⁵But if the slave declares, "I love my master, and my wife and children: I do not wish to go free," ⁶his master shall take him before God. He shall be brought to the door or the doorpost,

and his master shall pierce his ear with an awl; and he shall then
remain his slave for life. (Exod 21:2–6)

This law occasions what is perhaps the greatest understatement in the
long history of biblical interpretation. "We are surprised," remarks our
Latin American liberation theologian, George Pixley, "to discover that
there were slaves in the new revolutionary society."[20] Surprise on the
part of exegetes usually indicates an error in their preconception of the
text. In this case, the error, by no means unique to Pixley, is that early
Israel was a revolutionary society and exemplified egalitarianism and
primitive communism.

If Pixley and those on whom he builds were right, then the history of
biblical interpretation would present us with an even greater surprise:
How can it be that in Christendom slavery was so often justified precisely by reference to the Bible? Here, the precedent in Pixley's native
land in the nineteenth century is most instructive. For some theologians
in the American South in the decade before the Civil War were, like
Pixley and other liberationist exegetes, at pains to show that the social
and political order that claimed their allegiance had already been announced and even mandated in holy writ — except that their ideal was
an order that most assuredly has a place for slavery. James Smylie of Mis-
sissippi, for example, writing in 1836, noted that slavery is not just some
piece of superseded Jewish law, but, rather, is mentioned twice and
without censure in the Decalogue itself. "If God foresaw, or intended,
that servitude should expire with the Mosaic ritual," wrote Smylie, "the
authority of masters would, probably, not be recognized in a law, intended to be perpetual; nor would there have been, as is the fact, a
recognition made of servants, as property." Frederick A. Ross, a Presbyterian minister from Huntsville, Alabama, went even further. Noting, on
the eve of the War between the States, that the King James Version of
Lev 25:44–46 uses the verb "shall" rather than "may" in speaking of the
acquisition of Gentiles to be lifetime slaves, Ross held that "God *commanded* [the Israelites] to be slave-holders. He *made it* the law of their
social state." Nor did the New Testament offer any more hope to religiously inclined abolitionists. John England, the Roman Catholic bishop
of Charleston, South Carolina, pointed out that Jesus made use in his
parables of the master-slave relationship without once condemning the
institution.[21] He might also have noted that the apostle Paul, though he
wrote that in Christ there is neither slave nor free (Gal 3:28), maintained
that if one was a slave when he received his call, he should remain in

that state (1 Cor 7:17–24). In his shortest extant letter, Paul does seem to have asked Philemon to free his slave Onesimus, but not because of humanitarian concerns; rather, the apostle needed the slave's help during his own imprisonment (Phlm 11–16).[22] I see no reason to think that Paul would ever have objected to the advice attributed to him in Eph 6:5 — "Slaves, obey your earthly masters with fear and trembling, single-mindedly, as serving Christ."[23] This was, according to Eugene D. Genovese, "the favorite text of the white preachers" in those days. But some of them were equally drawn to 1 Pet 2:18–19: "Servants, accept the authority of your masters with all due submission, not only when they are kind and considerate, but even when they are perverse. For it is a fine thing if a man endures the pain of undeserved suffering because God is in his thoughts."[24]

In sum, the New Testament is no more a charter for the "new revolutionary society" than is the Hebrew Bible. And, in fact, in some ways, it is a step backward. For when the legislation of the Torah is thought to have been suspended through Christ, the substantial protections that it extends to Hebrew slaves also disappear, and the slaves have nothing more reliable to which to appeal than their masters' Christian love and whatever protections the law of the pagan state might happen to provide. Even the modest hope of emancipation in the seventh year could disappear — and did!

To the arguments of the proslavery theologians, the Christian abolitionists, of course, had their answers ready. In his great tract *The Bible Against Slavery* (originally published in 1839, reprinted in 1864), Theodore Dwight Weld pointed out the differences between slavery in biblical Israel and in the American South. In the Bible "servants who were 'bought' *sold themselves*" as a way of discharging their debts;[25] they were not kidnapped as were the African ancestors of the American slaves. In fact, biblical law specifically forbids kidnapping a person, whether to sell or to keep (Exod 21:16) — the very basis of what was to become the South's "peculiar institution." Those unfortunates who did sell themselves into debt slavery were paid for their labors and, as Lev 25:49 makes clear, when they had accumulated sufficient capital, they could redeem themselves, that is, buy themselves out of slavery, as the American blacks could not, since they were defined as property.[26] Furthermore, Weld claimed, if you add up all the Sabbaths and other holy days plus the Sabbatical and Jubilee Years during which the fields lay fallow, you find that slaves were actually free from labor for over twenty-three years out of every fifty![27] Finally, given the vast differences between biblical servitude and slavery as it was known in antebellum America, Weld felt justified in going so far as to say that the Hebrew term *'ebed* should be translated not as "slave," but as "servant," for the Hebrew language, like Hebrew society, was unfamiliar with the institution of slavery, for which Weld's opponents thought they had found biblical authorization.[28]

As sympathetic as we all are to Weld's humanitarian goal, we still must recognize that he badly overstated his case, as even some of his fellow abolitionists felt the need to concede.[29] To mention only one problem, Weld did not adequately reckon with the fact that in biblical law, Gentile slaves, unlike their Israelite coworkers, did not have to be released in their seventh year of service or in the Jubilee (Exod 21:1; Deut 15:12; Lev 25:44–46); it is not even clear that they were to rest on the Sabbath. Proslavery theologians like Ross held that the black person in white America had the same status as the Gentile in ancient Israel and could therefore justly be subjected to the same brutality. It is surely true that throughout the Hebrew Bible, there is a passionate concern to avert the victimization of the *gēr*, a term usually translated as "sojourner," "stranger," or "resident alien." Though *gēr* later comes to denote a convert, in the Bible it refers either to an Israelite dwelling outside his tribal patrimony (e.g., 2 Chr 15:9) or to a non-Israelite dwelling in Israel (e.g., 2 Chr 2:16). Even if we assume that the prohibition on victimizing the *gēr* applies to these foreigners in Israel, it is still the case that their enslavement was not thought to be inevitably offensive to God (see 1 Chr 22:2; 2 Chr 2:17). The cold fact is that in the Hebrew Bible, slavery was not reckoned as inherently exploitative or victimizing. Our conclusion must thus be that despite Weld's title and his unquestionably humane motives, he did not at all succeed in showing that the Bible was against slavery. All he proved was that the brutal and dehumanizing form of slavery in the American South did not correspond to the biblical pattern. Even so, the question could have remained open whether white masters should regard their black slaves as Israelites or as Gentiles, since the periodic emancipation of slaves applied only to the former. Of course, if the Christian church wished to consider itself the new Israel and if both masters and slaves were Christians, then the answer is obvious: to the extent that Old Testament law is incumbent upon Christians, then the masters should have treated their Christian blacks according to the relatively more humane norms applicable to Israelite slaves. Even this, however, is not an argument for the abolition of slavery, but only for its reform, and it still holds out the unwelcome prospect that a slave who rejected baptism could have been justly and legally subjected to the harsher set of norms.

There is one important difference between Israelite and American slavery that Weld did not mention, perhaps because it could have played into the hands of his opponents. Bondage to pharaoh was not domestic slavery, but state slavery. As Michael Walzer nicely puts it, the Israelites in Egypt "were not the victims of the market, but of the state."[30] State slavery, unlike domestic, is roundly condemned in the Hebrew Bible. Consider that it was King Solomon's imposition of forced labor upon the populace in order to conduct his massive state building projects that ultimately precipitated the split of his united monarchy of Israel and Judah (1 Kgs 5:27–30; 12:1–19). When his son and successor Rehoboam sent Adoniram, the officer in charge of forced labor, to the north, the northerners stoned Adoniram to death and thus launched their revolt (1 Kgs 12:18–19). The chapter in which this happens has significant points of contact with Exodus 1.[31] It is this antipathy to forced labor that stands behind much and perhaps most of the criticism of monarchy in the Hebrew Bible. The kind of liberation typified by the exodus from Egypt represents a transition from a regime of centralized government and state domination to one in which authority is located in village elders administering traditional law within a clan structure. In these narratives, one important end-result of the exodus is political and social decentralization and local control. If this is a point that would have embarrassed a Northern abolitionist like Weld, it should devastate an exegete of Marxist sympathies like Pixley. For if there is one thing that the Communist revolutionaries to whom Pixley likens Moses could not tolerate, it was the persistence of traditional modes of association outside state control (that is, until that happy day when the state withers away, and even then, what succeeds it is nothing like those traditional modes of association).

Let us now take a moment to draw together the threads of our inquiry that have been spun so far. I have argued that the ongoing significance of the exodus does not lie in its putative status as an instance of liberation in the quasi-Marxist sense in which that term is now used in many Christian seminaries and by the elites of liberal churches. The early chapters of the book of Exodus do not speak of a social revolution or a class struggle; close inspection shows that they do not even speak of the overthrow of pharaoh. The exodus does not change the social structure of Egypt one whit. Instead, the subject of these chapters is the miraculous escape to their native and promised land of foreigners who had been impressed into state slavery.[32] Even in the more general, non-Marxist sense of "emancipation," the term "liberation" as a description of the exodus from Egypt is problematic (though, as we shall see, not necessarily to be discarded). The society that the book of Exodus mandates is still one in which there are slaves, some for a limited period, others for life. If this seems a denial of the exodus from Egypt itself, as it does to Pixley and, I daresay, to most other liberation theologians, it must be borne in mind that most references to the exodus in the Hebrew Bible make no reference to slavery at all. The Bible is more likely to refer to the God who brought Israel out of Egypt only, omitting that familiar appositive, "the house of bondage" (Exod 20:2). This fits with Walzer's observation that "the memory of the Exodus is more often invoked on behalf of aliens than on behalf of slaves."[33] "You shall not oppress a stranger [*gēr*]," demands the Book of the Covenant, "for you know the feelings of the stranger, having yourselves been strangers in the land of Egypt" (Exod 23:9). The implication would seem to be that the exodus is more directly about the repatriation of aliens than the emancipation of slaves. If this is true, then the best twentieth-century analogues to Moses are not domestic revolutionaries like Lenin, Tito, Mao, Ho, and Castro, but leaders like the Zionist heroes Herzl, Weizmann, and Ben-Gurion, who made possible the ingathering of an exiled people to their ancient homeland. But to speak of exile rather than enslavement as that for which the exodus provided relief is to endorse the conception that comes into being only in Pixley's putative third stage: the exodus as an instance of *national* liberation rather than of class-based rebellion.

Confronted with the fact that the message of the text is not what they wish, interpreters of all sorts are tempted to ignore those elements of the Bible that speak against the desired message and to concentrate only on those that can be made to seem to speak for it. I call this "the temptation of selective attention." We have already seen one variety of it in Pixley's relegation of so much of the *text* to the category of ideology and his preference for the underlying *history* of sociopolitical revolution that some scholars reconstruct. One justification for selective attention is the claim that the undesired parts of scripture are only remnants of ancient Near Eastern cultures, whereas the desired parts are the unique innovation of Israel. In other words, the enduring message of the text is limited to those features we find appealing. Those we find unappealing are historical accidents, with which we can dispense without incurring any loss in our understanding of the overall text. The potential for self-flattery in this technique is considerable: "we," that is, the Jews or the church, are good; "they," the ancient Near East or the Jewish matrix of Christianity, respectively, are bad.[34]

One problem with this self-flattering technique is that it cannot reckon with the presence of the desired element in the cultural background, especially when it is absent or deficient in scripture. Consider, for example, the Code of Hammurabi, a Babylonian legal collection several hundred years older than the earliest parts of the Bible. This code limits debt slavery to three years, whereas the Hebrew Bible limits it either to six or to forty-nine years.[35] Hammurabi also requires that those who ransom persons taken captive while on official missions abroad be reimbursed from the treasury of the temple or the state[36] — a norm that may in some way underlie God's commitment to redeem Israel from slavery in Egypt.[37] It is, in short, too convenient to portray Mesopotamian society as brutal and degrading and biblical law as a time-conditioned effort to mitigate the brutality and degradation. Rather, honest investigation of the Bible requires us to recognize that the parts we like and the parts we do not are *both* biblical and that *both* these components have roots and parallels in the larger ancient Near Eastern world.

A second danger in concentrating only on those features we find desirable is in that by doing so, we implicitly deny the existence of structural connections within the body of material that we are interpreting. If, as is so often the case today, "liberation" is defined as simply the antonym of "subjugation," then the question ought to arise as to how these antonymic realities could coexist, indeed interpenetrate, in the same text and in the same culture. Or could it be that they are not so far apart after all, that the two have a tangent that the description of them as polar opposites disguises? If such interconnections do indeed exist, then there is a great danger to the interpreter in a premature moralism in which distasteful features are simply denounced as valueless or dismissed as accidental. The question of liberation and subjugation in the book of Exodus is a case in point. The embarrassing fact that the Bible was long invoked in support of both slavery and its abolition not only suggests that it is misleading to identify the biblical message with liberation without nuance; it also suggests that the stark dichotomies of freedom versus slavery and liberation versus subjugation may be inadequate to accommodate biblical thinking on these issues. Nothing tests the adequacy of our categories so effectively as a serious consideration of the arguments of those interpreters whose values we find offensive. Though not much good can be said about the proslavery theologians of the Old South, for example, they have done us one service: by drawing attention to the fact that the Bible, within limits, allows one person to be the property of another, they have, as I hope to show, provided a clue to the message of the exodus that those who dichotomize liberation and subjugation are all too inclined to miss. For in important ways, the relationship of God to Israel in the Hebrew Bible is patterned upon the very institution whose existence surprises the liberationist commentator George V. Pixley and, I daresay, most other sensitive readers in our time.

• II •

To determine the categories in which the exodus should be conceived, we first go most profitably to the Song of the Sea, the great hymn that Israel sings under the direction of Moses and Miriam just after the elite troops of pharaoh have been drowned (Exod 15:1–21). It is telling but rarely remarked that neither slavery nor freedom is so much as mentioned there.[38] Instead, the song commemorates the victory of YHWH, the God of Israel, in a battle with pharaoh's charioteers at the Sea of Reeds, the safe passage of YHWH's redeemed to his temple mountain, and their acclamation of him as their eternal king:

> [17]You brought them and planted[39] them in Your own mountain,
> The place You made to dwell in, LORD,
> The sanctuary, O LORD, which Your hands established.
> [18]The LORD will reign for ever and ever. (Exod 15:17–18)

This connection of God's kingship with his victory over the angry waters and the establishment of his temple is a familiar pattern in the Hebrew Bible. The three elements are tied together most tightly in the exquisite little poem that is Psalm 93:

> [1]The LORD has become king,[40]
> He is robed in grandeur;
> the LORD is robed,
> He is girded with strength.
> The world stands firm;
> it cannot be shaken.

> [2]Your throne stands firm from of old;
>   from eternity You have existed.
> [3]The ocean sounds, O LORD,
>   the ocean sounds its thunder,
>   the ocean sounds its pounding.
> [4]Above the thunder of the mighty waters,
>   more majestic than the breakers of the sea
>   is the LORD, majestic on high.
> [5]Your decrees are indeed enduring;
>   holiness befits Your house,
>   O LORD, for all times.

This poem presents us with a threefold pattern of (1) victory over the sea, (2) kingship, and (3) temple. The best parallel to the pattern, and perhaps its ultimate source, is the Babylonian creation epic, the *Enuma elish*. This is the story of the young god Marduk's victory over Tiamat, the primordial sea monster, a victory that resulted not only in creation, but also in Marduk's achieving unquestioned supremacy over the other gods, symbolized by the construction of his royal city, Babylon, and his palace, the great temple Esagila. Geographically closer to Israel is the very similar Canaanite story of the god Baal's victory over the sea (Yamm), the object of much attention in recent years.[41]

The outstanding difference between the Song of Sea and these other Israelite, Mesopotamian, and Canaanite parallels is that in the song, the sea is not the enemy, but rather the weapon that the victorious deity employs against the real adversary, pharaoh. This is not a case of victory *over* the sea, but victory *at* the sea over a historical enemy. Nonetheless, the Song of the Sea remains an acclamation of this God's incomparability and supremacy within the pantheon — "Who is like You, O LORD, among the gods!" (Exod 15:11)[42] — and a ratification of his kingship and his right to a palace fit for a God, that is, a temple. Within the narrative shape of the book of Exodus, the Song of the Sea simply culminates a long process in which the God of Israel demonstrates that he is unique, and his power supreme, even over the incarnate god of the Egyptians, the pharaoh. According to Exod 9:14, God brought about the plagues so that pharaoh "may know that there is none like [YHWH] in all the world." It is that message of God's supremacy and incomparability that Israel is charged to pass on from generation to generation (Exod 10:1–2).

This pattern of victory and acclamation is known among scholars of ancient Near Eastern religion as "enthronement."[43] This, then, is the first message of the exodus: the exodus is a story of the *enthronement* of YHWH and the glad acceptance of his endless reign by his redeemed, the whole House of Israel.

To understand the second aspect of the meaning of the exodus, we go to another familiar passage:

> [20]When, in time to come, your children ask you, "What mean the decrees, laws, and rules that the LORD our God has enjoined upon you?" [21]you shall say to your children, "We were slaves to Pharaoh in Egypt and the LORD freed us from Egypt with a mighty hand. [22]The LORD wrought before our eyes marvelous destructive signs and portents in Egypt, against Pharaoh and all his household; [23]and us He freed from there that He might take us and give us the land that He had promised on oath to our fathers. [24]Then the LORD commanded us to observe all these laws, to revere the LORD our God, for our lasting good and for our survival, as is now the case. [25]It will be therefore to our merit before the LORD our God to observe faithfully this whole Instruction, as He has commanded us." (Deut 6:20–25)

These words are known to contemporary Jews from the Passover Haggadah, in which the wise son is said to ask the great question of v. 20: Why do you Jews do all these strange things? The answer is that the Passover seder commemorates and relives the exodus. In the biblical context, however, "the decrees, laws, and rules" to which v. 20 refers are not the laws of Passover, still less those of the paschal banquet. They refer, instead, to everything in "this whole Instruction" (v. 25), the whole pattern of observance that defines the Israelite's life and gives it meaning. The exodus provides the ground for obedience; it specifies God's claim upon Israel.

To understand how, we must go back to the moment between the destruction of pharaoh's army and the revelation at Mount Sinai, to God's opening address to Israel at that sacred spot:

> [4]You have seen what I did to the Egyptians, how I bore you on eagle's wings and brought you to Me. [5]Now then, if you will obey Me faithfully and keep My covenant, you shall be My treasured possession among all the peoples. Indeed, all the earth is Mine,

⁶but you shall be to Me a kingdom of priests and a holy nation.
(Exod 19:4–6)

In this text, the relationship of obedience to YHWH and faithful observance of his directives is given a name: covenant. The roots of covenant
so conceived lie in ancient Near Eastern suzerainty treaties, that is, in
documents that authorize an alliance between a great emperor (the
suzerain) and the king of a lesser state (the vassal). In some of these
treaties, the suzerain cites his past benefactions of the vassal. In well-
nigh all of them, the suzerain promises protection and support to the
vassal if the latter remains loyal, and the vassal swears to uphold the stipulations that his lord imposes.[44] With this pattern in mind, we come to
see the meaning of YHWH's opening statement: "[y]ou have seen what
I did to the Egyptians" (v. 4). The exodus serves as YHWH's outstanding
act of benevolence toward Israel — his great benefaction. The basis of
Israel's obedience to God lies in their gratitude for his deliverance as
they faced slavery and death in Egypt and at the sea. It is through that
act of deliverance that he acquired them, becoming their lord even as
they became his subjects (Exod 15:16).

The second aspect of the meaning of the exodus, then, is that the
exodus constitutes the basis of *covenant.* It provides the rationale for
Israel's observance of their divine lord's commandments. These norms
are practiced not simply because they are right, but because they have
been commanded by Israel's loving and delivering lord and master,
YHWH their God. The commandments derive their authority from the
relationship in which they are embedded, and it is this relationship that
ensures that their observance will be marked by love and gratitude.

Earlier, I had occasion to remark that Leviticus 25 forbids one Israelite to subject another to the sort of slavery inflicted by pharaoh.
It might be thought that the reason for the prohibition is that, having
been redeemed from Egypt, Israel is to remain free. In fact, however,
the truth is almost the opposite:

> For it is to Me that the Israelites are servants [*'ăbādîm* = slaves]:
> they are My servants, whom I freed from the land of Egypt, I the
> LORD your God. (Lev 25:55)

The limitation on Israelite slavery is owing to YHWH's prior claim upon
them: he, and no one else, is their master. For similar reasons, the same
chapter of Torah stipulates that land may not be sold in perpetuity: it belongs to God and the Israelites are but "strangers resident with [Him]"

(Lev 25:23–24). The image that Leviticus 25 evokes is thus that of the land of Israel as a huge temple estate, worked by people who are in the simultaneously exalted and humble role of slaves consecrated to their God, humble because they are only slaves, exalted because they have been chosen for service to the lord of the universe.

The ancient Near Eastern background of this image lies in the right of a king to free cities from state labor, military conscription, and the like by dedicating them to a god. In the twenty-fifth century B.C.E., for example, the Sumerian king Entemena liberated four cities and "restored them to the hands of the gods." In the twenty-second century B.C.E., King Manish-tushu freed thirty-eight towns by dedicating them to the god Shamash. In the fourteenth century, the Kassite king Kirigalzu liberated the citizens of Babylon from state labor "for the sake of the god Marduk."[45] In each case, liberation comes not through simple emancipation, but through dedication and consecration. Whether in Mesopotamia or in Israel, the gods' slaves may be no one else's.

This idea of liberation through a change of masters shows how misleading it is to summarize the exodus through the popular slogan, "Let My people go." The full form of the challenge is actually *šallaḥ 'et-'ammî wĕyaʿabdûnî*, "Let My people go that they may serve Me."[46] The emphasis, I think, falls on that last word: that they may serve *Me* and no one else. The point of the exodus is not freedom in the sense of self-determination, but *service*, the service of the loving, redeeming, and delivering God of Israel, rather than the state and its proud king. The paradox should not be overlooked that if you rid biblical theology of slavery altogether, you will miss one important basis for the biblical efforts to mitigate slavery.

Dedication in the sense of *consecration* is, then, the third message of the exodus: Israel is free of degrading bondage because they have been dedicated and consecrated to the service of their God.

We have now developed three meanings of the exodus — *enthronement, covenant,* and *dedication.* The differences between them in idiom and in legal background should not be allowed to obscure what they have in common. In their various ways, enthronement, covenant, and dedication all signify God's proprietorship of Israel and Israel's inescapable subjugation to its God. Proprietorship and subjugation are clear enough in the cases of enthronement, the language of which is monarchical, and of dedication, the language of which involves the issue of property. It is less clear in the case of covenant, the language of which sometimes stresses free choice — the choice of the vassal to enter into the alliance with his suzerain. "I call heaven and earth to witness against you this day," thunders Moses in Deuteronomy. "I have put before you life and death, blessing and curse. Choose life — if you and your offspring would live — by loving the LORD your God, heeding His commands, and holding fast to Him" (Deut 30:19). The vassal's consent to service is indeed essential and constitutes a crucial difference between service to pharaoh and the covenantal service of YHWH. Pharaoh never gives Israel the opportunity to declare of him what they unanimously declare of YHWH: "All that the LORD has spoken we will do!" (Exod 19:8). Important though consent to covenant be, however, it must not be overlooked that there is no alternative to it. No one in the Hebrew Bible ever turns down an offer of covenant with God and lives to tell of it.[47] The alternative to the life of obedience that Moses offers is death through disobedience. In fact, one point of the exodus story is that Israel would have perished not only in Egypt but also at Sinai had it not been for covenant, in this case, the prior covenant with Abraham, Isaac, and Jacob (Exod 32:13–14). By the time Israel gets to Sinai, they have already learned that covenant means the difference between life and death. They are hardly in a position to say "no" to their suzerain, for now he has proven himself their redeemer as well. Indeed, the role of the suzerain and that of the redeemer are, in the biblical vision, ultimately inseparable.

I have been stressing the element of subjugation, Israel's inescapable subjugation to YHWH, because in the contemporary context, the term "liberation" can suggest something very different from what the Bible intends: it can suggest *self-determination.* For many people today liberation means in essence an expansion of choices: the more options you have, the freer you are. Concentration on the movement out of bondage in Egypt can leave the impression that the Torah, too, endorses the modern Western agenda of self-determination in its various forms, just as concentration on covenant, a form of contractual relationship, can leave the false impression that the Torah endorses the currently popular idea that the only obligations that persons have are those they have voluntarily assumed, there being no morality independent of human will. But, as we have seen, the biblical story of the exodus is not couched in the vocabulary of freedom at all. Rather, it serves to undergird a set of obligations to the divine sovereign, who is Israel's king, their lord in covenant, and the deity to whose service they have been dedicated and consecrated. As John Howard Yoder puts it, in the case of the kind of liberation that the exodus represents, "*what for* matters more than *what from.*"[48] And the *"what for"* is not simply human equality and justice in community, as a Marxist understanding of liberation might suggest. Indeed, as our example of the death of the firstborn showed, the norms that Israel has been liberated to observe sometimes involve such non-egalitarian provisions as emoluments for the hereditary priest-hood. This is because the *"what for"* of Israel's liberation has a vertical as well as a horizontal dimension. It is spiritual, not just social, and involves many practices that are not presented as interpersonal at all, but as the mysterious stipulations of the divine king. What underlies such practices is an act of collective submission that goes far beyond the mutual submission of individuals to each other in a just and loving community.

The term "liberty," therefore, can indeed describe the result of re-demption of the sort typified by the exodus, but only if some crucial semantic distinctions are maintained.[49] One of the several meanings of "liberty" in Western thought is government by law rather than by a tyrant. If this is what we identify as the result of the exodus for Israel, then "liberty" and the process that produces it, "liberation," are appro-priate terms for the biblical process. We must, of course, recognize that the sole source of law in the Pentateuch is God, so that the ultimate allegiance of the populace is to him as their lord and redeemer rather than to the legal order as an autonomous entity. If, however, "liberty" be taken to mean the self-government of the populace, as has also of-ten been the case in Western thought, then the exodus must be seen as profoundly *opposed* to liberty and liberation. For liberty so con-ceived cannot allow for the collective act of subjugation upon which the relationship of YHWH and Israel is founded and which is variously thematized as enthronement, covenant, and dedication/consecration.

I have been stressing that the Hebrew Bible does not conceive the exodus as a move from slavery to freedom, either freedom in the older, liberal sense of emancipation from external constraint for the purpose of self-determination, or freedom in the newer, Marxist sense of lib-eration from oppression and alienation for the purpose of equality, solidarity, and community. It might be rejoined, however, that in tan-naitic as opposed to biblical Judaism we find the exodus conceived in precisely this way, as a move "from slavery to freedom," *mē'abdût lĕḥērût*, in the words of the first-century patriarch Rabban Gamaliel II, which have long been incorporated in the Passover Haggadah. In fact, Rabban Gamaliel ruled that in every generation each Jew is to regard himself as if he personally had come out of Egypt (*M. Pes.* 10:5). But what did Rabban Gamaliel mean by "freedom"? He lived, it will be recalled, at the end of the first century of the common era, between the two great Jewish revolts against the Roman Empire. Since I know of no evidence that would associate this patriarch with Jewish insurrectionist movements, I must assume that "freedom" to him was not a code word for the overthrow of the brutal imperialism of Rome and the establishment of political independence. It is more likely that by "freedom" he meant the opportunity for Israel to serve YHWH, or, in the words he is actually quoted as using, to accept "the Kingdom of Heaven" (*M. Ber.* 2:5). This freedom is not only spiritual; it has material requirements and doubtless could not have been fully realized amidst the degrading bondage to the pharaoh. But the spiritual component, evident in the positive acceptance of the Kingdom of Heaven, is essential, I submit, to the rabbinic concept of freedom. This is suggested not only by the two comments of Rabban Gamaliel II, but by a few other rabbinic remarks that connect Torah and freedom. Rabban Yochanan ben Zakkai, of the previous generation, for example, is said to have made this comment about the law that requires the master to bring the Hebrew slave who declines freedom to the door or the doorpost and there to bore his ear with an awl (Exod 21:6; Deut 15:17):

> Why was the ear singled out from all the other limbs of the body? The Holy One, blessed be He, said, This ear, which heard my voice on Mount Sinai when I proclaimed, *For unto me the children of Israel are servants, they are my servants* [Lev 25:55], and not servants of servants, and yet this [man] went and acquired a master for himself — let it be bored! (*b. Qidd.* 22b)

About five generations later, this midrash is said to have been repeated by Rabbi Simeon son of Rabbi Judah the Patriarch, only with the exodus taking the place of Mount Sinai as the point at which Lev 25:55 was proclaimed:

> The Holy One, blessed be He, said, The door and the doorpost, which were witnesses in Egypt when I passed over the lintel and the doorposts and proclaimed, *For unto me the children of Israel are servants, they are my servants* [Lev 25:55], and not servants of servants, and so I brought them from bondage to freedom, yet this [man] went and acquired a master for himself — let him be bored in their presence! (*b. Qidd.* 22b)[50]

In Rabbi Yochanan ben Zakkai's version, service or slavery (the word is again the same) to God, revealed and established on Mount Sinai, is the worthy alternative to service or slavery to another man. He who chooses slavery proves himself deaf to Sinai.[51] In Rabbi Simeon son of Judah the Patriarch's version of the same midrash, God's proclamation that the Israelites are to be his servants (or slaves) is retrojected into the night of the exodus itself, and that service or slavery to him is explicitly identified with the transition _mē'abdût lĕḥērût_, "from slavery to freedom." In both cases, the distinguishing mark of freedom is not the absence of subjugation, but the one to whom Israel is subjugated and the nature of life _sub iugo_, "under the yoke." Israel's freedom lies in their subjugation to YHWH, which, in turn, is realized in their glad acceptance of what the Mishnah calls "the yoke of the Kingdom of Heaven" (e.g., _M. Ber._ 2:3), manifest in the life of Torah and commandments. As Rabbi Joshua ben Levi, a Palestinian authority of the third century C.E., remarks about the Decalogue "incised [_ḥārût_] upon the tablets" (Exod 32:16), "Don't read 'incised' [_ḥārût_] but rather 'freedom' [_ḥērût_, a word that differs in only one vowel], for no one is free except one who involves himself in the study of Torah" (_M. Abot_ 6:2).

This rabbinic association of Torah with freedom is, in a sense, the diametric opposite of the familiar Pauline view that the Law represents one form of the slavery from which the Christian has been set free. For Paul, the covenant of Mount Sinai is associated not with the freedom of Sarah but with the servitude of the bondswoman Hagar, and the Christian — or at least the Gentile Christian — who accepts the Torah and its commandments trades freedom for slavery. "Stand firm, then," Paul warns his correspondents in Gal 5:1, "and refuse to be tied to the yoke of slavery again."[52] It is tempting to conclude that the rabbinic connection of Torah with freedom is a deliberate counterpoint to the Pauline theology at issue. For the effect of the midrash about the slave's ear, in either formulation quoted above, is to prevent the sort of separation of the freedom of exodus from the service of Sinai characteristic of Paul's thinking. Indeed, the effect of the second version, attributed to the third-century Rabbi Simeon son of Rabbi Judah the Patriarch, is to make Lev 25:55 the keynote of the night of emancipation itself: the transition from slavery to freedom is the transition from one form of service to another, from the service of pharaoh to the service of God.

As opposite as the rabbinic and the Pauline theologies are in one sense, in another they are quite congruent. For Paul's hostility to Torah must not be mistaken for a general antinomianism, nor must his advocacy of freedom be taken for a denial of objective norms.[53] "You, who once were slaves of sin," Paul writes in Rom 6:17–18, "have yielded whole-hearted obedience to the pattern of teaching to which you were made subject, and, emancipated from sin, have become slaves of righteousness." And so, the movement of the Christian's life, like that of the Jew's, is not a movement from slavery to freedom as these terms are now generally understood in secular circles. Rather, it is a movement from one form of slavery to another, to a form of slavery that, paradoxically, emancipates and liberates. Though Judaism and Christianity came to differ sharply and irreconcilably over the issue that we might call "Torah versus Christ," classically they have stood together in their refusal to affirm either liberation or service alone. The slaves of pharaoh/sin have become the slaves of YHWH/righteousness. Hence, in their very different ways, Judaism and Christianity affirm both the liberation that results in service and the service that brings about liberation. In so doing, each shows itself a worthy heir of the tradition at whose foundation lies the exodus from Egypt.

The Pauline identification of the Torah with slavery has reverberated throughout the history of the study of Christendom's Old Testament. One form of this reverberation has been a tendency to drive a wedge between emancipation from Egypt and the actual regime established at Sinai. Indeed, to drive this wedge has been a major goal of much Old Testament scholarship, and not just "Old Testament theology," in this century.[54] In the nineteenth century, no less a thinker than Hegel could describe Judaism as "a direct slavery, an obedience without joy, without pleasure or love . . . the most senseless bondage," "bondage to external commands."[55] Among the many points that Hegel's attempt to describe Judaism misses is that the mastery of YHWH over Israel is based not on enslavement, but on its opposite, YHWH's *redemption* of his people from the house of bondage. Pharaoh acquired Israel because of his own insecurities: "Look, the Israelite people are much too numerous for us. Let us deal shrewdly with them, so that they may not increase; otherwise in the event of war they may join our enemies in fighting against us" (Exod 1:9–10). YHWH, in contrast, acquired Israel and its service because of his mysterious love for them and his unmotivated oath to the Patriarchs:

> [6]For you are my people consecrated to the LORD your God: of all the peoples on earth the LORD God chose you to be His treasured people. [7]It is not because you are the most numerous of

peoples that the LORD set His heart on you and chose you — indeed, you are the smallest of peoples; [8]but it was because the LORD favored you and kept the oath He made to your fathers that the LORD freed you with a mighty hand and rescued you from the house of bondage, from the power of Pharaoh, king of Egypt. (Deut 7:6–8)

In Leviticus 25, as we have seen, it is precisely this connection of service to redemption that mandates a social order fundamentally different from Egypt's, one in which slavery is not abolished, to be sure, but circumscribed by humanitarian constraints. The Israelite slave is to be given one year out of every seven free of work in the fields (vv. 2–6). The impoverished kinsman, who faces enslavement, must be redeemed (vv. 25–34, 47–55). Loans are to be free of interest (vv. 35–38); one Israelite is not to profit from another's distress. If poverty forces a member of the community to sell himself into slavery, he is still not to be treated as a slave (vv. 39–43), that is, "ruthlessly," using the same word that Exod 1:13–14 employed to describe pharaoh's abuse of Israel (*běpārek*, v. 43). In the fiftieth year, the Jubilee, all Israelite slaves are freed, and lands that have had to be sold since the last Jubilee revert to the clans that originally owned them, thus giving the new freeman an economic base and preventing the sort of victimization of the ex-slave that has marked so much of the black experience in America.

The exodus thus cannot justly be taken to authorize liberation in the sense of freedom from external constraints or the attainment of self-determination. Neither should it be taken, however, as another example of senseless bondage, to use Hegel's term. Israel's service of the God who took it out of the land of Egypt is rooted in gratitude for his mysterious love and generosity. Hegel missed the paradoxical point that the *service* (or "slavery") of the God of Israel is based on *redemption* from slavery. Liberation theologians are more likely to miss the other half of the same paradox: the redemption from slavery follows not from the perceived needs of the members of the human community, but from the mysterious intentions and promises of their redeemer, into whose service they enter. Once again, service and redemption are inseparable, and liberation and a certain kind of subjugation are not antonymic but synonymous.

David Daube has argued that a number of details in the exodus story are best seen against the background of the laws of slavery in the Torah. For example, three times we are told of God's disposing the Egyptians favorably toward the Israelites so that the slaves go out with great wealth and not in poverty (Exod 3:21–22; 11:2–3; 12:25–36). Daube connects these strange verses to the requirement in Deuteronomy that the master not let his emancipated slave leave empty-handed, but "furnish him out of the flock, threshing floor, and vat" (Deut 15:12–14).[56] If, as I think highly likely, laws like this one do underlie the depiction of Israel's servitude in Egypt, then the effect is to make pharaoh into a Simon Legree: he becomes the archetype of the impious slave-driver, and his dehumanizing regime becomes the foil for God's liberated kingdom. The implication of this, in turn, is that pharaoh's deepest problem is his refusal to conform to the laws decreed by the real master of the universe, the God of Israel, whom he brusquely and arrogantly dismisses (Exod 5:1–2). Pharaoh's refusal to acknowledge his own creaturely subjugation to God seals his doom.

• III •

We have seen that the motivation for God's deliverance of Israel from Egypt does not lie in any principled opposition to slavery. At most, biblical law is opposed to inflicting brutal bondage upon Israel, as pharaoh does; it does not forbid the same brutality when it is inflicted upon the Gentile slave, and no exegetical sleight of hand can make this double standard disappear. Indeed, the question can be asked whether God would have freed pharaoh's slaves at all if they had not happened to be the descendants of Abraham, Isaac, and Jacob, to whom God had promised a land of their own. Here it is essential to avoid two extremes, each of which oversimplifies the issue, as extremes are wont to do. One extreme ignores the particularistic dimension, the chosenness of Israel, altogether and subtly universalizes the exodus story, as if all Egypt's slaves were manumitted in the exodus, if not all the world's slaves. The other extreme ignores the universalistic dimension of the exodus, the connection of the exodus with the character of the God who brings it about, as if only the Patriarchal Covenant enabled him to be moved by the pain and suffering of those in great affliction. In short, an adequate theology must reckon both with the chosenness of Israel and with what the liberation theologians tend to call the preferential option for the poor.

The following text shows that the two motivations are indeed intertwined in God's determination to help Israel in Egypt:

²³A long time after that, the king of Egypt died. The Israelites were groaning under the bondage and cried out; and their cry for help from bondage rose up to God. ²⁴God heard their moaning, and God remembered His covenant with Abraham and Isaac and Jacob. ²⁵God looked upon the Israelites, and God took notice of them. (Exod 2:23–25)

On the one hand, God's taking notice of Israel (and therefore commissioning Moses in the next chapter) is a consequence of the Patriarchal Covenant, with its unconditional promise of land for the descendants of Abraham, Isaac, and Jacob. The point is not that it is Israel's *suffering* that brings about the exodus, but that it is *Israel* that suffers — Israel, God's "treasured people," "the people consecrated to [Him]" (Deut 7:6). Suffering alone does not qualify a people for an exodus. Even in Egypt, no other slaves are redeemed, only Israel. It is this element of particularism in the exodus story that prevents it from becoming nothing more than an example of universalism and humanitarianism — or should, if exegetes and preachers are paying attention to the text. On the other hand, what attracts God's attention and causes him to remember his long-neglected covenant is Israel's groaning, crying, and moaning in bondage. These reach God independently of his remembering the covenant and even *before* he does so. The point here is that the pain of *any* slave can evoke sympathy in God; slaves need not be members of the covenantal community for God to be affected by their plea. It is this element of universalism that prevents the story of the exodus from degenerating into a religio-ethnic parochialism without a larger ethical message — just another tale of national liberation, though couched in theological language.

In the thinking of liberation theologians whom we mentioned at the outset of our discussion, the universalistic dimension of the text, its ethical message, or at least a certain version of it, overwhelms the particularistic dimension altogether, as when Croatto calls the exodus "a liberative plan for all peoples," or Brown perceives in it a God who "intervene[s] to free the poor and oppressed," or Pixley sees it as an insurrection that merged with a class struggle.[57] The problem with these liberationist views is not that they indicate that the God of Israel sympathizes and often sides with the oppressed, the poor, and the suffering. The problem is that these views do not reckon sufficiently with the cold fact that the biblical criteria for inclusion among those who benefit from the exodus are not poverty, oppression, suffering, or anything of the kind. The criterion is singular — descent from a common ancestor, Jacob/Israel son of Isaac son of Abraham. Throughout the Hebrew Bible, Israel is portrayed as a natural family, a kin-group and not a voluntary association, a mystical sodality, or, as these liberationists would have it, a socioeconomic class or political movement. It is not incidental that the book of Exodus begins with a genealogy.[58] God's preferential option for the poor can indeed be detected in the story of the exodus, in other parts of the Hebrew Bible,[59] and in the Jewish ethical tradition, where its application is, as we are about to see, by no means limited to the Jewish poor and oppressed. But the chosenness of Israel is even more pervasive in the Hebrew Bible and carries with it numerous and weighty legal implications both there and in the ongoing Jewish tradition. As important as these two concepts are, the preferential option for the poor and the chosenness of Israel are not to be *equated,* and, though both can be heard in the story of the exodus, it is the chosenness of Israel that dominates there. For though God hears the groaning, crying, and moaning of the afflicted slaves, it is his memory of the still unfulfilled covenant with Abraham, Isaac, and Jacob that motivates him to send them the great deliverer Moses.

No interpretation of the exodus, then, can be faithful to the biblical text if it fails to reckon with both these factors. Any interpretation that portrays the biblical message as liberation in the sense of manumission is doubly wrong — first, because it fails to reckon with God's ownership of Israel, which is at least akin to a master-slave relationship and is, in some formulations, identical with it, and, second, because it overlooks the acceptance of slavery as a social institution in the Hebrew Bible (and in the New Testament). Theoretically, it is possible to uphold God's mastership over Israel without upholding the morality of slavery in human society: the Israelite is to have a master but no slave. This position goes beyond that of the Hebrew Bible and, *pace* some abolitionists, should not be read into it. But it does build on major points of biblical theology, for it affirms both the chosenness of Israel and the preferential option for the poor and, more importantly, does not allow either to overwhelm the other.

This theoretical possibility comes close to realization in the concluding section of the laws of slavery in the *Mishneh Torah* of Maimonides (1138–1204), probably the greatest of Jewish codifiers:

> It is permitted to work a gentile slave harshly. And although such is the law, kindness and wisdom dictate that a man be merciful,

pursue justice, and not make his yoke on his slave too heavy or afflict him. Rather, he should give him to eat and drink from every type of food and beverage. The early sages used to give their slaves portions from every type of dish that they ate and to serve their animals and slaves before themselves. For the Bible says:

> As the eyes of slaves follow their master's hand,
> as the eyes of a slave-girl follow the hand of her mistress,
> [so our eyes are toward the LORD our God,
> awaiting His favor]. [Ps 123:2]

Therefore the master must not humiliate the slave physically or verbally: scripture delivered them into slavery, not into disgrace. Nor should he scream angrily at him very much, but, rather, he should speak with him calmly and listen to his grievances. This is made explicit in the discussion of Job's good ways, for which he was praised:

> Did I ever brush aside the case of my servants, man or maid,
> When they made a complaint against me?
> . . . .
> Did not He who made me in my mother's belly make him?
> Did not One form us both in the womb? [Job 31:13–15]

Cruelty and harshness are found only among idolatrous gentiles. But as for the descendants of Abraham our father, who are Israel, to whom the Holy One (blessed by He) caused the goodness of the Torah to flow and upon whom He enjoined just and compassionate laws and statutes — they are compassionate toward everyone. Thus, in reference to the attributes of the Holy One (blessed be He), which he commanded us to imitate, the Bible says, "and His mercy is upon all His works" [Ps 145:9]. And all who are merciful receive mercy [from God (*b. Shab.* 151b)], as it is written, "[The LORD] will give you mercy and be merciful to you and make you increase." [Deut 13:18] (*Hilkhot 'Avadim* 9:8)

Maimonides's first sentence succinctly and unflinchingly states the law as he has received it: "It is permitted to work a gentile slave harshly." But the rest of the paragraph enlists the humanitarian dimension of the traditions of biblical and rabbinic Judaism and of Maimonides's own philosophy in an effort to mitigate the severity of this most inhumane legacy of traditional law. For a Jew to treat his Gentile slave harshly, though within the letter of the law, is to act unkindly and foolishly; to spurn both mercy and justice; to ignore the precedent of rabbinic practice itself; to miss the biblical affirmation of the fatherhood of God over the whole human family; to act like an idolater; to fail indeed to observe the great command to imitate God himself, which for Maimonides meant to imitate God's ways, which are merciful and not severe; and, lastly, to act against self-interest by obstructing the wellsprings of divine mercy. Maimonides piles clause upon clause, citation upon citation, precisely because of the formidability of the challenge, for the law he wishes to nullify is too well-rooted to be easily dislodged. Instead, every manner of weapon that the tradition affords must be marshaled against it. The end-result is an affirmation of the broad ethical and theological aspects of the tradition over the narrowly legal aspect: the brutal treatment of the Gentile slave is legal but unconscionable. What this complex position loses in simplicity it gains in honesty and fidelity to the tradition. For though the offensive feature is transcended, it is never denied, ignored, disguised, or explained away. On this point, many liberation theologians could stand to be instructed by Maimonides's example.

· IV ·

The replacement of the people Israel with the poor and oppressed that we have seen in several liberationist interpretations of the exodus follows a long tradition. Who is or is not a member of the people Israel has seldom, if ever, been self-evident, at least since the close of the biblical period itself. For eighteen and a half centuries the rabbinic tradition has followed the biblical precedent in respecting the natural, familial definition, though with a matrilineal criterion: a Jew is a person born of a Jewish mother or converted according to Jewish law and with a commitment to observe it.[60] Christianity, not surprisingly, has identified Israel with the church, that is, with the mystical body of Christ (though on occasion it has allowed the Jews some continuing role, usually subordinate, in its economy of salvation). Contrary to what some Christians think, this identification does *not* universalize the identity of Israel. Most of the human race has never been Christian, just as it has never been Jewish, and in the first century of the common era, when this identification of Israel with the church was first made, Christians were a tiny minority of the world's population and knew it. Sometimes particular

Jewish or Christian sects have laid claim to the status of Israel and applied the biblical story to themselves in this way with varying degrees of identification. Thus the Puritans tended to think of New England as the new land of Israel, as names like Bethel, Hebron, and New Canaan (all of them in Connecticut) still suggest. In modern times, as the force of Christianity has receded, still other definitions of Israel have been propounded. In the last century, for example, the Anglo-Israelite movement argued that the "British are the true Jews":

> Originally the Jews had been a blond people very similar to the modern Anglo-Saxons. After the crucifixion of Christ, according to one exegete, the physiognomy of the Jews had greatly altered for the worse.... But the Jews who were members of the ten tribes retained their blondness and their beauty. The Anglo-Saxons were the true Jews, God's chosen people.[61]

If the Anglo-Israelite movement thought that blonds are the true Jews, the opposite identification is suggested in the Reverend Martin Luther King, Jr.'s last speech, on April 3, 1968, in Memphis, Tennessee:

> I just want to do God's will. And He's allowed me to go up the mountain, and I have looked over, and I've seen the promised land. I may not get there with you. But I want you to know tonight, that we, as a people, will get to the promised land.[62]

But it would be a grievous error to see in these, Rev. King's last public words, the black equivalent of the Anglo-Israelites' assumption of the name and status of Israel. One key difference is that King identified with Israel in its suffering and not just in its triumph. His words do not seek to claim a superior status for his own people but rather greater understanding of their affliction. The same sense of humility can be heard in his own poetic, understated identification with Moses not in the latter's moment of revelation or military victory but in his last moment, his moment of denial, as he hears God announce that he is to die outside the Promised Land (Num 27:12–23; Deut 3:23–28; 34:1–4).

There is, however, a more pertinent sense in which King's last speech differs from the identification with Israel of the Anglo-Israelite movement, and this is in the very nature of the two hermeneutical moves. I am referring to the all-important difference between *projection* and *appropriation*. The Anglo-Israelites *rewrote history* so as to project themselves into the paradigmatic past: the original Jews were fair and blond, the people presently known by that name being only a decadent and degenerate form of their ancestors. The direction of King's hermeneutical move is the reverse. He does not project his own group into the past; he *brings the past, the story of Israel, to bear upon the present*, using the powerful archetype of Moses' life and death to convey the meaning of his own life and times. What makes the archetype so appropriate is the obvious analogy of the American black experience of slavery and emancipation and the experience of ancient Israel, an analogy with a rich and venerable resonance in the history of black spirituality in America. It is this affinity that imparted such poignancy and such power to Rev. King's evocation of Moses as he gazes upon the Promised Land, which God has forbidden him to enter. Because of this fit between ancient Jewish and modern American black experience, Rev. King's use of Moses will long be remembered, whereas the Anglo-Israelites' identification of modern Anglo-Saxons with ancient Jews has already been justly forgotten.

It should now be clear in which category Pixley's particular liberationist perspective on the exodus falls. Pixley does not content himself with an *analogy* between Israel in Egypt and the impoverished peoples of Latin America with whom he identifies. Instead, he makes use of historical-critical research (of disputed value) to reconstruct a past that fits his Christian Marxist convictions better than the manifest text of the Bible does. This is a past in which the people Israel has been *replaced* by the poor and the oppressed, first by a heterogeneous underclass in Egypt and then by a band of rebellious peasants who, though they came to call themselves "Israel," were really Canaanites and linked to each other not by kinship ties but by social class and revolutionary activity. Grounded in a historical claim rather than in analogy, Pixley's hermeneutic is thus closer to that of the Anglo-Israelites than to the more restrained and yet more potent use of the Bible by Martin Luther King, Jr.

Liberationist supersessionism of the sort represented by Pixley's commentary on Exodus is not identical to the old Christian supersessionism, in which the Jews, conceived as the "carnal Israel" or the "old Israel," are replaced by the church, conceived as the "spiritual" or "new Israel." In fact, the two supersessionisms are mutually exclusive, since many Christians are not poor, suffering, or oppressed. But in dispossessing the Jews of what they consider their own story, in denying the natural familial character of early Israel altogether *even in the Hebrew Bible itself,* this type of liberationism, whether intentionally or not, taps into wells of Christian Jew-hatred that are as deep as they are ancient.

Nor, given the fate of Jewish life under Communist regimes, does Pixley give Jews comfort by comparing Moses to Lenin, Tito, Mao, Ho Chi Minh, and Castro. Though Marxism is not the sole source of the Jewish fate in Communist lands, it bears mention that Karl Marx expected the disappearance of Jewry and Judaism after the revolution and is thus the author of his own particular brand of supersessionism. Now it is true that Marx considered all religion to be an epiphenomenon upon the true motive force of history, which is economic, and therefore expected *all* religions, like all class divisions, to disappear together with the alienation that they reflect but cannot cure. But it is also the case that Marx saw in Judaism the epitome of capitalism and the bourgeoisie, and it has been pointed out that he "initially presented his historical diagnosis, which became the kernel of his socialist thought, as a sequel to a polemic on the Jewish question."[63] In fact, Marx's later image of capitalist society is a partial generalization of the anti-Jewish stereotypes to which he had long subscribed. Consider these words from his early essay, "Zur Judenfrage":

> What is the worldly basis of Judaism? *Practical* need, *self-interest.*
> What is the worldly cult of the Jew? *Haggling.*
> What is his worldly god? *Money.* Very well! Emancipation from haggling and money, that is from the practical and tangible Judaism, might well be the self-emancipation of our age.[64]

In liberation theology of the sort represented by Pixley's commentary on Exodus, we find a strange confluence of these two currents of anti-Jewish thinking, the Christian and the Communist. The Christian current is seen in his reading the Israelite nation out of the biblical story, which is assumed to apply actually to another category of people, not another nation, but a community whose primary principle of association lies in something other than consanguinity. The Communist current is seen in his replacement of Israel not with those with faith in Jesus Christ, but with a social class, originally the heterogeneous underclass of Egypt, which then links up with disaffected Canaanite peoples who had come to be known as "Israel." Whatever other challenges liberation theology may pose to traditional Christianity and to traditional Marxism, on the question of the Jews, Judaism, and Zionism, it generally seems to continue those traditions, in part because of the supersessionism that the two traditions in some measure share.[65]

• V •

We began this discussion with the question: In what sense ought the exodus to be seen as an instance of liberation? The importance of liberation theology in recent decades has forced us to spend much of our time providing a negative answer: the exodus as described in the biblical text is not an instance of liberation in the sense of a social revolution in pursuit of equality and solidarity. Whatever one may wish to speculate about the Moses of *history* — and *all* reconstructions of the exodus are exceedingly speculative — the Moses of the *text* is not appropriately compared to Lenin and others in the Marxist revolutionary tradition. But this does not mean that the exodus is not about liberation. The liberation of which the exodus is the paradigmatic instance is a liberation from degrading bondage for the endless service of the God who remembers his covenant, redeems from exile and oppression, and gives commandments through which the chosen community is sanctified. Whether the life of obedience in Torah in which the exodus eventuates is genuine liberation is a question that goes beyond the scope of our inquiry. If the past is a sound guide to the future, there will continue to be Jews who, in word and deed, answer the question emphatically in the affirmative.

Notes

CHAPTER 1

1. The translation is from Jacob Z. Lauterbach, ed., *Mekilta de-Rabbi Ish-mael*, 3 vols. (Philadelphia: Jewish Publication Society, 1933), 1:62.

2. This law refers only to the positive commandment, the commandment to eat unleavened bread. The negative commandment, the prohibition on leavening, applies, of course, throughout Passover.

3. See Yehezkel Kaufmann, *History of Israelite Religion* (in Hebrew), 8 vols. in 4 books (Jerusalem: Bialik, 1937–56; Tel Aviv: Dvir, 1976 [7th printing]), 4:327–28.

4. Volumes are spoken by the title of the collection of essays, *Scripture in Context*, ed. W. W. Hallo et al. (Pittsburgh: Pickwick Press, 1980).

5. An example, motivated by theological concerns, is Brevard S. Childs. See especially his *Introduction to the Old Testament as Scripture* (Philadelphia: Fortress Press; London: SCM Press, 1979). See also below, pp. 79–81 and pp. 120–122.

6. Benedict de Spinoza, *A Theologico-Political Treatise and a Political Treatise* (New York: Dover Publications, 1951), 106. The *Tractatus Theologico-Politicus* was first published in 1670. See also below, pp. 91–96.

7. See Hans Dieter Betz, "The Hermeneutical Principles of the Sermon on the Mount (Matt 5:17–20)," in *Essays on the Sermon on the Mount* (Philadelphia: Fortress Press, 1985), 37–53. I find it difficult, however, to accept that "commandments" in v. 19 refers to something different from "law" in v. 18, as Betz maintains.

8. Roland Bainton, *Here I Stand: A Life of Martin Luther* (Nashville and New York: Abingdon-Cokesbury Press, 1950), 185.

9. See also B. A. Gerrish, "The Word of God and Words of Scripture: Luther and Calvin on Biblical Authority," in *The Old Protestantism and the New* (Chicago: University of Chicago Press, 1982), 51–68.

10. James M. Robinson, "Jesus: From Easter to Valentinus (or to the Apostles' Creed)," *JBL* 101 (1982): 37.

11. A. H. J. Gunneweg, *Understanding the Old Testament*, OTL (Philadelphia: Westminster Press, 1978), 40.

161

12. Julius Wellhausen, *Prolegomena to the History of Ancient Israel* (Edinburgh: A. and C. Black, 1885; rpt.: Gloucester, Mass.: Peter Smith, 1973), 80. The original (1878) version of the *Prolegomena* was entitled simply *Geschichte Israels* (History of Israel) (vol. 1).

13. Ibid., 108. The negative judgment upon postbiblical Judaism through its association with landlessness and trade is something Wellhausen shared with a number of nineteenth-century thinkers, including some early Zionists and Karl Marx. On the general question of the attitude of liberal Christians toward Jews in the Second Reich, see Uriel Tal, *Christians and Jews in Germany* (Ithaca, N.Y., and London: Cornell University Press, 1975), 160–222. On the pervasiveness of anti-Jewish tendencies in German biblical scholarship, see Charlotte Klein, *Anti-Judaism in Christian Theology* (London: SPCK, 1978); Rolf Rendtorff, "Die Hebräische Bibel als Grundlage christlich-theologischer Aussagen über das Judentum," in *Jüdische Existenz und die Erneuerung der christlichen Theologie*, ed. M. Stöhr, ACJD 11 (Munich: Chr. Kaiser Verlag, 1981), 32–47; idem, "The Jewish Bible and Its Anti-Jewish Interpretation," *CJR* 16/1 (1983): 3–20; Joseph Blenkinsopp, "Old Testament Theology and the Jewish-Christian Connection," *JSOT* 28 (1984): 3–15.

14. Wellhausen, *Prolegomena*, 410.

15. Ibid., 405 n. 1. The use of death language to describe Judaism was hardly unique to Wellhausen among Christians in Germany in the last century. Schleiermacher, e.g., described Judaism as "a dead religion" (*eine tote Religion*) whose practitioners sit lamenting in the presence of their "imperishable mummy" (*unverweslichen Mumie*). Friedrich Schleiermacher, *Über die Religion: Reden an die Gebildeten unter ihren Verächtern* (Göttingen: Vandenhoeck & Ruprecht, 1926), 176. The book was originally published in 1799.

16. Julius Wellhausen, *Die Pharisäer und die Sadducäer* (Greifswald: Bamberg, 1874), 17.

17. E.g., Frank Moore Cross, *Canaanite Myth and Hebrew Epic* (Cambridge, Mass.: Harvard University Press, 1973), 82.

18. G. W. F. Hegel, *Der Geist des Christentums und sein Schicksal*, TKT 12 (Gütersloh: Gütersloher Verlagshaus Gerd Mohn, 1970), 63. The essay was written in 1798–99. These German theologians' use of the language of death (see n. 15 above) and excrement to describe Judaism was an eerie prefiguration of important aspects of the Holocaust. Note, e.g., that the inmates of the death camps were forced to live in their own feces. See the chapter on "Excremental Assault" in Terence Des Pres, *The Survivor: An Anatomy of Life in the Death Camps* (New York: Oxford University Press, 1976), 51–71. One inmate reported, "They had condemned us to die in our own filth, to drown in mud, in our own excrement" (p. 62). See also Richard L. Rubenstein, "Religion and the Origins of the Death Camps: A Psychoanalytic Interpretation," in *After Auschwitz* (Indianapolis: Bobbs-Merrill Co., 1966), 1–44. The Holocaust was many different and contradictory things. Enacted theology is one of them.

19. The interpretation of Wellhausen as a Hegelian has been effectively attacked by Lothar Perlitt, *Vatke und Wellhausen*, BZAW 94 (Berlin: Töpelmann, 1965), 206–43.

20. Julius Wellhausen, *Israelitische und jüdische Geschichte*, 2d ed., (Berlin: Georg Reimer, 1895), 356.

21. See Rudolf Smend, "Wellhausen und das Judentum," *ZTK* 79 (1982): 263.

22. Wellhausen, *Prolegomena*, 3–4. Note the "ghost" language again.

23. The translation here essentially follows the *New English Bible*, except that I have put in the definite article and capitalized "Law" throughout, since the context indicates that Paul is speaking of the Mosaic Torah. It is essential to note, however, that Paul does not always distinguish between the Mosaic Torah and other forms of "law."

24. This is not to deny that the Lutheran-Romantic reading of Paul may be a misinterpretation. See Krister Stendahl, "The Apostle Paul and the Introspective Conscience of the West," *HTR* 56 (1963): 199–215; rpt. in *Paul among Jews and Gentiles* (Philadelphia: Fortress Press, 1976), 78–96.

25. See Moshe Weinfeld, "Getting at the Roots of Wellhausen's Understanding of the Law of Israel on the 100th Anniversary of the *Prolegomena*," Institute for Advanced Studies, The Hebrew University, report no. 14/79 (Jerusalem: Hebrew University, 1979); and idem, "Old Testament — the Discipline and Its Goals," VTSup 32 (1981): 423–34.

26. Walther Eichrodt, *Theology of the Old Testament* (Philadelphia: Westminster Press, 1961), 1:31–32; originally published in 1933–39.

27. See Jon D. Levenson, *The Death and Resurrection of the Beloved Son: The Sublimation of Child Sacrifice in Judaism and Christianity* (New Haven, Conn.: Yale University Press, 1993).

28. See Jan Assmann, "Die Zeugung des Sohnes," in *Funktionen und Leistungen des Mythos: Drei Altorientalische Beispiele*, ed. Jan Assmann et al., OBO 48 (Göttingen: Vandenhoeck & Ruprecht; Freiburg: Universitätsverlag, 1982), 13–61.

29. See Frank Moore Cross, "'ēl," *Theological Dictionary of the Old Testament*, ed. G. Johannes Botterweck and Helmer Ringgren, rev. ed. (Grand Rapids: Wm. B. Eerdmans Publishing Co., 1977), 1:248. Michael David Coogan, *Stories from Ancient Canaan* (Philadelphia: Westminster Press, 1978), 87, 113; and Levenson, *The Death*.

30. See E. E. Urbach, *The Sages* (Jerusalem: Magnes, 1975), 1:525–41.

31. Eichrodt, *Theology*, 1:26.

32. Ibid., 1:133.

33. Ibid., 2:348 n. 1.

34. Ibid., 1:168.

35. Ibid., 1:218.

36. One wonders how Eichrodt would have reacted had he read Abraham Joshua Heschel, *The Sabbath* (New York: Farrar, Straus & Giroux, 1951).

37. Eichrodt, *Theology*, 1:249.

38. Ibid., 1:249 n. 3. I have here corrected the English translation, which mistakenly inserts "his" before "works." Unable to procure the sixth edition of the *Theologie* (from which the translation was made), I have checked the fifth (Stuttgart: Ehrenfried Klotz, 1957), 1:161 n. 96. Eichrodt's concluding comment in the note probably suggested the innocent change to the translator.

On the text of the logion, see S. Safrai, "And All Is According to the Majority of Deeds" (in Hebrew), *Tarbiz* 53 (1983): 33–40. Safrai chooses a textual variant that reads "but *not* according to the majority of deeds." This variant destroys the exquisitely paradoxical structure of Aqiba's statement. But if accepted, it would be yet another example of the rabbinic theology of grace — the very theology whose existence Christian theologians in the same mold as Eichrodt tend to deny.

39. See Smend, "Wellhausen," 256–57. On the pernicious effects of the ignorance of rabbinic literature on New Testament scholars, see E. P. Sanders, *Paul and Palestinian Judaism* (Philadelphia: Fortress Press, 1977), 33–59. On the underlying and more general sociopsychological dynamics, see Jon D. Levenson, "Is There a Counterpart in the Hebrew Bible to New Testament Anti-Semitism?" *JES* 22 (1985): 242–60.

40. Gerhard von Rad, *Old Testament Theology* (New York: Harper & Row, 1965), 2:319.

41. Ibid., 2:322.

42. Ibid., 2:325.

43. Ibid., 2:428.

44. Ibid., 2:321.

45. Childs, *Introduction,* 669. Childs correctly notes that the same criticisms apply to Hartmut Gese. See his *Essays on Biblical Theology* (Minneapolis: Augsburg Publishing House, 1981). Gese sees the elucidation of continuities, in this case the continuities of the Old Testament and the New, as a central task of the theologian. I would add that neither he nor von Rad reckons with the fact that the "heresies" (e.g., Gnosticism) are also in continuity with the past and can be, as Robinson points out (see n. 10 above), as ancient as the "normative" position. Since heresy and orthodoxy can be part of the same *culture,* cultural affinities cannot be an adequate criterion for determining the validity of a theology. Thus, Gese's great efforts to establish the Hebraic character of the New Testament, even if valid, fail to achieve his larger theological goal.

46. Von Rad, *Old Testament,* 1:201.

47. See Paul J. Achtemeier, "An Apocalyptic Shift in Early Christian Tradition," *CBQ* 45 (1983): 231–48, and, more generally, E. P. Sanders, *Jesus and Judaism* (Philadelphia: Fortress Press, 1985).

48. Von Rad, *Old Testament,* 2:428–29.

49. See John A. Miles, "Radical Editing: Redaktionsgeschichte and the Aesthetic of Willed Confusion," in *Traditions in Transformation,* ed. Baruch Halpern and Jon D. Levenson (Winona Lake, Ind.: Eisenbrauns, 1981), 9–31.

50. Gerhard von Rad, "The Form-Critical Problem of the Hexateuch," in *The Problem of the Hexateuch and Other Essays* (New York: McGraw-Hill Book Co., 1966), 53–54.

51. Ibid.

52. Albrecht Alt, "The Origins of Israelite Law," in *Essays on Old Testament History and Religion* (Garden City, N.Y.: Doubleday & Co., 1968), 101–71. The essay was originally published in 1934.

53. George E. Mendenhall, "The Conflict Between Value Systems and Social Control," in *Unity and Diversity,* ed. H. Goedicke and J. J. M. Roberts; Johns

Hopkins Near Eastern Studies (Baltimore: Johns Hopkins University Press, 1975), 174–75.

54. See the discussion and bibliography in Childs, *Introduction*, 109–27, esp. 124–29. See also Weinfeld, "Getting at the Roots"; Jon D. Levenson, "The Theologies of Commandment in Biblical Israel," *HTR* 73 (1980): 17–33; and idem, *Sinai and Zion* (Minneapolis: Winston Press, 1985), 35–56.

55. See also von Rad's attempt to offer a historical-critical argument for Paul's interpretation of Gen 15:6 in Gal 3:6 in von Rad, "Faith Reckoned as Righteousness," in *The Problem*, 125–30. On the failure of this attempt, see below, pp. 57–61 and 102–104.

56. Mendenhall's christological concerns are patent: "The permanent symbol of the necessity as well as the reality of that rule of God is the crucifixion of Jesus" (Mendenhall, "The Conflict," 178). Is this the view in the Hebrew Bible? On the contemporary political context of Mendenhall's position, see Richard L. Rubenstein, "The Besieged Community in Ancient and Modern Times," *MQR* 22 (1983): 457–58.

57. Martin Hengel, *Judaism and Hellenism* (Philadelphia: Fortress Press, 1974), 300.

58. Hans Dieter Betz, *Galatians*, Hermeneia (Philadelphia: Fortress Press, 1979), 139.

59. See pp. 40–45.

60. Friedrich Baumgärtel, "The Hermeneutical Problem of the Old Testament," in *Essays on Old Testament Hermeneutics*, ed. Claus Westermann (Richmond: John Knox Press, 1963), 135.

61. Gunneweg, *Understanding*, 222.

62. Relativism is no less problematic for philosophy and ultimately self-refuting. On the contemporary debate, see Richard J. Bernstein, *Beyond Objectivism and Relativism: Science, Hermeneutics, and Praxis* (Philadelphia: University of Pennsylvania Press, 1983). If, indeed, as Bernstein says, a position beyond these antinomies is emerging, it should help those wishing to live in both the religious and the historical-critical worlds without imposing one paradigm upon the other. In the terms of his dichotomy, both the traditionalist and the historical critic are objectivist. They believe that religious faith or historical reconstruction, respectively, provide us secure knowledge of what the text really means (although not all religions are equally universalistic/imperialistic in their truth claims). The religious and methodological pluralism of programs in biblical studies in recent decades promotes a contrasting relativism. Whether the pluralism can endure without producing interpretive anarchy is still open to doubt.

CHAPTER 2

1. Yehezkel Kaufmann, *The Religion of Israel* (Chicago: University of Chicago Press, 1960); Nahum M. Sarna, *Understanding Genesis* (New York: Jewish Theological Seminary of America and McGraw-Hill Book Co., 1966).

2. Walther Eichrodt, *Theology of the Old Testament*, 2 vols., OTL (Philadelphia: Westminster Press, 1961); Gerhard von Rad, *Old Testament Theology*, 2 vols. (New York: Harper & Row, 1962).

3. Robert C. Dentan, *Preface to Old Testament Theology*, rev. ed. (New York: Seabury Press, 1963), 81. In his bibliography, Dentan lists the works as follows:

Buber, Martin: *The Prophetic Faith*. New York: Macmillan Co., 1949.
Herberg, Will: "Faith as Heilsgeschichte: The Meaning of Redemptive History in Human Existence," *The Christian Scholar* 39 (1956): 25–31.
Heschel, Abraham J.: *The Prophets* (Chaps. 9–17 on prophetic theology). New York: Harper & Row, 1962.
————: *Theology of Ancient Judaism*. London and New York: Soncino Press, 5722/ 1962 (in Hebrew).

4. David Neumark, *The Philosophy of the Bible* (Cincinnati: Ark Publishing, 1918).

5. On the discipline in general, see Norman W. Porteous, "Old Testament Theology," in *The Old Testament and Modern Study*, ed. H. H. Rowley (Oxford: Clarendon Press, 1951), 311–45; Dentan, *Preface*; H. J. Kraus, *Die Biblische Theologie: Ihre Geschichte und Problematik* (Neukirchen-Vluyn: Neukirchener Verlag, 1970); Gerhard Hasel, *Old Testament Theology: Basic Issues in the Current Debate*, rev. ed. (Grand Rapids: Wm. B. Eerdmans Publishing Co., 1982); George W. Coats, "Theology of the Hebrew Bible," in *The Hebrew Bible and Its Modern Interpreters*, ed. Douglas A. Knight and Gene M. Tucker (Philadelphia: Fortress Press; Chico, Calif.: Scholars Press, 1985), 239–62.

6. Dentan, *Preface*, 87, 90.

7. John Bright, *The Authority of the Old Testament* (Nashville: Abingdon Press, 1967), 113–14.

8. Quoted in Dentan, *Preface*, 22–23.

9. Ibid., 92.

10. Ibid., 64, 93.

11. Bright, *Authority*, 122. See also p. 126.

12. Ibid., 136. Cf. John Bright, *A History of Israel*, 3d ed. (Philadelphia: Westminster Press, 1981), 148–62.

13. Bright, *Authority*, 136.

14. See Glendon E. Bryce, *A Legacy of Wisdom* (Lewisburg, Pa.: Bucknell University Press, 1979).

15. Dentan, *Preface*, 108 (the words quoted are the title of a section).

16. See chapter 3 below.

17. Dentan, *Preface*, 116.

18. Hasel, *Old Testament Theology*, 173.

19. Moshe H. Goshen-Gottstein, "Jewish Biblical Theology and the Study of Biblical Religion" (in Hebrew), *Tarbiz* 50 (1980/81): 45; see also pp. 48–49 n. 24. Also noteworthy are his essays "Christianity, Judaism, and Modern Bible Study," VTSup 28 (1975): 69–88, esp. 81–88, and "Tanakh Theology: The Religion of the Old Testament and the Place of Jewish Biblical Theology," in *Ancient Israelite Religion*, ed. Patrick D. Miller, Jr., et al. (Philadelphia: Fortress Press, 1987), 617–44.

20. Dentan, *Preface*, 23.

21. Goshen-Gottstein, "Jewish Biblical Theology," 54.

22. Ibid., 47.

23. Dentan, *Preface*, 15, 94, 98.

24. Ibid., 90, 94.

25. Cf. Friedrich Baumgärtel, "The Hermeneutical Problem of the Old Testament," in *Essays in Old Testament Hermeneutics*, ed. Claus Westermann (Richmond: John Knox Press, 1963), 135, and A. H. J. Gunneweg, *Understanding the Old Testament*, OTL (Philadelphia: Westminster Press, 1978), 222.

26. Porteous, "Old Testament Theology," 344.

27. See Neumark, *Philosophy*, xiv.

28. See Hasel, *Old Testament Theology*, 145–67.

29. See Rosemary Ruether, *Faith and Fratricide* (New York: Seabury Press, 1974). The New Testament writings often depict the Jews and Judaism as hypocritical, pedantic, carnal, literalistic, misanthropic, godless, christocidal, diabolical, or some combination of these. See, e.g., 1 Thes 2:14–16; 2 Cor 3:4–16; Rom 2:17–29; Matt 6:1–18; 27:25; John 5:23; 8:44.

30. For a fuller discussion see Charlotte Klein, *Anti-Judaism in Christian Theology* (London: SPCK, 1978), esp. 15–66; Rolf Rendtorff, "Die Hebräische Bibel als Grundlage christlich-theologischer Aussagen über das Judentum," in *Jüdische Existenz und die Erneuerung der christlichen Theologie*, ed. M. Stöhr, ACJD 11 (Munich: Chr. Kaiser Verlag, 1981), 33–47; idem, "The Jewish Bible and Its Anti-Jewish Interpretation," *CJR* 16/1 (1983): 3–20; and Joseph Blenkinsopp, "Old Testament Theology and the Jewish-Christian Connection," *JSOT* 28 (1984): 3–15.

31. Eichrodt, *Theology*, 1:26.

32. Ibid., 1:133.

33. E.g., Abraham Joshua Heschel, *The Sabbath* (New York: Farrar, Straus & Giroux, 1951).

34. Eichrodt, *Theology*, 2:348 n. 1.

35. Ibid., 1:168 and 2:218.

36. Von Rad, *Old Testament Theology*, 2:321. The English translation takes some liberties with von Rad's wording here, but the sense is not materially affected.

37. Blenkinsopp, "Old Testament Theology," 6.

38. See the work of Klein and the two works of Rendtorff referred to in n. 30.

39. Bright, *History*, 464.

40. For an exposé, see John Pawlikowski, *Christ in the Light of the Christian-Jewish Dialogue* (Ramsey, N.J.: Paulist Press, 1982), 59–73; John P. Meier, "The Bible as a Source for Theology," *PCTSA* 43 (1988): 1–14; Susannah Heschel, "Anti-Judaism in Christian Feminist Theology," *Tikkun* 5/3 (May/June 1990): 25–28, 95–97; and see below, pp. 155–158.

41. Julius Wellhausen, *Prolegomena to the History of Ancient Israel* (Edinburgh: A. and C. Black, 1885; rpt.: Gloucester, Mass.: Peter Smith, 1973), 410. The original (1878) version of the *Prolegomena* was entitled simply *Geschichte Israels* (History of Israel) (vol. 1).

42. Ibid., 405 n. 1.

43. Ibid., 108.

44. Joseph Blenkinsopp, *Prophecy and Canon,* UNDCSJCA 3 (Notre Dame, Ind.: University of Notre Dame Press, 1977), 20. On the Christian penchant for describing Judaism and the Jews as dead, see p. 11, above, and n. 18 of chap. 1, above.

45. Ibid.

46. On the theological roots of Wellhausen's anti-Jewish reading of the Old Testament, see pp. 12–15, above.

47. Solomon Schechter, "Higher Criticism — Higher Anti-Semitism," in *Seminary Addresses and Other Papers* (Cincinnati: Ark Publishing, 1915), 36–37.

48. Ibid., 38. On the background, see Naomi W. Cohen, "The Challenges of Darwinism and Biblical Criticism to American Judaism," *MJ* 4 (1984): 121–57, esp. 133–34.

49. See below, pp. 84–88.

50. S. David Sperling, "Judaism and Modern Biblical Research," in *Biblical Studies: Meeting Ground of Jews and Christians,* ed. Lawrence Boadt et al. (Ramsey, N.J.: Paulist Press, 1980), 39.

51. Solomon Schechter, *Aspects of Rabbinic Theology: Major Concepts of the Talmud* (New York: Schocken Books, 1961). The book first appeared in 1909.

52. Yehezkel Kaufmann, *History of Israelite Religion* (in Hebrew), 8 vols. in 4 books (Jerusalem: Bialik, 1937–56; Tel Aviv: Dvir, 1976 [10th impression]).

53. See Kaufmann, *Religion of Israel* (see n. 1 above), and also his *The Religion of Israel,* vol. 4: *From the Babylonian Captivity to the End of Prophecy* (New York: Union of American Hebrew Congregations, 1970).

54. See Kaufmann, *Religion of Israel* (see n. 1 above) (the Hebrew has no author index).

55. See Albrecht Alt, *Essays on Old Testament History and Religion* (Garden City, N.Y.: Doubleday & Co., 1967).

56. Quoted in Robert C. Johnson, *Authority in Protestant Theology* (Philadelphia: Westminster Press, 1959), 26–27. Johnson notes that the reference to goats is from a polemic of 1520/21 against Hieronymus Emser, whose "treatise had borne his coat of arms, elaborately adorned with the head of a long-horned goat."

57. Ibid., 48.

58. Dentan, *Preface,* 87.

59. The *lex talionis* appears in Exod 21:23–25; Lev 24:19–20; and Deut 19:21. Its meaning and implementation in biblical times are matters of dispute.

60. Quoted in William B. Silverman, *Basic Reform Judaism* (New York: Philosophical Library, 1970), 44.

61. See Neumark, *Philosophy.* The fact that Neumark taught at the Hebrew Union College is significant.

62. Yosef Hayim Yerushalmi, *Zakhor: Jewish History and Jewish Memory* (Seattle: University of Washington Press, 1982), 85–86.

63. Ibid., 86.

64. See pp. 10–15, above.

65. For an accessible overview, see Edward Norden, "Counting the Jews," *Commentary* 92/4 (October 1991): 36–43, esp. 42.

66. In private conversation, October 21, 1983.

67. Bright, *Authority*, 152–53.

68. Erich Auerbach, *Mimesis: The Representation of Reality in Western Literature* (Princeton, N.J.: Princeton University, 1953), 48–49.

69. Susan A. Handelman, *The Slayers of Moses: The Emergence of Rabbinic Interpretation in Modern Literary Theory* (Albany, N.Y.: State University of New York Press, 1982), 19.

70. Gershom Scholem, "Revelation and Tradition as Religious Categories in Judaism," in *The Messianic Idea in Judaism and Other Essays on Jewish Spirituality* (New York: Schocken Books, 1971), 289.

71. See Hasel, *Old Testament Theology*, 117–47, esp. 119–21.

72. G. Ernest Wright, *God Who Acts: Biblical Theology as Recital*, SBT 8 (London: SCM Press, 1952).

73. Hasel, *Old Testament Theology*, 120–21.

74. Ibid., 135–36.

75. Ibid., 82–83.

76. John L. McKenzie, *A Theology of the Old Testament* (Garden City, N.Y.: Doubleday & Co., 1974), 334.

77. See Marvin A. Sweeney, "Tanakh Versus Old Testament," forthcoming in Rolf Knierim festschrift, BZAW (1994).

78. Gerhard von Rad, "Faith Reckoned as Righteousness," in *The Problem of the Hexateuch and Other Essays* (New York: McGraw-Hill Book Co., 1966), 125. The same ideas appear in Gerhard von Rad, *Genesis: A Commentary,* OTL (Philadelphia: Westminster Press, 1972), 184–85.

79. Von Rad, "Faith," 126.

80. Ibid., 127.

81. Ibid., 128–29.

82. Ibid., 129.

83. Ibid., 130.

84. All New Testament translations in this chapter are taken from the *New English Bible* (New York: Oxford University Press, 1970), except that I have capitalized "Law" here because Paul is writing specifically about the Mosaic Torah.

85. Von Rad, "Faith," 129.

86. Philo Judaeus, *De Abrahamo,* Les Oeuvres de Philon D'Alexandrie, ed. J. Gorez (Paris: Cerf, 1966), 129 (§262).

87. Ibid., 132 (§275).

88. On the ideas of Abraham in first-century Judaism and Christianity, see Samuel Sandmel, *Philo's Place in Judaism: A Study of Conceptions of Abraham in Jewish Literature,* augmented ed. (New York: KTAV Publishing House, 1971); and Hans Dieter Betz, *Galatians,* Hermeneia (Philadelphia: Fortress Press, 1979), 139–40.

89. David H. Kelsey, "Protestant Attitudes Regarding Methods of Biblical Interpretation," in *Scripture in the Jewish and Christian Traditions,* ed. Frederick Greenspahn (Nashville: Abingdon Press, 1982), 138.

90. *Luther's Works,* vol. 3: *Lectures on Genesis, Chapters 15–20,* ed. Jaroslav Pelikan (St. Louis: Concordia Publishing House, 1961), 19.

91. Ibid., 21.
92. Ramban to Gen 15:6.
93. Note also how the lament begins in Jer 12:1.

CHAPTER 3

1. This is my own translation from the Hebrew provided in *The Authorized Daily Prayer Book*, ed. Joseph H. Hertz, rev. ed. (New York: Bloch, 1948), 6.

2. Ibid., 252. This, again, is my own translation.

3. Maimonides's commentary on the Mishnah can be found in traditional volumes of Talmud. This one is taken from Bavli, *Sanhedrin* (Jerusalem: Sifre Qodesh, n.d.), 15:247.

4. Shalom Rosenberg, "Biblical Research in Recent Orthodox Jewish Thought" (in Hebrew), in *The Bible and Us*, ed. Uriel Simon (Tel Aviv: Dvir, 5739/1979), 90. All translations herein are my responsibility. See also Jakob J. Petuchowski, "The Supposed Dogma of the Mosaic Authorship of the Pentateuch," *Hibbert Journal* 57 (1959): 356–60, esp. 360; Abraham Joshua Heschel, *Torah from Heaven* (in Hebrew) (London and New York: Soncino, 5722/1962), esp. 2:71–99; and Louis Jacobs, *Principles of the Jewish Faith* (New York: Basic Books, 1964), 216–301.

5. The biblical citation is Num 15:31.

6. See also *b. Baba Batra* 88b–89a; and Heschel, *Torah*, 2:181–83.

7. See, e.g., Hartwig Hirschfeld, "Mohammedan Criticism of the Bible," *JQR*, o.s. 13 (1901): 222–40.

8. Rosenberg, "Biblical Research," 90–91.

9. Ibid., 91.

10. See n. 4 above, esp. the bibliographic excursus in Jacobs, *Principles*, 301. The question of whether an Orthodox thinker remains Orthodox after accepting a nonfundamentalist understanding of the process of composition of the Torah is, of course, complex and controverted.

11. Asher Weiser, ed., *Commentaries on the Torah of Rabbi Abraham ibn Ezra* (in Hebrew) (Jerusalem: Mossad Harav Kook, 1977), 1:51.

12. Nahum M. Sarna, "The Modern Study of the Bible in the Framework of Jewish Studies," in *Proceedings of the Eighth World Congress of Jewish Studies* (Jerusalem: World Union of Jewish Studies, 1983), 22.

13. Weiser, *Commentaries*, 314–15.

14. Joseph Bonfils (Tov Elem), *Tsaphenat Pa'aneah*, ed. D. Herzog (Heidelberg: Carl Winter, 1911), 91–92. Compare the attitude of St. Gregory (ca. 540–604), as presented by Beryl Smalley: "Spiritual instruction was what his audience needed, simple for the clergy and people, more advanced for the religious. The problems of biblical scholarship did not concern them. It was 'very superfluous' to inquire into the authorship of the book of Job; enough to know that the Holy Spirit was its real author; 'if we were reading the words of some great man with his epistle in our hand, yet were to inquire by what pen they were written, it would be an absurdity' " (Beryl Smalley, *The Study of the Bible in the Middle Ages* [New York: Philosophical Library, 1952], 33).

15. Sarna, "Modern Study," 24.

16. Ibid., 21, 20, 27.

17. See Leo Strauss, *Philosophy and Law* (Philadelphia: Jewish Publication Society, 5747/1987), 43: "[W]hile for the modern Enlightenment the truths of Revelation are at the same time the truths of a healthy common sense, and thus are accessible to all men without further ado, according to the teaching of the medieval rationalists, only the philosophers can recognize the truths of Revelation by themselves and even they can do so only after strenuous, protracted preparations." (The book was originally published as *Philosophie und Gesetz* in 1935.)

18. Moshe Greenberg, *On the Bible and Judaism,* ed. Abraham Shapiro (in Hebrew) (Tel Aviv: Am Oved, 1984), 275.

19. Menahem Haran, "Midrashic and Literal Exegesis and the Critical Method in Biblical Research," in *Studies in Bible,* ed. Sara Japhet, SH 31 (Jerusalem: Magnes, 1986), 36–37.

20. James Barr, *Holy Scripture* (Philadelphia: Westminster Press, 1983), 37.

21. See Brevard S. Childs, *Biblical Theology in Crisis* (Philadelphia: Westminster Press, 1970); idem, *Introduction to the Old Testament as Scripture* (Philadelphia: Fortress Press, 1979); and idem, *Old Testament Theology in a Canonical Context* (Philadelphia: Fortress Press, 1986).

22. Paul D. Hanson, "The Theological Significance of Contradiction Within the Book of the Covenant," in *Canon and Authority: Essays in Old Testament Religion and Theology,* ed. George W. Coats and Burke O. Long (Philadelphia: Fortress Press, 1977), 110–31. See also his fuller statements of the method and its theological underpinnings in Paul D. Hanson, *Dynamic Transcendence* (Philadelphia: Fortress Press, 1978), and *The Diversity of Scripture,* OBT 11 (Philadelphia: Fortress Press, 1982).

23. Hanson, "Theological Significance," 116–17.

24. Anyone under the impression that Paul's social attitudes and ethics were advanced for his day is invited to consult G. E. M. de Ste. Croix, *The Class Struggle in the Ancient Greek World* (Ithaca, N.Y.: Cornell University Press, 1981), 103–11, 418–25.

25. Hanson, "Theological Significance," 123, 127.

26. Ibid., 131.

27. John Barton, *Reading the Old Testament: Method in Biblical Study* (Philadelphia: Westminster Press, 1984), 94.

28. Martin Luther, "Preface to the Epistles of Saint James and Saint Jude," in *Works of Martin Luther* (Philadelphia: A. J. Holman and Castle, 1932), 6:478.

29. If such a concession is to be made — and the holistic reading of the text requires it — then it becomes clear that God's deliverance of Israel from bondage is not owing to any opposition to slavery per se but to his faithfulness to his oath to their Patriarchs to give them the land of Canaan (Exod 2:23–25; Deut 7:8). It should also be noticed that the law of the Hebrew slave forbids that he be worked "ruthlessly" (*běpārek/běperek,* Lev 25:43, 46, 53), using the same word that describes the Egyptian mistreatment of Israel in Exod 1:13–14. In sum, there are not two attitudes here at all but one theology, which insists that the

Israelite slave be treated mildly and in a way that recognizes his special status as a member of the covenant people. See below, pp. 135–140 and 151–153.

30. Paul's position is, of course, more radical than Hanson's, for whereas the latter can allow for some laws of continuing value (those that manifest or advance liberation), Paul shifts the vehicle of injunction generally away from commandments and laws onto the Spirit and love. It is important to note that the basis of Paul's supersessionism is apocalyptic dispensationalism, whereas the basis of Hanson's is liberal progressivism and egalitarianism. Hanson's theology thus replicates Pauline apocalyptic only in a naturalized, humanized, and liberalized form.

31. William B. Silverman, *Basic Reform Judaism* (New York: Philosophical Library, 1970), 44.

32. R. J. Zwi Werblowsky, "Judaism, or the Religion of Israel," in *The Concise Encyclopaedia of Living Faiths*, ed. R. C. Zaehner (London: Hutchinson, 1959), 46–47.

33. See Otto Eissfeldt, *The Old Testament: An Introduction* (New York: Harper & Row, 1965), 219–23.

34. See the variant way of reasoning to the same conclusion in *Mek. Nezikin* 2 (English translation: Jacob Z. Lauterbach, ed., *Mekilta de-Rabbi Ishmael* [Philadelphia: Jewish Publication Society, 1935], 3:17).

35. Barr, *Holy Scripture*, 67.

36. Benjamin Jowett, "On the Interpretation of Scripture," in *The Interpretation of Scripture and Other Essays* (London: George Routledge & Sons; New York: E. P. Dutton, n.d.), 36. (The essay was published in 1860). See also James Barr, "Jowett and the Reading of the Bible 'Like Any Other Book,'" *HBT* 4/5 (1982–83): 1–44. Barr is correct that Jowett's main concern was "the sense of the text itself" rather than "historical investigation" (p. 9), but he fails to see that Jowett's limitation of the sense of the text to its authors' intended meaning introduces serious complications of the sort that Childs's method is attempting to address.

37. See Barr, *Holy Scripture*, 66, 94, where it is assumed that the canonical perspective will be that of the patristic compilers of the (Christian) canon.

38. Barton, *Reading*, 78.

39. James L. Mays, "Historical and Canonical: Recent Discussion about the Old Testament and Christian Faith," in *Magnalia Dei*, ed. Frank Moore Cross et al. (Garden City, N.Y.: Doubleday & Co., 1976), 524. In a Jewish framework, another moment must be added to these three, the context defined by the rabbinic tradition, including the medieval pursuit of the *peshat*. I find unpersuasive Barr's argument (*Holy Scripture*, 65) that relativizing the author's meaning is possible only if we accept a stance of full-blown cultural relativism incompatible with traditional religious commitments. The legacy of medieval multisense and multipurpose exegesis speaks strongly against this. It is regrettable that Childs's formulations do not always acknowledge the multicontextuality of the Hebrew Bible but sometimes and inconsistently bespeak a hermeneutical monism. For an analysis of this and a defense of a pluralistic reconstruction of Childs's "canonical method," see Mark G. Brett, *Biblical Criticism in Crisis?* (Cambridge: Cambridge University Press, 1991).

40. David Rosen, ed., *Complete Commentary of Rashbam on the Torah* (in Hebrew) (Breslau: David Schottlaender, 5642/1882), 114. See also Rashbam's statement of principle in his comment to Gen 37:2 (p. 49).

41. On the roots of this curious but essential aspect of Jewish thought, see David Weiss Halivni, *Midrash, Mishnah, and Gemara* (Cambridge, Mass., and London: Harvard University Press, 1986), esp. 105–15; and idem, *Peshat and Derash* (New York and Oxford: Oxford University Press, 1991), esp. 101–25.

42. These are not necessarily the same (see Brevard S. Childs, "The Sensus Literalis of Scripture: An Ancient and Modern Problem," in *Beiträge zur Alttestament Theologie,* ed. Herbert Donner et al. [Göttingen: Vandenhoeck & Ruprecht, 1977], 80–93). Rashbam may be said to have pursued the literal sense (*peshat*), but like the other medieval commentators, he failed to draw *historical* conclusions from his novel exegesis. His relevance to this discussion lies not in the precise categories that he used but in his ability to recognize the multi-contextuality of scripture, avoiding, as Jowett, e.g., could not, the temptation to regard the text as univocal. The contradiction between historical and literary analysis ought now to push biblical hermeneutics toward a modern analogue to the medieval concept of multiple senses of scripture. The shape of this new philosophy of interpretation is as yet unclear. It is safe to say, however, that it will be different from classical historical criticism and from the deconstructionist idea of total semantic indeterminacy, a nihilistic notion fundamentally at odds with the religious affirmation at the foundation of medieval Jewish biblical interpretation.

43. See Smalley, *The Study,* esp. 102–5, 110–11, 149–72, 189–93, 225–36, 364–66; and Herman Hailperin, *Rashi and the Christian Scholars* (Pittsburgh: University of Pittsburgh Press, 1963), esp. 103–34.

44. It is especially important for those who engage in the literary study of the Bible to remember that the contours of the book have been defined in important ways by theological forces. Neither the older historical criticism nor the newer aesthetic analysis can claim to be religiously neutral when they must, in fact, accept a definition of "Bible" that has been bequeathed to them by Jewish or Christian communities. Those who wish to stand "before the text" rather than to penetrate "behind it" need to be reminded that what they consider to be the text is itself a function of their attachments to a community and its antecedent history. In recognizing this, Childs's overtly confessional method is considerably more advanced in its self-awareness than some of its philosophical analogues, which presume a false universalism (see his brief remarks on Paul Ricouer in *Introduction,* 77).

45. See pp. 56–61 and 102–4.

46. For this celebrated distinction, see Krister Stendahl, "Biblical Theology, Contemporary," in *The Interpreter's Dictionary of the Bible,* ed. George Arthur Buttrick et al. (New York and Nashville: Abingdon Press, 1962), 419–20.

47. See Barr, *Holy Scripture,* 1–6.

48. In Israel, even in earlier times, there was, of course, in some circles an increasing awareness of the changes that book-centeredness induces. This is evident in the phenomenon of harmonization of law in the Hebrew Bible it-

self (see Michael Fishbane, *Biblical Interpretation in Ancient Israel* [Oxford: Oxford University Press, 1985], esp. 220–28).

49. See Jon D. Levenson, *Theology of the Program of Restoration of Ezekiel 40–48*, HSM 10 (Missoula, Mont.: Scholars Press, 1976), 37–53.

CHAPTER 4

1. Lawrence Boadt et al., eds., *Biblical Studies: Meeting Ground of Jews and Christians* (Mahwah, N.J.: Paulist Press, 1980).

2. Ibid., 3–4.

3. Ibid., 5.

4. Solomon Schechter, "Higher Criticism — Higher Anti-Semitism," in *Seminary Addresses and Other Papers* (Cincinnati: Ark Publishing, 1915), 36–47.

5. Chaim Potok, *In the Beginning* (New York: Alfred A. Knopf, 1975), 399.

6. James L. Kugel, "Biblical Studies and Jewish Studies," *AJSN* 36 (Fall 1986): 22.

7. Jon D. Levenson, *Sinai and Zion* (Minneapolis: Winston Press, 1985), 203–4 n. 21.

8. Kugel, "Biblical Studies," 22.

9. See Jon D. Levenson, "Hebrew Bible in Colleges and Universities," *RE* 81 (1986): 37–44.

10. "Damit endete das schauerliche Nachspiel der Geschichte Israels" (Martin Noth, *Geschichte Israels*, 3d ed. [Göttingen: Vandenhoeck & Ruprecht, 1956], 406. English trans.: *The History of Israel*, 2d ed. [New York: Harper & Row, 1960], 454). (The first edition of Noth's book was issued in 1950.)

11. Noth, *History*, 4–5.

12. Ibid., 7.

13. See John Bright, *A History of Israel*, 3d ed. (Philadelphia: Westminster Press, 1981), 463–64; and J. Alberto Soggin, *A History of Ancient Israel* (Philadelphia: Westminster Press, 1985), 336–37. It is still odd, however, that Soggin closes his book with a brief mention of the Diaspora, as if Jewry did not continue in the Land of Israel in large numbers for several centuries after 135 C.E., when his narrative ends.

14. Noth, *History*, 7.

15. Kugel, "Biblical Studies," 22.

16. Ibid., 24.

17. Ibid., 22.

18. Peter Burke, *The Renaissance Sense of the Past* (New York: St. Martin's Press, 1969), 1.

19. Ibid., 3.

20. See pp. 66–71, above.

21. *Tsaphenat Pa'aneah* to Gen 12:6. Joseph Bonfils (Tov Elem), *Tsaphenat Pa'aneah*, ed. D. Herzog (Heidelberg: Carl Winter, 1911), 92.

22. E.g., Nahum M. Sarna, "The Modern Study of the Bible in the Framework of Jewish Studies," in *Proceedings of the Eighth World Congress of Jewish Studies* (Jerusalem: World Union of Jewish Studies, 1983), 22–24; and Frederick E.

Greenspahn, "Biblical Scholars, Medieval and Modern," in *Judaic Perspectives on Ancient Israel*, ed. Jacob Neusner et al. (Philadelphia: Fortress Press, 1987), 245–58.

23. Burke, *Renaissance*, 23–24.

24. Ibid., 5, 32–33.

25. Ibid., 50–54.

26. Ibid., 55.

27. Ibid., 58–59.

28. Cited in ibid., 61.

29. Moshe Greenberg, "Exegesis," in *Contemporary Jewish Religious Thought*, ed. Arthur A. Cohen and Paul Mendes-Flohr (New York: Charles Scribner's Sons, 1986), 215.

30. Benedict de Spinoza, *A Theologico-Political Tractate and a Political Treatise* (New York: Dover Publications, 1951), 100. The *Tractatus Theologico-Politicus* was originally published in 1670.

31. Ibid., 119.

32. Ibid., 108.

33. Ibid., 55.

34. Ibid., 238.

35. See, e.g., Norman Gottwald, *The Tribes of YHWH* (Maryknoll, NY: Orbis Books, 1979).

36. See above, pp. 10–15, 18–21, 26–27. It is significant that some efforts to counter the anti-Jewish interpretation have to rely on the practice of non-rabbinic groups. See, e.g., Bernadette J. Brooten, *Women Leaders in the Ancient Synagogue*, BJS 8 (Decatur, Ga.: Scholars Press, 1982). The position she holds — that the desired values did indeed appear among Jews in late antiquity, but among those groups that the rabbinic movement supplanted — is no consolation to those Jews seeking to uphold the dignity of the rabbinic tradition.

37. Spinoza, *Theologico-Political Tractate*, 14.

38. Ibid., 27.

39. Ibid., 119.

40. See Michael L. Morgan, "Scriptural Religion in Spinoza's *Tractatus Theologico-Politicus*" (draft manuscript graciously sent to me by the author), 16.

41. Benjamin Jowett, "On the Interpretation of Scripture," in *The Interpretation of Scripture and Other Essays* (London: George Routledge & Sons; New York: E. P. Dutton, n.d). See also James Barr, "Jowett and the Reading of the Bible 'Like Any Other Book,'" *HBT* 4/5 (1982–83): 1–44.

42. Spinoza, *Theologico-Political Tractate*, 101.

43. Ibid., 103.

44. Morgan, "Scriptural Religion," 1–2.

45. Richard H. Popkin, *The History of Skepticism from Erasmus to Spinoza*, rev. ed. (Berkeley, Calif.: University of California Press, 1979), 3.

46. Ibid., 299.

47. Leo Strauss, *Spinoza's Critique of Religion* (New York: Schocken Books, 1965), 116, 120.

48. Spinoza, *Theologico-Political Tractate*, 103.

49. Ibid., 9.

50. Ibid., 8.

51. E.g., Moses Maimonides, *The Guide for the Perplexed,* trans. M. Friedländer, 2d ed. (New York: Dover Publications, 1956), 75–78 (= bk. 1, chap. 54).

52. See below, pp. 111–117, and chap. 6.

53. See Thomas Hobbes, *Leviathan* (London: Oxford University Press, 1909), 291–302 (= chap. 33). The *Leviathan* was published in 1651.

54. Lewis Samuel Feuer, *Spinoza and the Rise of Liberalism* (Boston: Beacon Press, 1958), 143.

55. Yirmiyahu Yovel, "Marrano Patterns in Spinoza," in *Proceedings of the First Italian International Congress on Spinoza* (Naples: Bibliopolis, 1985), 466. See also Edward Feld, "Spinoza the Jew," *MJ* 9 (1989): 101–19.

56. Yovel, "Marrano," 473.

57. Feuer, *Spinoza,* 121.

58. Spinoza, *Theologico-Political Tractate,* chaps. 17 and 18. See Feuer, *Spinoza,* 131–35.

59. E.g., Niccolò Machiavelli, *The Prince,* in *The Prince and the Discourses* (New York: Modern Library, 1950), chaps. 4 and 24.

60. Quoted in Rudolf Smend, "Wellhausen and his *Prolegomena to the History of Israel,*" *Semeia* 25 (1983): 6.

61. See Ben C. Ollenburger, "What Krister Stendahl Meant — A Normative Critique of 'Descriptive Biblical Theology,'" *HBT* 8/1 (June 1986): 61–98.

62. See Wilfred Cantwell Smith, "The Study of Religion and the Study of the Bible," in *JAAR* 39 (1971): 132: "The courses actually available, and the training of men actually available to teach them, are on the whole calculated to turn a fundamentalist into a liberal." On the problem in general, see chap. 5, below.

63. Boadt et al., *Biblical Studies,* 3–4; Potok, *In the Beginning,* 399.

64. Cf. David C. Steinmetz, "Superiority of Pre-Critical Exegesis," *TT* 37 (1980): 38: "Until the historical-critical method becomes critical of its own theoretical foundations and develops a hermeneutical theory adequate to the nature of the text which it is interpreting, it will remain restricted — as it deserves to be — to the guild and the academy, where the question of truth can endlessly be deferred."

65. Spinoza, *Theologico-Political Tractate,* 103. But what I call "trivializing antiquarianism" has forgotten Spinoza's purpose in this, "that we may not confound precepts which are eternal with those which serve a temporary purpose." The distinction was not hard to make for Spinoza, since those precepts that conformed to his philosophy (there were not many) were simply presumed to be eternal and those that did not, to be historically contingent. This has remained the usual method of religious liberals to this day, and it accounts in no small measure for the relative lack of interest in scripture in liberal communities.

66. Jowett, "Interpretation," 36.

67. Hans W. Frei, *The Eclipse of Biblical Narrative* (New Haven and London: Yale University Press, 1974), 6.

68. Ibid., 28.

69. Ibid., 8.

70. Walther Eichrodt, *Theology of the Old Testament*, trans. J. Baker, 2 vols. (Philadelphia: Westminster Press, 1961), 1:31. The first German edition was published in 1933. On the contradiction between Eichrodt's two goals, see above, pp. 16–21.

71. Ibid., 1:26. See Levenson, "Hebrew Bible in Colleges," 37–40.

72. Boadt et al., *Biblical Studies*, 5.

73. Most notably Childs, whose "canonical method" relativizes historical criticism without denying its value within the domain of history. See his *Biblical Theology in Crisis* (Philadelphia: Westminster Press, 1970); idem, *Introduction to the Old Testament as Scripture* (Philadelphia: Fortress Press, 1979); and idem, *Old Testament Theology in a Canonical Context* (Philadelphia: Fortress Press, 1986).

74. Northrop Frye, *The Great Code* (New York: Harcourt Brace Jovanovich, 1981), xiii.

75. Robert Alter, *The Art of Biblical Narrative* (New York: Basic Books, 1981; Philadelphia: Jewish Publication Society, 1983), ix.

76. Ibid., 21.

77. All biblical quotes here are taken from *Tanakh* (Philadelphia: Jewish Publication Society, 1988).

78. Moshe Weinfeld, "The Covenant of Grant in the Old Testament and in the Ancient Near East," *JAOS* 90 (1970): 85. The terminology here is misleading, in that Weinfeld's "grant" would itself appear to be a species of treaty, i.e., a treaty with an unconditional component.

79. See above, pp. 56–61.

80. See chap. 3.

CHAPTER 5

1. Wilfred Cantwell Smith, "The Study of Religion and the Study of the Bible," *JAAR* 39 (1971): 134.

2. Ibid., 132.

3. Ibid.

4. John Barton, *Reading the Old Testament* (Philadelphia: Westminster Press, 1984), 172.

5. Tzvetan Todorov, "Crimes Against Humanities," *The New Republic*, July 3, 1989, 30.

6. Robert B. Coote and Mary P. Coote, *Power, Politics, and the Making of the Bible* (Minneapolis: Fortress Press, 1990), 3.

7. Ibid., 4.

8. Ibid., 21.

9. Ibid., 29.

10. Ibid., 30.

11. Ibid., 38.

12. Ibid., 41–42.

13. Ibid., 42.

14. Ibid., 116.

15. Ibid., 119.

16. Ibid., 121.

17. Ibid., 144.

18. Benedict de Spinoza, *A Theological-Political Tractate and a Political Treatise* (New York: Dover Publications, 1951), 8. The *Tractatus Theologico-Politicus* was published originally in 1670. See also above, pp. 91–96.

19. Catherine Bell, *Ritual Theory, Ritual Practice* (New York and Oxford: Oxford University Press, 1992), 194.

20. Ibid., 199–200.

21. Leszek Kolakowski, *Religion* (New York and Oxford: Oxford University Press, 1982), 15–16.

22. See Paul V. Mankowski, "Academic Religion: Playground of the Vandals," *First Things* 23 (May 1992): 31–37.

23. Bell, *Ritual Theory*, 6.

24. Ibid., 30–31.

25. See Peter L. Berger, *A Rumor of Angels* (Garden City, N.Y.: Doubleday & Co., 1969), 31–53, esp. 45: "When everything has been subsumed under the relativizing categories in question (those of history, of the sociology of knowledge, or what-have-you), the question of truth reasserts itself in almost pristine simplicity. Once we know that all human affirmations are subject to scientifically graspable socio-historical processes, *which affirmations are true and which are false?*"

26. Allan Bloom, *The Closing of the American Mind* (New York: Simon and Schuster, 1987), 218–19.

27. Leo Strauss, *Natural Right and History* (Chicago and London: University of Chicago Press, 1950), 25.

28. Quoted from Arthur Hertzberg, *The French Enlightenment and the Jews* (New York: Schocken Books, 1968), 360.

29. See Glenn W. Olsen, *Deconstructing the University* (Salt Lake City: Division of Continuing Education, University of Utah, 1991), esp. 11: "If I were to put the matter sharply, I would be tempted to say that the first amendment meant that only a Protestant notion of voluntary religion may be practiced in the United States, that, ecclesiologically speaking, the other religions, Catholicism, Judaism, etc., must adjust themselves to being, ecclesiologically, Protestant. But to put the matter this way would not be fair to Puritanism and other forms of eighteenth and nineteenth century Protestantism, which wanted a public life for Christianity."

30. John J. Collins, "Is a Critical Biblical Theology Possible?" in *The Hebrew Bible and Its Interpreters,* ed. William Henry Propp et al. (Winona Lake, Ind.: Eisenbrauns, 1990), 2. Troeltsch's essay is "Über historische und dogmatische Methode in der Theologie," in *Gesammelte Schriften* (Tübingen: J. C. B. Mohr, 1913), 2:729–53.

31. Collins, "Critical Biblical Theology," 3. Collins draws this formulation from Van A. Harvey, *The Historian and the Believer* (Philadelphia: Westminster Press, 1966), 103. Harvey argues that "[t]he revolution in historical method occurred only when integrity was identified with loyalty to the methodological procedures of the intellectual community, when historians agreed on general

canons of inquiry" (p. 103). It must be noted, however, that, there being many intellectual communities, not all of them historicistic or naturalistic, the transference of loyalties of which Harvey speaks represents something other than merely a felt need to be intellectually responsible. It must also be noted that the extent of agreement among historians about "general canons of inquiry" has declined markedly in the three decades since Harvey wrote these words.

32. Strauss, *Natural Right,* 25.

33. Collins, "Critical Biblical Theology," 7.

34. On the problems with the Enlightenment goal of eradicating tradition and replacing it with reason and science, see Hans-Georg Gadamer, *Truth and Method* (New York: Crossroad, 1975), esp. 235–74; and Alasdair MacIntyre, *After Virtue* (Notre Dame, Ind.: University of Notre Dame Press, 1981).

35. Brevard S. Childs, *Biblical Theology in Crisis* (Philadelphia: Westminster Press, 1970), 99. On Childs's method, see also his *Introduction to the Old Testament as Scripture* (Philadelphia: Fortress Press, 1979), and idem, *Old Testament Theology in a Canonical Context* (Philadelphia: Fortress Press, 1985).

36. Collins, "Critical Biblical Theology," 6.

37. Brevard S. Childs, *The Book of Exodus* (Philadelphia: Westminster Press, 1974).

38. See Todorov, "Crimes," 30: "It is at the moment of their creation that works are the most political and the most particular. But we also have the right to ask what they mean to us, above and beyond the circumstances in which they were created." But be aware that this is not a question with which historical-critical scholars are generally comfortable. The preservation of meaningfulness requires a check on the historical contextualism that Todorov rightly associates with politicizing interpretation.

39. Barton, *Reading,* 172.

40. See chap. 1, above.

41. E.g., see William G. Dever, "Syro-Palestinian and Biblical Archaeology," in *The Hebrew Bible and Its Modern Interpreters,* ed. Douglas A. Knight and Gene M. Tucker (Philadelphia: Fortress Press; Chico, Calif.: Scholars Press, 1985), 31–74; and idem, *Recent Archaeological Discoveries and Biblical Research* (Seattle and London: University of Washington Press, 1990), 3–36. Note esp. *Recent Archaeological Discoveries,* 26: "Worse still, some biblical scholars actively opposed the growth of Palestinian archaeology as an independent, professional discipline, and thus found themselves left behind." Instead, Dever calls for a relationship between biblical studies and Syro-Palestinian archaeology that is "a true dialogue, one that will respect the integrity of both disciplines and profit from the specialized knowledge of each" (ibid., 32). If Syro-Palestinian archaeology is to be genuinely independent, however, it will need to justify itself over against other areas of archaeology by reference to something other than its mutually enriching dialogue with biblical studies.

42. For the difference this makes, see Marvin A. Sweeney, "Tanakh Versus Old Testament," forthcoming in BZAW.

CHAPTER 6

1. J. Severino Croatto, *Exodus: A Hermeneutic of Freedom* (Maryknoll, N.Y.: Orbis Books, 1981), 28, 15.

2. Robert McAfee Brown, *Theology in a New Key: Responding to Liberation Themes* (Philadelphia: Westminster Press, 1978), 88, 90.

3. George V. Pixley, *On Exodus: A Liberation Perspective* (Maryknoll, N.Y.: Orbis Books, 1987), xviii–xx.

4. Ibid., 25. See also Gustavo Gutiérrez, *A Theology of Liberation* (Maryknoll, N.Y.: Orbis Books, 1973), 155–160; and Gerhard Sauter, " 'Exodus' und 'Befreiung' als theologische Metaphern," *ET* 38 (1978): 554–56.

5. Pixley, *On Exodus*, 37.

6. Ibid., xiv.

7. Ibid., 39.

8. Ibid., xix.

9. Ibid., 117.

10. Unless otherwise noted, all quotations from the Hebrew Bible in this essay are taken from *Tanakh* (Philadelphia: Jewish Publication Society, 5746/1985).

11. Pixley, *On Exodus*, 80.

12. On the modern historical-critical preference for the reconstructed history over the manifest text, see above, pp. 10–15.

13. Pixley, *On Exodus*, 121; see also 164.

14. Ibid., 81.

15. Lincoln Steffens, *Moses in Red: The Revolt of Israel as a Typical Revolution* (Philadelphia: Dorrance, 1926), 21.

16. Ibid., 28.

17. The only real textual support is an obscure expression consisting of two Hebrew words in Exod 12:38, *'ēreb rab,* conventionally rendered "a mixed multitude." The parallel in Neh 13:3, however, suggests that the term ought perhaps to be rendered "a large number of people of mixed blood." Cf. Ezra 9:2 and Lev 24:10–23.

18. The theory is most fully set forth in Norman Gottwald, *The Tribes of YHWH* (Maryknoll, N.Y.: Orbis Books, 1979).

19. See Baruch Halpern, *The Emergence of Israel in Canaan*, SBLMS 29 (Chico, Calif.: Scholars Press, 1983), esp. 239–61; and Israel Finkelstein, *The Archaeology of the Israelite Settlement* (Jerusalem: Israel Exploration Society, 1988).

20. Pixley, *On Exodus*, 169.

21. H. Shelton Smith, *In His Image, But: Racism in Southern Religion, 1780–1910* (Durham, N.C.: Duke University Press, 1972), 132–33.

22. On Paul's intensely conservative social thought, see G. E. M. de St. Croix, *The Class Struggle in the Ancient Greek World* (Ithaca, N.Y.: Cornell University Press, 1981), 103–11, 418–25.

23. All quotations from the New Testament in this essay are taken from the *New English Bible* (New York: Oxford University Press, 1970).

24. See Eugene D. Genovese, *Roll, Jordan, Roll* (New York: Pantheon, 1974), 208.

25. Theodore Dwight Weld, *The Bible Against Slavery* (Pittsburgh: United Presbyterian Board of Education, 1964; Detroit: Negro History Press, 1970), 38. The tract was originally published in the *Anti-Slavery Quarterly Magazine*, 1839.

26. Ibid., 22–30.

27. Ibid., 44.

28. Ibid., 106.

29. See Robert Abzug, *Passionate Liberator: Theodore Dwight Weld and the Dilemma of Reform* (New York and Oxford: Oxford University Press, 1980), 162.

30. Michael Walzer, *Exodus and Revolution* (New York: Basic Books, 1985), 30.

31. See Richard Elliot Friedman, "The Recession of Biblical Source Criticism," in *The Future of Biblical Studies: The Hebrew Scriptures*, ed. Richard Elliot Friedman and H. G. M. Williamson (Atlanta: Scholars Press, 1987), 87, in which Friedman notes the oddity of the term for taskmasters in Exodus 1 (*śārê missîm* rather than *nōgĕśîm*) and connects this with 1 Kings 12.

32. See John Howard Yoder, "Probing the Meaning of Liberation," *Sojourners* 5/7 (Sept. 1976): 26–29, esp. 28: "To transpose the motif of liberation out of that distinct historical framework and thereby away from the distinct historical identity of the God of Abraham, Isaac, and Jacob, into some kind of general theistic affirmation of liberation, is to separate the biblical message from its foundation."

33. Walzer, *Exodus*, 31.

34. See above, pp. 71–74.

35. James B. Pritchard, ed., *Ancient Near Eastern Texts Relating to the Old Testament*, 3rd ed. (Princeton, N.J.: Princeton University Press, 1969), 170–71. Cf. Exod 21:2–6; Deut 15:12–18; Lev 25:39–43.

36. Pritchard, *Ancient Near Eastern Texts*, 167 (para. 32).

37. See David Daube, *The Exodus Pattern in the Bible*, All Souls Studies 2 (London: Faber and Faber, 1963), 39.

38. See James Barr, "The Bible as a Political Document," in *The Scope and Authority of the Bible* (Philadelphia: Westminster Press, 1980), 107–8.

39. I depart from *Tanakh* here in order to capture the likely preterite use of these ostensible imperfects. See Frank Moore Cross, *Canaanite Myth and Hebrew Epic* (Cambridge, Mass.: Harvard University Press, 1973), 125.

40. This departs from *Tanakh* in order to reflect the likely inchoative nuance of *mālāk*. See Sigmund Mowinckel, *The Psalms in Israel's Worship* (New York and Nashville: Abingdon Press, 1967), 1:107–9.

41. See Cross, *Canaanite Myth*, 112–44, and Jon D. Levenson, *Creation and the Persistence of Evil* (San Francisco: Harper & Row, 1988), 3–50.

42. "Gods" has been substituted for "celestials" (*Tanakh*) in the interest of accuracy.

43. See Sigmund Mowinckel, *Psalmenstudien II: Das Thronbesteigungsfest YHWHs und der Ursprung der Eschatologie*, SNVAO (Kristiana, Norway: J. Dybwad, 1921).

44. See Dennis J. McCarthy, *Treaty and Covenant*, AnBib 21A (Rome: Biblical Institute Press, 1978), and Jon D. Levenson, *Sinai and Zion* (San Francisco: Harper & Row, 1987), 23–86.

45. Moshe Weinfeld, *Justice and Righteousness in Israel and the Nations* (in Hebrew) (Jerusalem: Magnes, 1985), 134. Weinfeld acknowledges a debt to an unpublished work of Yochanan Muffs that suggested some of these connections (p. 139 n. 28).

46. Exod 7:16, 26; 8:16; 9:1, 13; 10:3. I again depart from *Tanakh* in the interest of precision.

47. See Jon D. Levenson, "Covenant and Consent," in *The Judeo-Christian Tradition and the U.S. Constitution: Proceedings of a Conference at Annenberg Research Institute*, November 16–17, 1987, ed. David Goldenberger (Philadelphia: Annenberg Research Institute, 1987), 71–82.

48. Yoder, "Probing," 28.

49. On the variety of meanings of "liberty," see the enlightening discussion in John Phillip Reid, *The Concept of Liberty in the Age of the American Revolution* (Chicago: University of Chicago Press, 1988).

50. The translation, including that of the biblical citation, is from *Kiddushin*, trans. H. Freedman (London: Soncino, 1966).

51. On slavery in rabbinic Jewish thought and law, see Ephraim E. Urbach, "The Laws Regarding Slavery," in *Papers of the [London] Institute of Jewish Studies*, ed. J. G. Weiss (Jerusalem: Magnes, 1964), 1–94.

52. See above, pp. 11–15, 56–61, and 102–104.

53. On this, see E. P. Sanders, *Paul and Palestinian Judaism* (Philadelphia: Fortress Press, 1977), 431–556.

54. See chaps. 1 and 2, above.

55. Georg Wilhelm Friedrich Hegel, "The Spirit of Christianity and Its Fate," in *Early Theological Writings* (Chicago: University of Chicago Press, 1948), 191, 202, 206, 208. The essay was written in 1798–99. On this, see Levenson, "Covenant and Consent."

56. Daube, *The Exodus*, 55–61, esp. 57.

57. See Croatto, *Exodus*, 15; Brown, *Theology*, 88, 90; Pixley, *On Exodus*, xviii–xx.

58. On the importance of Israel's identity as a biological family, see Michael Wyschogrod, *The Body of Faith* (New York: Seabury Press, 1983).

59. Note, however, that "the preferential option for the poor" in the Hebrew Bible falls in the domain of social policy. In the domain of judicial process it is strictly prohibited. See Exod 23:3 and Lev 19:15. The limited scope of the preferential option for the poor is nicely brought home when God's response to Israel's cry in bondage in Egypt (Exod 2:23–25) is juxtaposed to his response to an *Egyptian* slave's attempt to escape mistreatment by her *Israelite* mistress: "Go back to your mistress, and submit to her harsh treatment" (Gen 16:9).

60. See Shaye J. D. Cohen, "The Origins of the Matrilineal Principle in Rabbinic Law," *AJSR* 10 (1985): 19–53.

61. Thomas F. Gossett, *Race* (Dallas: Southern Methodist University Press, 1963), 190.

62. David J. Garrow, *Bearing the Cross* (New York: William Morrow, 1986), 621.

63. Jacob Katz, *From Prejudice to Destruction* (Cambridge, Mass.: Harvard University Press, 1980), 173.

64. Karl Marx, "Zur Judenfrage" (1844), as quoted in ibid., 173.

65. On the reappearance of classic Christian anti-Semitism in some liberationists, see John T. Pawlikowski, *Christ in the Light of the Christian-Jewish Dialogue* (New York and Ramsey, N.J.: Paulist Press, 1982), 59–73; John P. Meier, "The Bible as a Source for Theology," *PCTSA* 43 (1988): 1–14; and Susannah Heschel, "Anti-Judaism in Christian Feminist Theology," *Tikkun* 5/3 (May/June 1990): 25–28, 95–97.

Index of Authors

Index of Ancient Sources